AF522600

LAND, LABOUR AND POWER

Agrarian Crisis and the State in Bihar
(1937-52)

LAND, LABOUR AND POWER
Agrarian Crisis and the State in Bihar (1937-52)

USHA JHA

AAKAR BOOKS
DELHI

LAND, LABOUR AND POWER

Agrarian Crisis and the State in Bihar (1937-52)

First Published, 2003

ISBN 81-87879-07-6

Published by

AAKAR BOOKS

28-E, Pocket-IV, Mayur Vihar Phase-I, Delhi-110 091

Phone : 22795505 Telefax : 22795641

E-mail : aakarb@del2.vsnl.net.in

Laser Typesetting

Nidhi Laser Point, Shahdara, Delhi-110 032

Ph. : 22825424

Printed in India on behalf of M/s Aakar Books by

Arpit Printographers, B-7, Saraswati Complex,

Subhash Chowk, Laxmi Nagar, Delhi-110 092

PREFACE

An attempt has been made to study and analyse the agrarian problems of Bihar and the relevant policies of the State Government during the period 1937-52. It investigates into the various aspects of land question of the period, its tenures, rack-renting suppression of the rights of raiyats and perpetration of injustice on them, throwing them to the stokes-holes of serfdom prevalent in the state.

The main object of the study is to trace the significant developments in the agrarian life which ultimately marked a new dawn of equality, liberty and fraternity in the countryside. It has also tried to portray the policy of the Indian National Congress towards the land problems. The period is stirred with various agrarian movements, sometimes under the banner of Bihar Prantiya Kisan Sabha (BPKS) and sometimes spontaneously, which forced the Government to abolish the Zamindari system.

The entire study has been divided into seven chapters. The first chapter deals with the agrarian adversities of Bihar and the several measures that were taken to improve the situation. The curses did not abound only from natural calamities alone but also from man-made calamities which added to their severity. The second chapter emphasises the land system, the importance of the land, various changes in the land tenures and the need for a transformation. The third chapter discusses the attitude of the Indian National Congress towards the land problem and curses that led to the emergence of the Kisan Sabha. It also takes in view various meetings of the Congress General Secretaries as well as the Bihar Provincial Kisan Sabha and the All India Kisan Sabha. The fourth chapter highlights various agrarian movements during the period, forms of peasantry, the differentiation and class consciousness of peasantry. The fifth chapter abounds in great importance as it reveals the story of the abolition of Zamindari System. It also reveals the long drama of the enactment of several Tenancy Acts and their amendments. The sixth chapter discusses the impact of the abolition of Zamindari on social, economic, political and cultural lives of the villages as well as of the State. The last chapter is the concluding which includes some suggestions.

In the present study, primary and secondary sources of information have been used to provide authenticity to the findings of the study. Besides, unpublished records of the State Archives, Government of Bihar, official reports, proceedings of the Bihar Legislative Assembly and Council, annual budgets, memoirs of the then congressmen, contemporary newspapers and journals have been consulted for analysing critically the agrarian problems of Bihar during 1937-52.

I express my deep sense of gratitude to Prof. Ratneshwar Mishra, who always gave valuable suggestions and guidance the book could see the light of the day. My thanks also goes to Dr. R. Ram, Professor of History, Patna University for encouraging with constructive suggestions time and again. I am also obliged to Prof. D.D. Guru of A.N. Sinha Institute of Social Studies, who helped me by his encyclopaedic knowledge. I am sincerely thankful to the Principal, Head of the Department of History and other colleagues of my college.

I am deeply indebted to my parents, Dr. Chiranjeev Jha and Mrs. Shyama Jha and other family members, Rakesh Ranjan, Shri Yamunadhar Mishra and all other well-wishers for their words of encouragement, inspiration and assistance at various stages. Special mention must be made of my younger brother Ajay, who took great pains in correcting the type-script. Grateful acknowledgement is due to Dr. S.F. Rab. Deputy Librarian, Dr. P.P. Singh, Asstt. Librarian and Mr. Nehal

Ashraf, Professional Assistant of A.N. Sinha Institute of Social Studies, Patna for their co-operation in collecting the factual and statistical data. I am also thankful to the staff of the Bihar Assembly Library, Bihar Secretariat Library, the Bihar State Archives, Patna University Library, Sinha Library, Mazharul Haq Library K.P. Jaiswal Research Institute, and the L.N.M. Institute of Economic Development & Social Change.

Department of History **Usha Jha**
Sri Arbind Mahila College,
Magadh University
Bodh Gaya, Bihar

CONTENTS

CHAPTER 1

INTRODUCTION

In Bihar where three out of every four persons depend on agriculture, the importance of agriculture in the State economy cannot be understated. But it is a pity that inspite of its preponderating importance in our economy, agriculture has become a depressed industry. Dr. Clouston, a former Agricultural Advisor to the Government of India, has remarked:

> *"In India we have our depressed classes, we have too our depressed industries, and agriculture unfortunately is one of them. This is proved by the fact that yield per acre crops is comparatively low, which is barely one-third or one-fourth of the yield of other state like Punjab".*

Agrarian Curses of Bihar

The low yield of crops is the root of the poverty which is crushing the rural masses of Bihar. It has been the basic cause of the severity of food problem since 1937. Malnutrition and undernourishment often lead to low vitality and at times even to starvation deaths. On the economic front, its effect is directly felt on the purchasing power of our rural masses. Following consequences are directly correlated to a low yield rate:

(*i*) the home market for industrial goods shrinks,
(*ii*) industrial decay produced unemployment for the workers and the middle class people, and
(*iii*) the burden of rent, interest and taxes grow to such an

extent that the rural economy cracked up, in domination of the moneylender increased over the peasantry, and peasants were forced to sell their land which gets concentrated in the hands of the parasitic class of landlords. This in turn reduced the productivity of the soil.

Among the agrarian problems in Bihar during the period 1937-52 had been the adverse natural conditions and climatic fluctuations which were in some regions directly responsible for low unit yields. The density of population may not have any relation with the yield in such cases but natural factors do not entirely explain the fact that even the maximum in low unit regions fall below the optimum yield obtained in other regions of similar climatic conditions. The density of population depending upon agriculture in such cases has a direct bearing on the unit yield of the regions. The unit yield of cereals is lower in the agriculture-based economies than in more industrialised economies. Over population results in a disproportionate utilisation of land for cereals, unsatisfactory system of crop rotation and less possibility of recuperation of soil.

The obvious deduction, therefore, is that agriculture in Bihar had become a deficit economy, and to a great extent the Bihar cultivator laboured not for profit, for a net return but for subsistence. The overcrowding of the people on land, the lack of alternative means of securing a living, the difficulty of finding any avenue of escape and the early stage at which man is burdened with the dependants, combined to force the cultivator to grow food wherever he could and on whatever terms he could.

The causes of this situation may be stated as :

(1) the subsistence type of farming and consequent deficit in agricultural economy;
(2) poor equipment, inadequacy or obsolete nature of tools and inferior livestock;
(3) defective preparatory tillage;
(4) sub-division and fragmentation of holdings;
(5) lack of adequate credit facilities and the resultant indebtedness of the peasant and his poverty;

(6) large areas of land under cultivated wastes, insufficiency, irregularity and uncertain water supply;
(7) soil exhaustion due to continued cropping for hundreds and thousands of years without proper manuring either natural or artificial;
(8) the menace of soil erosion, which caused havoc to the land, and faulty methods of cultivation;
(9) lack of adequate supply of improved seeds;
(10) diseases of plants and the large incidence of insects and pests; and above all,
(11) the faulty land system.

These factors were responsible for deteriorating agrarian conditions in Bihar prior to independence, because the Colonial Agrarian Policy under the British rule was never peasant-oriented.

Over and above all these factors peasant farming in Bihar depends for its successful working not only on great perseverance but also on unwearied exercise of prudence, forethought and watchfulness, and the utilisation of the scientific knowledge of the means of production. The value of human factor is not to be overlooked in taking stock of the agricultural situation for communities and nations which have remained poor in the midst of rich surroundings, or fallen in decay or poverty inspite of the fertility of their soil and the abundance of their natural resources merely because the human factor was of poor quality or was allowed to deteriorate or run to waste. So far as this human resource or element is concerned, the seasonal variations rendered agriculture a precarious occupation, and the undue dependence of the cultivator on nature had engendered in him a spirit of depression, fatalism, and hopelessness to be rescued by external agencies. Very rightly it has been remarked that "to take the ordinary acts of husbandry, nowhere would one find better instances of keeping land scrupulously clean from weeds, of ingenuity in device of water-raising appliances, of knowledge of soils and there capabilities, as well as the exact time to sow and reap, as one would in Indian agriculture...".

"Crippled by a relentless climate, for generations scourged

by famine, pestilence, and war, his wealth at the mercy of every despot's whim, his cattle a prey to disease and drought, his crops periodically devasted by plight and flood, serving, too, not the gentle goddess that Nature is in the West but a volcanic force of terrific power and wild caprice, how can the Indian cultivator be anything but a fatalist. In such conditions progress is impossible, knowledge, skill, energy and capital must appear of little avail when man is infinitely weak and nature overwhelmingly strong".

In agrarian problems of Bihar, the question of technical assistance and education to the Bihar cultivator could not appear unless institutional changes provided the necessary economic basis for agriculture. Gradual worsening of debt position, violent price fluctuations, the middle traders' exhorbitant rates and exploitation and the landlord's apathy were some factors which discouraged the Bihar farmer to adopt new methods and techniques whose failure could ruin him and whose success benefit would everyone except him. Therefore, the measures required to trigger Bihar peasant incentives to betterment were security of tenure, stability, elimination of middle-traders, marketing facilities and credit institutions which, of course, were impossible under the condition of tug of war between the Colonial ruling class and the nationalist leaders of Bihar.

Agrarian problems in Bihar cropped up on the point of irrigation as well. In fact, agriculture depends upon adequate and regular supply of water. The scarcity, uncertainty or irregularity of water supply easily ranked high in worsening the conditions of Bihar. Annual rainfall was the main source of agriculture in Bihar. Unreliable advent of monsoon generally demoralised Bihar agriculturists. Yet the main sources of irrigation were wells, tanks, and reservoirs and few small canals dug up by the Indigo planters for their restricted use only. After the Indigo planters were compelled to leave Bihar as a consequence of the Champaran Agrarian Bills passed in 1918, the canals dug up by them were opened for general people. However, no fresh canals were dug up in Bihar by the British rulers during the period prior to independence. Even after independence of the country from the British colonial yoke,

Bihar farmers or peasantry could not improve their lot on account of the paucity of irrigation facilities for a long period.

In connection with irrigation research in India, Bihar lagged behind in comparison to other states. Great strides in irrigation research have been made in other states of India, the first in the field was Bombay where special Research Division was created in 1916 to investigate the problems of land drainage and reclamation. After 1945 the activities of the Central Research Station at Khadakvasla multiplied and problems were referred to it from many parts of the country. After Bombay, investigations in the problems of water-logging were started in Punjab in 1923, and a new Research Institute was set up after independence at Amritsar. Irrigation Research Station was established in Uttar Pradesh as early as in 1930. River Research Institute of West Bengal was set up in 1943. The Krishnaraj Sagar Research Station at Mysore was established in 1945. However, Bihar, inspite of having magnanimous rivers such as Ganga, Saryu, Gandak, Balan, Bhuthibalan, Bagmati Kamla, Kosi etc., lagged behind and added annual incidence of the sad plight of flood to the fate of agrarian prosperity of the State.

In respect of cattle wealth, Bihar, from the very beginning, has been in a privileged position due to its natural peculiarity and green surroundings. In this respect it has been commanding the second position in India. Uttar Pradesh being the first prior to independence and also prior to 1956. Cattle wealth was a great asset to the conventional method of cultivation in agrarian field. But side by side Bihar has been suffering from massive cattle death on account of epidemics and diseases for which little remedies were available.

Land Holdings in Bihar

India is a land of small peasants. The unit of holdings everywhere has been small and uneconomic. Various surveys undertaken in the country show that the average size of holdings has been very small. The Agricultural Labour Enquiry revealed that taking the country as whole, the cultivators holding below one acre were 17% of the total number; those between 1 and

2.5 acres were about 21% and those between 2.5 and 5 acres were another 21%. The average size of holdings varies from 5.3 acres in Assam to 4.1 acres in Bihar, to 5.3 acres in Uttar Pradesh and so on.

The progress of sub-division of holdings has been going on at a rapid pace for long throughout the country. Some surveys reveal that almost 67% of Uttar Pradesh, 63% in Bengal, 66% of the holdings in Andhra Pradesh, 64% in Punjab, 66% in Assam and 83% in Bihar were under 5 acres. In some villages in Bihar the largest percentage of holdings is below 2 acres. The problem of uneconomic holdings was further complicated by the practice of fragmentation of holdings. If a father had four sons and he died leaving four isolated fields of one acre each, the sons would not take one field each but one-fourth of each field, so that each field would be divided into four equal parts. This happened specially when lands were of different qualities and were situated in different localities. Fragmentation was accentuated by the expansion of cultivation irregularly over the waste, by commodification and the division of joint family property amongst a large number of distant relatives. As a result of fragmentation, the holdings of an agriculturist in Bihar did not consist of a single compact block of land but a number of small scattered plots over different parts of the village, often of a very irregular shape.

Some scholars have remarked with alarm the distress caused to the Bihar agriculturists through fragmentation. The average size of plots in some districts of Bihar was found to vary between 0.28 and 0.81 acre. In the densely populated parts such as the Ganga-Ghagra Doab, the eastern Uttar Pradesh and Bihar had gone to grotesque length. Thus the agrarian problems of Bihar during the period 1937-52 were the direct products of the agricultural curses which were actually the worst out-growth of a Joint Hindu Family.

Curses of Sub-division or Fragmentation

The fragmented and uneconomic holdings in Bihar led to agricultural deterioration and aggravated the poverty of the masses. The cultivation of an unduly small holding entailed waste in a variety of ways. This practice involved encroachment of the soil otherwise available for cultivation. It entailed waste of land in boundaries, hedges and ploughways. Sub-dívision also reduced the average size of holdings. When the holdings got smaller, the proportion of fixed cost to the total costs of cultivation increased. Some of the costs incurred by the farmer such as expenses of maintaining his family, a pair of bullocks and a few agricultural implements did not decrease proportionately when his holdings got smaller. The sub-division also meant a rise in variable costs. The costs of fencing per acre, of manure and of seed were all high when the farmer cultivated a small holding. Neither the improved tools nor the permanent improvement of any sort on land could be made because of the tiny size of the holdings in Bihar. In many tracts the inefficiency of agriculture was due more to the small size and scattered nature of the holding than to ignorance or want of alertness on the part of the peasants. Such holdings did not afford sufficient work for the cultivator and did leave him almost unemployed during most part of the year. Agricultural indebtedness was at once the cause and effect of the excessive division of holdings, and very often enforced idleness and indebtedness went together. When holdings were intensely fragmented, much time was lost naturally in moving from one plot to another, particularly at the time of sowing, watering, weeding and harvesting. Personal supervision was rendered difficult because unless the plot was large enough it did not pay to erect platforms for keeping an eye on the standing crop. Further, in a small family of farmer, the owner had to content himself with a morning and evening visit to his various fields and remainder plots were left to chance. Carriage of manure was easier and more economical if the land was in one block and so it was usual to manure the plots which were located near the heaps of cowdung manure. On the basis of present plight of the Bihar agriculturists, it may be assessed that the expenses of cultivation increased during pre-independent period after the formation of Bihar province (separated from Orissa in 1936) by 5.3% for every 500 meters of distance for manual labour and ploughing, from 20% to 25% for the transport of manure, from 15% to 32% for the transport of crops. The net yield, therefore, was bound to decrease with every increase in the distance from the village. Height of the plight of the Bihar agriculturists can be estimated with the hypothesis of ill-developed communication system in rural areas and in addition to this, usual callousness and malice of an average Bihar family in rural area were the worst cause which impeded the agrarian functioning at every stage in rainy season when a criminal sense of competition to water one's own field at the first instance arose in the mind of cultivator or the farmer.

Fragmentation of holdings also created difficulties in maintaining correct levels and making provision for surface drainage. When a land-owner held his land in scattered bits, he had naturally less incentive to spend money on the maintenance of proper drains to prevent waterlogging and on the construction of the embankments to check soil erosion. When the land became excessively fragmented, irrigation often became impracticable. Water could not be supplied so as to reach all the little parcels into which an individual holding was cut, and besides this, there was the difficulty of taking water by channels through other people's fields. The difficulties over the channel along which water had to be taken as well as its distribution led to much bickering and bad blood in the characteristic of Bihar, village life full of litigations and criminal incidences. Fragmentation also brought unavoidable chances of disputes regarding boundaries, rights of way, etc. leading the farmer to litigation of expensive nature.

Agrarian problems in Bihar had, in fact, all evils of small holdings. On the one hand it prevented the use of machinery and labour-saving devices and the other, on large holdings, they hindered the adoption of really intensive cultivation by hand labour which was of great advantage to small labourer. Difficulties in putting up fences, protection from stray cattle and from the depredation of thieves were common to excessive sub-division and fragmentation. The combined result of these was that it drove the land out of cultivation. This destroyed enterprise, resulted in enormous wastage of labour and led to a very large loss of land owing to boundaries, made it impossible to cultivate holdings.

These issues prevented the possibility of introducing the outsider cultivators or peasants on point of taking risk, with more money, as tenant farmers or as purchasers of a good agrarian property. Thus in all respects the curses of agrarian problems were formidable challenging the authorities for embarking on something new, which was not possible on account of the colonial exploitation of the British imperial rulers in pre-independence era and on account of the raw handed leaders surrounded by a bunch of problems cropped up out of the decaying feudal agrarian structure in post-independence era of the First Five Year Plan. Special Acts or legislation for consolidation were passed by several state or provincial governments during the period 1937-52, but so far, no such step was taken in Bihar. Peasant society in Bihar was dashed down the level of personal skirmishes sprouting out of agrarian issues. Dozens of Zamindars, big and small, perpetuated their strangleholds over the Bihar peasantry and in connivance with the corrupt bureaucracy in government offices they fared well at the cost of the agrarian tinkerings in Bihar.

Limitations of Bihar Peasant Workers

Among many limitations, poverty of the Bihar peasant worker became the chief hurdle in his way. Knowing well that a certain crop or a certain new fertilizer would be profitable to him in the end, the Bihar cultivator possessed the essential knowledge and the required skill but not the finance and the proper lead. The illiteracy of the Bihar cultivator was another hurdle in the way of agrarian improvement of Bihar. Physical inefficiency of the peasant in Bihar was yet another curse coming in the way of toning up agriculture. By his insanitary habits of living, he drew upon himself much avoidable physical sufferings, evils of low vitality and incapacity for persistent and strenuous labour and a sombre outlook towards life. Bihar cultivators frequently fell victims to malaria, cholera, plague, dysentery, tuberculosis, Kala-zar, hookworm, skin complaints and leprosy. A large number of these diseases invaded the cultivators due to ill-nourishment, starving condition and working in the field on empty stomachs and with half-naked bodies thus becoming easy prey to diseases. Besides these curses and crises, the Bihar peasant was also prone to litigations, improvidence and recklessness; and too fond of locking up his capital in jewellery and trinkets instead of devoting it to remunerative investment. The Bihar peasant also spent beyond his means on dowry-bound marriages and finally walked into the moneylenders parlour.

Views and sentiments of the peasants in Bihar were seldom shared by persons posted at the top posts in the administration. No viable change in the attitude of the administration was noticeable. Above all, the old system, traditions and outlook had not yet disappeared. Also, it was difficult for the bureaucrats to functions on the basis of trust and co-operation as between equals. Identification with the people was further made difficult by the fact that higher officers usually came from higher classes and castes in Indian society. Above all, the passive attitude of the rural community was also not changed by the non-official leaders of the people.

Evils of Agrarian Economy and their Social Roots in Bihar

One of the most disquieting features of the rural economy of Bihar was the growth in the number of agricultural proletariates. The growth of the agricultural labour population of Bihar, comprising owner cultivators, tenant cultivators, farm hands, field worker, agrarian serfs and unspecified class of workers was alarming. Transition to self-cultivation by the feudal and semi-feudal landlords meant the transformation of the feudal mode of production based on the appropriation of the surplus product in the form of rent into the capitalist mode of production based on the appropriation of surplus product in the form of surplus value (Profit). In other words, it meant the transformation of the tenant or the share cropper into an agricultural labourer, ready to sell his labour power to his landlord now turning into a capitalist enterpreneur. Since feudalism was not abolished root and branch, feudal exploitation continued to exist side by side with capitalist exploitation and got interturned with it. Hence, usury, bonded labour, share-cropping, caste and social oppression often characterised the sale of labour power by the agriculture labourers. Insatiable greed for profit acted at the motive force impelling the landlords towards eviction of more and more tenants and share-croppers by means of deceit and fraud, force and terror, fire and sword.

At the bottom of the agricultural ladder in Bihar were those labourers whose conditions were not different from those of serfs. Agricultural serfdom was prevalent in those parts of Bihar where the lower and depressed classes were most numerous. In fact, the ethnic composition of the village, which governed (and is yet governing) the social stratification, was responsible for the survival of the slavish conditions. Thus in *Chotanagpur* we had a large aboriginal population, and condition of the agriculture labourer was very much like that of a slave. The average labourer was frequently compelled in times of stress to mortgage his personal liberty, in return for a small sum of money which he needed at the moment. He agreed to serve the moneylender-landlord. The money was not repaid, nor was it desired to be repaid, but the borrower remained a lifelong bonded slave of his creditor-landlord. For his work he merely received an inadequate quantity of food and for all practical purposes was in the position of medieval serf. This agrarian serf labour was regularised in such a manner that some of the regions had special name for it for example, Kaimuti in South Bihar, Janauri or Jan or Asmi in North Bihar and so on. These serf agrarian labourers served in their masters' households. They received money for their marriage expenses giving an undertaking to serve till they paid off their debt. They were the Kamias or Janas or Bond-servants, who having borrowed money, bound themselves to perform whatever menial services were required of them by their landlord master. Those depressed castes who had no land or security, pledged their labour, whenever they wanted money as loan; and not only their labour but that of their dependents also. Very often it happened that the joint wages of the kamia or Jana and his wife were not sufficient to feed them and their children.

The system of exacting forced labour existed in all parts of Bihar. The Agricultural Enquiry Committee called *'Begar'* as "involuntary labour". Various forms of *'begar'* were prevalent in North India. They were *'Beth Begar'* under which labourers were forced to perform agricultural operation for two to five days. In this way there was ploughing (Hal Beth), weeding and watering (Kudal Beth), harvesting the crop (Dhan or Paddy Beth) thrashing the crop (Misani or smashing Beth). In Bihar, "an attached worker was usually advanced a sum of rupees fifty to one hundred at the beginning of the year until he returned the sum, he was not permitted to leave his employer-landlord. The inability of workers to repay the advance led to certain practices of exacting labour either at nominal wages or without them. Apart from the *'Begar'* there was a system of levying *abwabs* or illegal exactions which survived in Bihar and Bengal. It had reduced the cultivators to the state of semi-serfdom. Sometimes these exactions took the form of the marriage fees. Sometimes they were taxed for carrying on certain trades. These exactions deprived the Bihar peasantry of a large portion of their already meagre income. The *abwabs* were employed not only as an engine of financial extortion but of physical oppression. Besides, the process of gradual expropriation of the cultivators by the moneylender landlords drove the aboriginals into the ranks of servile tenants liable to forced labour and to the payment of illegal exactions. This type of agrarian serfdom thus lingered on even during the post independent era unto the time of the abolition of Zamindari in Bihar and its glimpses may be seen even today.

Land Tenures and their Effects

In the foregoing discussion of the causes of low productivity in agriculture, the system in which land was owned and cultivated in Bihar was also an important factor. There were two allied problems:

1. The problem of land tenures, i.e. the legal or customary system under which land was actually owned; and
2. The problem of land tenancy, i.e, the system under which land was actually cultivated and the product was divided between the owner and the cultivator.

In a study, the system of land tenure, we generally discuss

the question of ownership, sale or mortgage of land and how far these rights are recognised by law or custom. Land tenancy is concerned with the study of the question of security under which cultivators hold land and of the division of the product.

So far as the problem of land tenure is concerned, the land tenure system may reduce the standard of living of the peasant by imposing on him exorbitant rents or high interest rates, it may check investment because it offers him no security. It may lead to the prevalence of farms which are too small to be efficient units of production or too large to cultivate intensively. The importance of the study of Land Tenure is threefold :

Firstly, it is necessary from the point of view of the State, to locate the owner of land, because it is he from whom the State has to claim the land revenue.

Secondly, the effects of the system of land tenure are far-reaching on the productivity of land. For example, an owner cultivates his land with greater zeal and is more anxious to introduce permanent improvement into it than a tenant who has to share the fruits of his labour with an absentee landlord.

Thirdly, the social organisation of a country or state depends on its land tenure system because it determines the standard of living of the masses.

The impact of the vagaries of the world capitalist market was felt by the peasants of Bihar when, as a result of the great depression of 1929-30, the prices of staple foodgrains which had shown a steady rise after the First World War suddenly dropped. During 1929-35 a fall by 60% to 70% was common in many districts of Bengal and Bihar. The professionals never had it so good, for a person could be maintained at Rs. 2-3 per month in the early thirties, but the peasants were done away with. Whatever little earnings they had were wiped out, and in order to pay rents and defray their subsistence and other necessary expenses they had to borrow more and more. But the enormity of this severe slump was realised neither by the government nor by the Congress and Kisan Sabha. Although they made occasional references of its effects in their reports and other publications, neither the Congress nor the Kisan Sabha set up any Enquiry Committee to gauge the full effects and implications of this great crisis for the peasants. Apparently, they did not appreciate the working of the capitalist market laws and therefore made no attempt to understand their operations and implications at a critical stage in the context of Bihar. Since the leaders of both organisations participated in the Civil Disobedience Movement, they did not get any time to pay attention to this economic problem. But even when the movement petered out by 1932, no effort was made to probe into this problem which continued to afflict the peasant society of the state.

The economic crisis was followed by the earthquake of January 15, 1934. It resulted in the widespread devastation in the towns of Monghyr, Darbhanga and Muzaffarpur. Buildings made up of concrete and thatched roofs collapsed in the rural areas in North Bihar and peasants were badly affected by deep fissures caused in their lands by the earthquake. The effects of this natural calamity were so great that Mahatma Gandhi and Jawaharlal Nehru rushed to Bihar and the Congress set up a Provincial Relief Committee with Rajendra Prasad as its president and with headquarters at Patna. The Kisan Sabha set up several committees to look into the effects of the earthquake on the peasants, and one such committee, set up in Muzaffarpur, consisted of three prominent kisan leaders of the district.

The earthquake of 1934 was followed by the ravaging flood of 1935 in North Bihar. It caused widespread damage to crops, animals and houses, and the kisans lost their bhadai—the rainy season crop (from the month Bhado)—which is the staple crop in North Bihar. The Kisan Sabha pointed out the enormous difficulties faced by the kisans in paying rents and in maintaining themselves, but its demands fell on deaf ears.

We should 'therefore' bear in mind that the special nature of the agrarian problems was caused by the existence of the Zamindari system. The operation of the system in a colonial set-up brought to the kisan untold miseries which were intensified and made intolerable by the great depression followed by the earthquake and floods. The agrarian problems could be solved only by bringing about fundamental changes in the structure of rural society, whose features were determined by colonialism of which it was a victim. The Congress and the Kisan Sabha could be of agents of social change but it was much depended on the nature of their leadership and ideology.

Tenancy Legislation in Bihar

In Bihar, the economic depression after 1929 increased the clamour for tenancy reforms. The result was the passing of the Bihar Tenancy Amendment Acts of 1937 and 1938. These Acts significantly strengthened the position of the tenants:

Firstly, these Acts cancelled all enhancements of rents between 1911 and 1936 and reduced all rents computed between these years in proportion to fall in prices,

Secondly, these Acts limited the rate of interest chargeable on arrears of rent to 6.25%,

Thirdly, these Acts granted the right to transfer to occupancy tenants with the rights to dig wells and construct houses,

Fourthly, these Acts conferred occupancy rights on under-ryots who had held the same land for 12 years, and

lastly, the Acts abolished the *Salami* payable to the Landlords.

The Bihar Restoration of the Bakashat Lands and Reduction of Arrears Rent Act of 1938 provided for restoration to the ryot of the land sold during the depression in execution of a decree for arrears of rent and for reduction of the arrears of rent in view of the circumstances of the ryot affected by fall in prices.

The Chotanagpur Tenancy Amendement Act of 1934, removed and relaxed the restrictions of transfer of occupancy holdings in Chotanagpur and their division by partition and distribution rent, it also laid down conditions under which a reduction of rent on occupancy holdings could be demanded and provisions for governing the realisation of arrears of rent. The other Acts are Champaran Agrarian Amendment Act of 1938, the Bihar Tenancy Amendment Act of 1940, etc.

The Bihar Government, like Bengal, did not appoint a committee to enquire into the problems connected with the abolition of Zamindari. It took decision on the basis of office memoranda. In pursuance of its policy it was passed an Act known as the Bihar State Acquisition of Zamindari Bill, 1947.

When the Congress assumed the reins of office in 1939, substantial reforms in tenancy were effected. The first popular ministry had aroused great expectations at the time of installation. There were kisan agitations. There was even a mammoth kisan march to Patna, the capital of the State. Naturally, the powers that be, could not remain indifferent to the burning issue of the day. As a result, the Bihar Tenancy Amendment Acts of 1937 and 1938 were passed to give a quietus to the kisan unrest. These Acts cancelled all enhancements of rents made during the years of 1911-1936. Rents were reduced to 25% generally in proportion to the fall in prices in the same period. There was a provision for the total or partial remission of rents where the soil had deteriorated as a consequence of sand deposits or for other reasons. The Act of 1938 went further and abolished the system of kind rents, prohibited rent enhancements during the next 15 years, withdrew the Zamindar's right to claim damages against rent arrears to 6.25% and conferred hereditary rights on such tenants as had occupied lands for 12 years and provided against their eviction.

Thereafter, the Bihar Tenancy Amendment Acts of 1946, 1947, 1948, 1950 and 1958 have been passed. The uniform object of these amendments has been to bend the provisions of the Bihar Tenancy Act of 1885 in favour of the kisans. The Amendement Act of 1946 inserted a new section, 178 C, which provided that where rent, in occupancy holding was payable in kind by division of produce, the landlord shall not be entitled to a share in the straw or *Bhoosa* as rent out of the produce of that holding. These provisions were made applicable to any suits or appeals pending for recovery of arrears of rent on the date the Act came into force. The Amendment Act XIV of 1946 amended Section 40 of the Bihar Tenancy Act of 1885 relating to the computation of rent payable in kind by an occupancy ryot. It provided that the officer should determine the computed rent, having regard to the average value of rent actually received by the landlord during the five years before the first day of Aswin, 1347 Fasali year.

The Amending Act XXII of 1947 amended several sections of

the Bihar Tenancy Act of 1885. The main changes introduced in the Act were: *Firstly*, one new section 21A was inserted regarding the settlement of the Bakasht lands. The *'Bakasht'* land means any land other than the proprietor's private lands as defined in Section 120 of the Bihar Tenancy Act, 1885, which is for the time being in the cultivating possession of a proprietor. *Secondly*, it provided that every person whether he is a settled raiyat of a village or not is entitled to the money rent calculated for the entire holding is reduced in the same proportion as the area of the land held by the under-raiyat bears to the total area of the holding. In case of produce rent, the landlord is not entitled to recover rent from the under-raiyat exceeding 7/20th of the produce. The landlord is also not entitled to any share in the straw or Bhoosa as rent out of the produce of such land. A protected tenant (i.e. a tenant who is a member of the scheduled castes, scheduled tribes and backward classes) cannot transfer his rights in his tenure, holding or tenancy by private sale, gift, will, mortgage, lease or any contract or agreement to persons who are not members of scheduled castes, scheduled tribes or backward classes, except by an application to the Collector in certain cases. The Collectors have been given the power to set aside improper transfers by tenure holders, raiyats or under-raiyats.

In the present century the simmerings of peasants discontent in Bihar found their first effective expression in the Champaran movement led by Mohandas Karamchand Gandhi in 1917 against the indigo planters. The kisans offered satyagraha against oppressions of white planters who, with the support and at the connivance of district and other local authorities, compelled the peasants to plant indigo and paid a very low price for it. The Champaran Satyagrah not only led to the withdrawal of white indigo planters from Champaran but also paved the way for their departure from other parts of Bihar. The movement brought forward some kisan leaders in other districts. They launched agitations for wresting concessions from the local landlords who behaved almost in the same manner as the white sahibs. One such case was that of Swami Vidyanand who in 1919-20 organised protest movement against the oppressions of the Darbhanga Raj and its amlas. He claimed to be Gandhi's disciple and seems to have felt the impact of Gandhi on Champaran.

In order to mollify the peasants and give them some relief, several attempts were made in the Bihar Legislative Council in 1920, to introduce Tenancy Amendement Bills. But since the Council was largely dominated by the Zamindars they could not be passed. So effective was the domination of the Zamindars that under their influence in 1929 the Bihar Home Secretary Sifton (who later became the Governor of the province) introduced a bill, detrimental to the interests of the tenants. This brought to the fore the urgency of setting up an organisation of the peasants and subsequently led to the establishment of the Bihar Kisan Sabha in 1929. Another factor which prepared the ground for the establishment of the Sabha was the whirlwind tour of Sardar Vallabhbhai Patel who in his public meetings always spoke about the conditions of the kisans and repeatedly narrated the story of the Bardoli Struggle of 1928. Not the least important was the third factor. The coming of the great depression which made the kisans realise the necessity of coming together to fight the onslaught of the Zamindars and apathy of the Government. Accordingly, in November 1929, at the Sonepur Mela—one of the largest cattle fair in Asia—where the kisans congregate annually in huge numbers, the Bihar Provincial Kisan Sabha was set up with Swami Sahajanand Saraswati as its President and Shree Krishna Sinha (who became the premier of Bihar in 1937) as its secretary. Rajendra Prasad and almost all the leading Congressmen of Bihar became its members. The Kisan Sabha offered vigorous opposition to Sifton's bill for which it held a meeting in January, 1930. So strong was its resistance that Sifton withdrew the bill from the Council on this ground. Thus for the first time the Government recognised not only the existence of the Sabha but also the indispensability of its support in matters of tenancy.

Since the members of the Bihar Kisan Sabha and the Congress happened to be the same, the Kisan Sabha could not function actively for two years on account of the Civil Disobedience Movement. Meanwhile, taking advantage of this situation and government repression against Congressmen, the Zamindars set up an organisation called United Party towards the end of 1932, and tried to recruit the kisans in it, but the game failed, and by the beginning of 1933, the Kisan Sabha again came to the forefront. To protect the interests of the Zamindars and to give some semblance of relief to the kisans, a bill was drawn up under the inspiration of Shyamanandan Sahay, a shrewd leader of the Zamindars (Baghi estate) from Muzaffarpur. In order to secure the seal of approval from the kisans a meeting of the so-called Bihar Provincial Kisan Sabha, which was hastily set up as a paper body and presumably as parallel to the one, already established in 1929, was organised on January 15, 1935. Although the Zamindars, at this meeting, were represented by the Raja of Surajpur who was a highly educated Zamindar and Dr. Sachidanand Sinha, an England-educated Zamindar of Victorian taste who became the first President of the Constituent Assembly of India, their tactics did not work because of the sudden appearance of Swami Sahajanand Saraswati who exposed the farcical character of this meeting.

The Bihar Provincial Kisan Sabha set up in 1929 continued to be the only state body of the kisans. It organised a conference of the kisans on March 22, 1933 which attacked the so-called agreement between the kisans and the Zamindars regarding the Bill of 1933. But inspite of the Kisans Sabha's opposition, the bill introduced in 1933 was passed in September 1934. Because of the Zamindar's dominance in the Council the kisans lobby could mobilise only 12 votes in favour of the reduction of rent which was opposed by 51 members.

But the kisan movement did not abate. The redoubtable Swami undertook a whirlwind tour in the state, and once the bill came on the anvil, hundreds of meetings were held between 1933 and 1935 against the bill which later became an Act, and in these meetings the grievances of the kisans and the oppressions of the Zamindars were highlighted. The intensity of the movement can be gauged from the fact that some 500 meetings were held in 10 districts only. Out of these, three provincial kisan conferences were held in 1933, 1934 and 1935 in Bihta (Patna), Gaya and Hajipur. Apart from these, other conferences and meetings were organised. They numbered 117 in 1933, 109 in 1934 and 20 in 1935. All these were attended by

Sahajanand, the President of the Provincial Kisan Sabha himself. There were atleast other 150 meetings in which Sahajanand could not go but were attended by other leaders of the Sabha. At all these meetings the kisans came in thousands. If one makes a rough calculation of the meetings held, then on an average one meeting took place everyday for about two and a half years till November 1935, all over the province. This in itself was a record for the whole of India.

Some of these meetings were largely attended and it estimated that between 60,000 and 1,00,000 kisans demonstrated before the Collector of Gaya on September 20, 1933, at the instance of Swami Sahajanand demanding reduction in rent. All these meetings and demonstrations demanded the cancellation of the arrears of rent and the reduction of rent by half. The Kisan Sabha also instituted several enquiries into the conditions of the kisans. A committee consisting of Jamuna Karjee, Sahajanand, Jugul Kishore Singh and Jadunandan Sharma was set up to enquire into the conditions of the Kisans in Gaya district. They visited hundreds of villages in twenty zamindaries and prepared a long report, the gist of which was published in 80 pages and was called *'Gaya ke kisanon ki karoon Kahani'* that is, *"Pitiable story of the Gaya kisans"*. The Enquiry revealed that fortyfive types of illegal exactions were made by the Zamindars. A similar exercise was undertaken by Rambriksha Benipuri with regard to Masaurhi Pargana in Patna district. Benipuri prepared a long list of illegal collections in connection with rent in cash and produce and various kinds of begar or forced labour. Again, the Bihar Provincial Kisan Sabha set up several enquiry committees to probe into the conditions of the kisans affected by the earthquake of January 15, 1934 which not only destroyed houses but also rendered a good portion of cultivable land useless by causing fissures and by covering fields with sand. A committee consisting of Rambriksha Benipuri, Kishori Prasanna Singh and Awadheshwar Prasad Singh enquired into the conditions in Muzaffarpur district which was one of the worst earthquake hit areas.

From the Report of the Bihar Provincial Kisan Sabha for

November 1929—November 1935, published by its secretary Awadheshwar Prasad Singh, who was graduate and a rich peasant, it is clear that in the early 1930s the Kisan Sabha tried its best to make up with the Zamindars and to wrest as much concessions from them as possible on the basis of goodwill and understanding. They did not doubt the good intentions of the Zamindars and thought that if the fact was brought to their notice they would act for their tenants. Therefore, whatever reforms the Kisan Sabha wanted to introduce, was within the framework of the Zamindari system. Their attempts to carry out this policy met with repeated failures. In regard to the tenancy bill of 1933 Swami Sahajanand suggested to the Raja of Surajpura, the Secretary of the United Party representing the Zamindars, that a committee of ten, consisting of five representatives each of the United Party and of the Kisan Sabha be authorised to take the final decision about the contents of the bill and this decision be binding on everybody. But the Raja and the other Zamindars did not accept it and the kisans received a rebuff. In the same connection Rajendra Prasad wrote to the Maharaja of Darbhanga: "The real difficulty, as I apprehended in bringing about better relations, is that the Zamindars do not seem prepared to recognise any organisation like the Kisan Sabha as representing the kisans and insist upon their nominees representing them". Again, Swami Sahajanand placed before the Raja of Amawan, his own casteman, a long list of the grievances of the kisans in the 60 villages of his Zamindari which he himself had enquired into, and wrote to him for taking appropriate action. He also talked to the Raja in the presence of his manager for three hours but nothing turned out to be fruitful.

The Government's apathy was not less deplorable. When in September 1933, nearly 60,000 to 1,00,000 kisans congregated before the Collector of Gaya demanding rent reduction, the Superintendent of Police in consultation with the Collector wrote to the Swami: "The rent is a matter between the landlord and the raiyat and the Collector could not possibly give the tenant any relief." What was worse, the Swami and other kisan leaders, under Section 144, were prohibited from speaking. The Swami did not break the law, because he apprehended that the kisans would be unduly provoked and the situation would go out of control. Since then there were numerous occasions till November 1935, when Sahajanand and other prominent kisan leaders were not allowed to speak.

The bitter experience in dealing with Zamindars and the Government made the kisan leaders rethink their position. On June 10, 1934 the Provincial Kisan Council defined the Fundamental Rights of the kisans, pointed out the weakness of Tenancy Laws in this light and declared that those laws which were not framed on the basis of these rights would not be acceptable to the kisans. The Fundamental Rights clearly stated that the actual tiller was the owner of the land. But for a good part of 1935 the Bihar Provincial Kisan Council did not ask for the abolition of the Zamindari System. This was because the provincial leadership was not sufficiently radicalised, and Sahajanand thought that if such a demand was made a good number of kisan workers who were Congressmen, would leave the Sabha and consequently would weaken it. He also thought that the Sabha had not acquired sufficient strength to enforce such a demand for ending the Zamindari System and expressed their dissatisfaction with the policy of the provincial leadership. For example, it was stated by the President of the third Muzaffarpur District Kisan Sabha Conference in October, 1935 that the Kisan Sabha was dominated by Congressmen and would continue to be so for some time. But he reminded his audience that this 'leadership from above' would not last long and that the kisans themselves would provide leadership which would completely identify itself with the kisan cause. This point was also emphasized by the Secretary, Bihar Provincial Kisan Sabha, who stated in November 1935 that the time will come when the leadership of the Kisan Movement would pass into the hands of the kisans which was always and under all circumstances desirable. In fact, already towards the end of 1935, District Kisan conferences had started asking for the abolition of the Zamindari System. Speaking at the Monghyr District Kisan Conference, Devbrata Shastri, editor of a Congress Hindi weekly called *Navashkti*, declared that unless the kisans of India were liberated from the clutches of the Zamindari System their real progress and welfare could not be achieved. From a similar position, Benipuri, another journalist and Hindi writer, asked for the abolition of the system. Since the Provincial Kisan Sabha had not said anything about the Zamindari System till then, the district conferences of Muzaffarpur, Patna, Gaya and Shahabad clearly recommended to the Provincial Sabha that the fundamental rights of the kisan should have no place for the existence of any exploiting class between the Government and the kisans.

The Bihar Provincial Kisan Sabha and its undisputed leader Swami Sahajanand could not ignore the resolution passed at the District Kisan Conferences for long. The leaders, including Sahajanand, were convinced that not much could be done to help the kisans within the framework of the Zamindari System. Towards the end of 1935, Sahajanand came to realise that "even a Zamindar made of clay would be as dangerous" as a living Zamindar. Therefore, in his presidential address delivered at the third session of the Provincial Kisan Sabha Conference at Hajipur in November, 1935, he invited his comrades to speak on the abolition of this system openly, although he himself did not try to impose his own view on them.

By the end of 1935, the Kisan Sabha also began to define its attitude toward political questions. It condemned the Act of 1935 as out and out reactionary act for it ignored the fundamental right of the Indians to self-determination. The Kisan Sabha called it a device to exploit the kisan and other poorer sections on the part of the British imperialism in collaboration with Zamindars and other classes which stood for the perpetuation of vested interests. The Sabha opposed the provision which enfranchised only propertied people and demanded adult suffrage. It may be added that according to the Act of 1935 only 11% of people were given the right to vote. Further it opposed the legislative assembly on the ground that it was an instrument to prevent the voice of the people from being heard and to consolidate the rights of the rich. This resolution of the Bihar Provincial Kisan Sabha was reiterated in numerous conferences of the kisans.

Once the resolution demanding the abolition of the Zamindari

System was passed in November, 1935, from 1936 onwards there was a marked change in the character of the Kisan Sabha. It started taking a militant posture and all talks of compromise that characterised its stance vis-a-vis the Zamindars earlier were now given up. The Kisan Sabha manifesto of 1936, stated very specifically that "if the Congress wishes to serve at the same time the interests of other classes, it may do so. But it may never do this at the cost of the interest of the starving millions of the peasantry". This can be attributed to several factors.

The objective for the rise of militancy in the Kisan Sabha in Bihar were created by a series of natural calamities. While nothing tangible had been done to remove the sufferings of the kisans on account of the great depression, the earthquake of January 15, 1934 added further to their miseries. The little relief given by the Congress or money advanced by the Government were cornered, in many cases, by the *amlas* of the Zamindars who were in no case prepared to forgo their rents. The earthquake was followed in quick succession by the devastating floods of 1934 and 1935 in North Bihar. All these factors combined to create an intolerable situation from which the kisans found it difficult to retrieve themselves by making petitions and applications.

In the context of the country as a whole the emergence of Jawaharlal Nehru as Congress President on the national scene played an important role in moulding the character of the Kisan Sabha. It was under his influence that in 1931 at the Karachi session of the Congress an "Economic programme" was adopted. There is no doubt that in the context of those days the programme represented was a radical trend. The demand included the reform of the system of land tenure, revenue and rent. The burden on agricultural land was to be equally adjusted; small peasants were to be given immediate relief by substantial reduction of rent and revenue paid by them, and a graded tax on net income from land above reasonable limit was to be imposed. There was also a promise of 'relief from agricultural indebtedness and control of usury—direct and indirect". It also asked for labour to be freed from serfdom or conditions bordering on serdom. Its last and the most important item was that it recognised the right of 'peasants and workers to form unions to protect their interest.'

In 1936, when Jawaharlal Nehru replaced the conservative Rajendra Prasad as Congress President, he openly talked of social justice in the Lucknow session of the Congress in April 1936 and declared that socialism was the panacea for all the ills of the country. He reiterated his position in the Faizpur Congress in December 1936.

More radical demands were put forward by the Congress Socialists. When the Civil Disobedience Movement was finally buried in the Patna meeting of the All India Congress Committee there were two types of reaction. The official Congress leadership began to talk of accepting office, while the radical Congressmen who stood for continued fight against colonialism, set up an organisation called the Congress Socialist Party. Their economic programme was definitely far more radical than that of the Karachi Congress. Amongst other demands, which are mentioned above, those which were most radical were—Transfer of all power to the producing masses . . . Elimination of princes and landlords and all other classes of exploiters without compensation; redistribution of land to peasant; encouragement and promotion of co-operative and collective farming by the state, etc."

The economic programme of the Congress and the Congress Socialists served as an eye-opener to the Kisan Sabha leaders. What is more important is that in 1934-35 Congress Socialist leaders joined the Kisan Sabha in good numbers and by the end of 1935 they made their voice heard. Their economic demands could in no way be achieved within the framework of the Zamindari System. There was a fundamental contradiction between the interest of the Zamindars and those of the peasants.

Together with these two factors the acceptance of the programme of the United Front by the Communists in 1936 acted as a catalyst in sharpening the Kisan Sabha's thinking. Hitherto the Communists were cut off from the mainstream of the national movement and were mainly engaged in organising the workers. Now with the coming up of the United Front they decided to work with Congress Socialist Party and other parties for organising peasants and industrial labourers. As the Communist Party was banned by the Government, its members had no option other than to accommodate themselves into the existing parties and organisations. Though there was hardly any large-scale Communist entry into the Bihar Provincial Kisan Sabha in 1936, individual Communists in some pockets such as Monghyr district worked in the Kisan Movement.

What further made 1936 important in the history of the peasant movement was the establishment of the All-India Kisan Sabha and its first session in April 1936, at Lucknow on the occasion of the Congress session presided over by Jawaharlal Nehru. The Sabha brought together the leftists and Kisan workers of Bihar, U.P., Andhra, Gujarat, Maharashtra and other parts of the country on the same platform and under the influence of the Kisan Sabha Conference, the Lucknow Congress asked the Provincial Congress Committees to look into the grievances of the kisans and to submit the reports of their Enquiry Committees to the All-India Congress Committee.

Any movement acquires militancy in stages. It starts with a very mild form of protest and indirect methods of struggle. If these fail to create any impact on the establishment then the movement becomes militant. An important factor in this process is the experience which the struggling people undergo. Failure of the earlier forms of protest serves as an experience to take to more militant forms. The same was the case with the Kisan Sabha. As stated earlier, the Kisan Sabha in the beginning had explored all possible avenues of compromise with the Zamindars. It also harboured the illusion that by doing so they could bring about a peaceful co-existence of the two. But with the failure of such efforts they understood the real character of the Zamindari System and turned to be its bitter critics.

There are some commendable works related with the Bihar Kisan Sabha and land problems of the State. Among them the work of Walter Hauser, entitled *the Bihar Provincial Kisan Sabha, 1929-1942 : A Study of Indian Peasant Movement* is a substantial one. This work contains five major chapters dealing with the condition of the land system of Bihar, organisation of Bihar Provincial Kisan Sabha, nature of the peasant unrest, national politics and the decay of the Bihar Kisan Sabha.

Walter Hauser, in his thesis has discussed the land system,

relation between the Zamindars and the peasants, the issues of Bakasht land and rent, the condition of the Bihar Kisan Sabha, its connection with the Non-cooperation Movment, land policy of the Bihar Government, rise of the Kisan movement, nature and development of the Kisan movement and its organisation, method and ideology' etc. In addition to these aspects, he has also dealt with the subjects such as the work of the Congress for the Bihar Provincial Kisan Sabha, attitude of the right wing towards the Bihar Kisan Sabha, effect of the election of 1937 on the Bihar Provincial Kisan Sabha, compromise and controversy, protest to compromise and the people's war etc. However, he got his own limitations in dealing with the subject honestly without being influenced by his social and political premises. In fact' the basic force of the peasant struggle in Bihar did not depend on the appeal of the ruling class under the leadership of the Congress Party and its nationalist feeling. It was based on the basic peasant unrest and its well-knit organisation. All the big talks in respect of the redressal of the demands of the peasants through hurriedly cooked up land legislation became fruitless when the formidable famine of 1943 broke out and no foodgrain could reach the real starving class in rural areas of Bihar and Bengal. Later the spirit of the peasant struggle did not end, but on the contrary, it advanced further with its enhanced vigour and reinforced organisational strength in different parts of the country. These points have been neglected by Walter Hauser. He has maintained a mystic silence over the tortuous roles of the landed gentry and the elite leaders of the period under review (1937-52). He has not only exposed the self-surrender-attitude of the so-called socialists before Gandhian philosophy, but he has also exaggerated their role in society.

Work of D. Thakur, entitled *Politics of Land Reform in India with Special Reference to Bihar*, of Rakesh Gupta, entitled *Bihar Peasantry and the Kisan Sabha* (1937-47), of Jagannath Mishra, entitled *Land Reforms in Bihar*, have dealt with issues of popular struggle of the peasants in Bihar and none of them has gone indepth into detailed discussion of the land policy of the Government of Bihar. Dr. Rajendra Prasad's papers edited by Valmiki Choudhary and large number of private papers of the

Darbhanga Raj have not been examined thoroughly in connection with the Bihar peasantry and the land policy of the Bihar Government.

The Second World War broke out in 1939. The Congress ministry resigned. A serious split took place in the Bihar Provincial Kisan Sabha. Among these events of importance no step was taken for the abolition of the Zamindari System. It became possible only when the Congress Party formed the Ministry in 1946. The Congress Party in its Election Manifesto, issued in December 1945, was specifically declared its view on the question of the abolition of intermediaries between the State and the actual tillers of the land. Main features of the Bihar Land Reforms Act, 1950 (A comparative study) may be perused for a detailed knowledge of the subject. Equally interesting is the study of the Land Reforms Act of 1950 which dealt with the issue of the abolition of landed intermediaries, although it did not touch the problems of the relations between the tenants and the landlords. Very accurately it has been mentioned that the Zamindar is dead, but long live the Zamindar in the new set up with a changed nomenclature (the Mukhia, the Sarpanch, the Mantri of the Samiti, etc.).

Notes & References

Klonov, V., quoted in *European Conference on Rural Life* (1939), Document No. 1 (League of Nations), p. 53.

Report of the Royal Commission on Agriculture in India (Linlithgow Commission), p. 433.

Voeleker, I.A., *"Report on the Improvement of Indian Agriculture"*. p. 10; R.C. Dutt, *"Economic History of India During Victorian Age."* (6th ed.) London, 1906, pp. 277-78.

First Five-year Plan; pp. 199-202; *Agricultural Legislation in India*, Vol. II.; *Consolidation of Holdings*, 1950, p. I.

Report of the Royal Commission on Agriculture.

Mukherjee, R.K., (ed.), *Economic Problems of India*. Vol I, 1940, Calcutta, pp. 110-111.

"Report of the Royal Commission on Agriculture 1928", pp. 130-144.

Singh, Indradeep, *"Maxism and the Peasantry"*, New Delhi 1982, p. 63.

Chotanagpur Tenancy Act, 1908 (Bengal Act of 1908) (As modified upto the 15th Nov. 1965), Patna, 1966.

Lorenzo, A.H., *"Agricultural Conditions in Northern India"*, 1948.

"*Agricultural Wages in India.*" Vol. I, 1966, New Delhi : Ministry of Food and Agriculture, 1966 Vol. 1.

"*Agricultural Labour Enquiry Committee*" New Delhi : Ministry of Food & Agriculture, Vol. I, p. 45.

U.N.O. : "*Land Reforms—Defects in Agrarian Structure as Obstacles to Economic Development*". 1951, p. 5.

Ph. D. Thesis, University of Chicago, 1961 (A Xerox copy of this thesis is available in the Library of A.N. Sinha Institute of Social Studies, Patna).

Mishra, Jagannath (ed.), "*Land Reforms in Bihar*", Patna, 1974, pp. 77-103.

CHAPTER 2

LAND SYSTEM AND THE NEED FOR A CHANGE

It is said that India lives in her villages. This is very true for Bihar, where over 82 per cent of the population lives in rural areas and depends on agriculture for its livelihood. The Gangetic plain of Bihar, particularly North Bihar, forms one of the richest and most fertile agricultural tracts in India and produces a great variety of crops. The Chotanagpur plateau, on the other hand, is a region of irregular surface and poor soil and is agriculturally far less productive than the plains.

Before presenting an analytical survey and observation of the land-system and the need for a change, it is essential to know about the geographical position of Bihar as well as the historical account with the importance of land.

Geographical Position of Bihar

The State of Bihar, situated between 21°.58′ 10″ and 27°.31′ 15″ north latitudes and 83° 19′ 50″ to 88° 17′ 40″ east longitudes with a population of 6,79,67,000 came under the British domination as a result of the battles of Plassey (1757) and Buxar (1764), though the British had already started trading in India about a century back. It remained a part of the Bengal Presidency upto April 11, 1912 when alongwith Orissa it was separated from Bengal, eventually Orissa too was separated from Bihar (1936-37) and some Bengali speaking areas of the district of Purnea and Manbhum were lost to West Bengal as a result of the States reorganisation in 1956.

Bihar covers a total area of 0.173 .9 and 6,99,14,173 of population of the country and the density of population per Sq.Km. is 402 whereas India's area in Sq.Km. is 3,287.3, its population is 68,51,84,692 and the density of population per Sq.Km. is 216.

The study is concerned with the rural problems, it is needed to emphasize the numbers of the villages from 1901 to 1961.

The following statement gives the number of inhabited villages as reported at successive censuses since 1901 :—

Number of Inhabited Villages : 1901-1961

St/Divi/Dist.	*Number of inhabited villages*						
	1961	*1951*	*1941*	*1931*	*1921*	*1911*	*1901*
1	*2*	*3*	*4*	*5*	*6*	*7*	*8*
Bihar (I)	**67,665**	**68,150**	**66,528**	**65,299**	**66,763**	**68,828**	**73,618**
Patna Division	13,328	13,119	12,980	13,103	13,054	13,211	18,338
Patna	2,335	2,288	2,260	2,315	2,319	2,342	4,952
Gaya	6,236	6,102	5,991	6,058	6,031	6,187	7,871
Shahabad	4,757	4,729	4,729	4,735	4,704	4,682	5,515
Tirhut Division	14,557	14,087	14,107	14,047	14,160	14,338	15,831
Saram	4,425	4,285	4,259	4,305	4,341	4,320	5,855
Champaran	2,642	2,622	2,612	2,548	2,554	2,651	2,623
Mazaffarpur	4,147	4,171	4,120	4,059	4,088	4,220	4,120
Darbhanga	3,143	3,009	3,107	3,135	3,177	3,147	3,233
Bhagalpur Division	20,903	21,984	20,445	19,287	20,207	18,977	17,378
Monghyr	3,464	3,073	3,311	2,610	2,768	2,530	2,516
Bhagalpur	2,489	2,291	2,224	1,955	2,564	2,468	3,063
Saharsa (2)	1,195	1,268	1,112	1,125	1,265	1,070	3,063
Purnea (3)	3,687	3,830	3,540	3,437	3,454	3,324	2,632
Santhal Pargna	10,068	11,522	10,258	10,160	10,156	9,585	9,167

1	2	3	4	5	6	7	8
Chotanagpur Divison	19,077	18,960	18,996	18,857	19,342	22,302	22,071
Palamau	3,194	320	3,110	3,134	3,120	3,101	3,184
Hazaribagh	6,162	6,129,	6,066	6,087	6,168,	8,399	8,848
Ranchi (4)	3,858	3,891	3,858	3,799	3,837	3,886	3,134
Dhanbad (5)	1,462	1,505	1,566	1,657	1,823	2,016	2,016
Singhbhum (6)	4,401	4,233	4,396	4,180	4,394	4,900	2,016

Source : *Census of India 1961* Vol. V. Bihar Part II-A General Publication Table.

The total number of villages inhabited or otherwise, is fixed. However, a certain amount of variation in the number of inhabited villages is possible because some may get deserted or denuded (e.g., by repairing action) while some others may become inhabited. However, it would be wrong to attribute all the variations in the above table to these causes only. In fact, the main cause as noted in the Census Report of 1931 as well as of 1951, is the failure of the local staff to adhere strictly to the definition of villages and their proneness to treat the larger hamlets as independent villages.

The total number of inhabited villages in Bihar, according to the 1961 figure is 67,665. It is less than the corresponding figure of 1951 by 485. With the growth of population one would normally expect an increase in the number of inhabited villages, from one census to another assuming, of course,

(i) that the definition of "village" has been strictly adhered to, and
(ii) that the loss in the number of inhabited villages due to natural calamities or other reasons has not been considerable.

A mere glance at the district figures would confirm this view generally, except in cases of Muzaffarpur, Saharsa, Purnea, Santhal Parganas, Palamau, Ranchi and Dhanbad. In Muzaffarpur and Palamau the difference is so small that it needs no explanation. In Saharsa, the decrease may be due to a considerable number of inhabited villages having fallen within the Kosi embankment and become depopulated. In Purnea, Santhal Pargana and Ranchi, the 1961 figures agree more closely with the figures of all other censuses except 1951, and it may be inferred that the big spurt in 1951 was perhaps due to a not-too-strict application of the definition of "villages." The decrease in the case of Dhanbad is explained by the fact that as many as 30 mauzas treated as rural in 1951 have been included in urban area.

A statement showing villages and towns in the State in 1961,

(1) the total number of mauzas borne on the Jurisdiction lists;
(2) the number of mauzas, *(a)* uninhabited, and *(b)* inhabited;
(3) the number of mauzas included in towns, *(a)* fully, and *(b)* partly; and
(4) the number of towns, is given below :—

Table 2.1
Villages and Towns in 1961

State/ District	*Total No. of mauzas borne or the thana Jurisdiction List*	*No. of mauzas uninhabited/ inhabited*		*Number of mauzas included in fully/Partly*		*Number of Towns*	*Total of columns 3.4.8.5*	*Difference*
1	2	3	4	5	6	7	8	9
Bihar	79,039	10,428	67,665	887	160	153	78,980	–59

Importance of Land

First of all it is necessary to throw light on the importance of the land. Many social philosophers have pointed out that the land is not created by man's efforts, yet it is the primary source of his existence. The importance of land lies in the fact, that it provides food, drink, cloth and other basic necessities, without which neither life nor civilisation is possible. It is evident says *"Van Der Post"* that society is dependent upon agriculture for its food and raw materials, for its clothing.

Due to its basic utility, all economists have been inclined to treat land as a special kind of property.

Land possesses many distinctive features. It is almost the only asset that improve with use. Shells, guns and battleships are rapidly wasting assets and so are minerals, factories and all kinds of machinery, but land is there still—the better and more valuable by sensible use. Unlike other terms of capital it is not evanescent or subject to wear and tear or depreciation, and therefore, need not be renewed or replaced.

"The relative inexhaustibility of the land", says Dr. Hsiao Tung Fei, "gives the people a relative security. Although there are bad years, the land never disillusions the people completely, since hope for plenty in the future always remains and is not infrequently realised. If we take the other kinds of productive work, we shall see that the risk involved is much greater".

The incentive to hold land is directly related to the sense of security. The following statement is very appropriately made by a villager about the land—"Land is there. You can see it everyday. Robbers cannot take it away. Thieves cannot steal it. Men die but land remains. "He again says, "the best thing to give one's son is land". It is a living property. Money will be used up but land never.

All Land Belongs to Gopal

Real Socialism has been handed down to us by our ancestors who taught "All land belongs to Gopal". This new slogan was given by Gandhiji. Gopal literally means shepherds. It also means God. In modern language it means the State i.e. the people. Similar was the theme of Rousseau's "Social contract. But unfortunately the land today does not belong to people is very much true.

The land was the main source of revenue in Bihar. In fully settled areas, revenue was raised directly from land. Therefore, it is requisite to analyse the land system, its tenure, revenue system, which was prevalent in Bihar.

Land System in different period

In ancient India, we get some clue of the land-taxation

referred to in the *'Dharma-Sutra'*. Kautilya in his *Arthasastra* has significantly pointed out that a king should always try to extend the area of his possession to his land and he should be inspired by the motto of *"Charuntam Mahim Jayet"* i.e. I shall conquer on all sides. Extension of possession over land has therefore been the kernel alongwith all political activities revealed in all ages in India. But Kautilya also pointed that mere possession or extension of possession over land would not serve the land, unless the land is properly cultivated, harvested and managed for the benefits of the people. He, therefore, detailed out three bases on which the land should be divided—its possession, control and its utility and guarantee for the benefit of the people. Needless to say that the rise and fall of Kingdom in India largely depended on the use or misuse of land. A ruler who successfully managed and controlled his land policy insured the stability of his dynasty. Who can deny that the stable economy of the Mauryas, Guptas, Vardhan dynasties as also of the Cholas largely depended on the sound management of land.

Before the Mughal times, we find Ala-ud-din (AD 1294-1315) imposing a half produce tax or *khiraj*. The unique position that Shershah occupied in the annals of Indian history was due to his reforming zeal in land management system. Keene has therefore rightly said: "No government showed so much wisdom as this pathan in the field of land management."

But the practically useful history of land revenue begins with the reign of Akbar. The central feature of the Akbarian settlement was the commutation of the grain share into a money payment. That method of grain division was employed, either between the native Raja and his subjects or between landlords and tenants, as in Bihar.

It may be concluded that during the rule of the Great Mughals, Indian ryots had enjoyed certain customary rights in the possession of lands. They could not be evicted from their holding by the Zamindars provided their dues were regularly paid. Besides, arbitrary fixation of the rents by the Zamindars was not possible, both rents and abwabs being guided by usual Jumma tumar.

Thus, the reign of Shershah and Akbar is remembered as far as land tenures are concerned. They did a lot for the well-being of the tenancy. Even a Farman of Aurangzeb, issued in the ninth year of his reign enjoins upon the sadar Kanungo's of Bihar the duty of ensuring the welfare of the ryots and warns them against committing a single act of opperession.

Under the later Mughals, their position seems to have deteriorated somewhat. The main cause of this deterioration was the imposition by the nawabs of a number of abwabs on the Zamindars. Mir Qasim during his short term of nawabship, aimed at thorough overhauling of the whole structure of the revenue administration.

Among other things, he also made it a settled policy to reduce the power of the Zamindars, who freely tyrannized and Amils and tahsildars were appointed in their place. The Zamindars at Monghyr were practically all imprisoned. Therefore during the Mughal period, the Zamindars were no better than tax collectors. The land actually belonged to the tiller of the soil.

The British came to upset all this. The East India Company took the Diwani of Bengal, Bihar and Orissa in 1765. It considered to recognise or confer a proprietory right in the lands and consequently to hand over to the proprietors, so recognised, the produce or money-rates paid by the non-proprietory cultivators; rates which would formally have been directly taken by the king's agents. The old customary revenue rates (with such local alterations as time and circumstances had brought about), thus becames the rents which proprietors got.

The right in the land was called "thhat" and the proprietors "thhatwan" : the term Zamindar has no meaning except its literal one—"anyone connected with land." Hence their early administrators recognised the Taluqdars as the prototypes of English landlords to subserve their political ends. But when they found that these Taluqdars were also undependable, Lord Dalhousie decreed that "the settlement should be made village by village with the parties actually in possession but without any recognition, either formal or informal, of their proprietory right so as to deal with the actual occupants of the soil."

The grant of Diwani to the East India Company did not improve at once the position either of the Zamindars or the tenants. In some cases the Zamindars were over assessed. To give but one instance, within two years of the Diwani grant, Suchet Ram, Amil at Purnea, was made to pay twentyfive lakhs of rupees from his district. This unusually heavy amount realised from the Zamindars drove them to exceed all limits of moderation in making their collections from the ryots.

At this time Bengal faced the deadliest famine. Considerable areas of Bihar, such as Purnea, Bhagalpur, Rajmahal, Darbhanga, Panchet, Patna and Gaya were victims of the terrible calamity. But no mercy was shown by the company's servants to the utterly destitute peasants, so much so that they were obliged to sell even their seeds requisite to the next harvest.

Then, again the ryots were required to provide supplies of grain for the military and Pargana sepoys. Alexander, supervisor of Bihar and Ducarel, supervisor of Purnea, strongly disapproved the way grain was exacted from the famished population.

The effect of the famine on the cultivation was simply devastating. In four pargana's of Purnea there was no harvest at all. Harwood reported that in Bhagalpur, the land did not return even half the usual produce of the year. The same was the condition of things in Darbhanga and Champaran.

With the arrival of Warren Hastings some measures were taken for the security of the farmers called as 'amilnama', for five years. Hastings proposed that the revenue should be farmed out to persons, preferably Zamindars, for life. For the protection of the ryots' interests, he said that, while he paid his rent, the Zamindars had no right to dispossess him, nor could the latter extract higher rent than the patta prescribed.

But this five year farming system proved thoroughly unsatisfactory settlement. Apart from the fact that under this farming system the ryots of Bihar were generally subjected to heavy rent payments. They had no freedom in the matter of cutting the crops. According to Brook this was followed more or less throughout Bihar, but more particularly in Shahabad. The defaulting ryots were put into the custody at the pleasure of the Zamindars or farmers.

Emergence of Permanent Settlement

On the failure of this system of annual farming, the 'Decennial Settlement' instituted by Lord Cornwallis in 1789, was completed in 1791 and was made permanent in 1793. It was introduced in Patna, Tirhut, Bhagalpur Sub-divisions, part of Hazaribagh, Manbhum districts and a few estates in Singhbhum and Ranchi and the Chotanagpur Sub-division in Bihar. The principle on which permanent settlement was based, was of two-fold the security of the government revenues and the security and protection of the subjects. It transformed the rural society because it created proprietory rights for the Zamindars and the ryots were placed at the mercy of the farmer.

Although Dr. Ranjit Guha, has tried to show that the permanent settlement was the outcome of the influence of French thinking on the British administrators at that time, yet from a careful perusal of the Bhagalpur documents it seems that the practical difficulties of the company in collecting revenue led to the introduction of permanent settlement.

Thus, the main purpose for its introduction was that the Company wanted a fixed amount without any botheration of accounting and collection. The Permanent Settlement gave the East India Company a fixed amount but no protection to the tenants. Now millions of tenants were placed at the mercy of the newly oriented class of Landlords.

Lord Lawrence described the proposal of Permanent Settlement as a step to improve the material condition of the people, to encourage the investment of money in the land, to promote the growth of a middle class in India and to stimulate the accumulation of capital and resource which would help the people in times of difficulties, droughts and distress. The above statement of Lawrence was true only in theory, not in practice. Whatever might be the justification for the Permanent Settlement in the context of the then socio-political situation, it bore a bitter fruit which destroyed the age old system of land management. The system created a host of irresponsible Zamindars and a second line of exploitators in the form of middlemen. They were mad after their own ends (interests) and hardly took any trouble for the improvement of agriculture. The effect of this sub-infeudation led to an immensely complex revenue system. As a matter of fact the Zamindari system placed the Government and the actual tiller of the soil on two opposite ends in midst which an army of intermediaries appeared. Thus, the British took away the ownership from the hands of the peasants and vested it in the state by the Permanent Settlement. They gave their right to the new class of landlords technically different from Zamindars of the Mughal days. It is difficult to imagine the agony and miseries of the millions of people, who in order to meet the daily increasing demands of their landlords, had to part with their land. There was no tie of love between the newly created class of landlords and the actual tillers. The property in the soil was formally declared to be vested in the landholders, but adequate provision was not made for the protection of the class of actual cultivators.

On the whole, the tenancy of Bihar, it may be said, was in 1833 scarcely better than in 1793. Indeed in some respect their position was even worse on account of forced labour extracted from a great many of them by the unscrupulous European Indigo planters. Sandwitched between the Zamindar and the planter, the poor ryot was utterly helpless, and reconciled only to the idea that suffering was the very condition of his existence. Not that the Government was apathetic to their lot but the slowness of administration, mistakes committed by authorities and the great attention paid to other aspects of the land revenue problems stood in the way of betterment of ryot's conditions. Some collectors posted in different districts of Bihar were also opposed to the Permanent Settlement. They contended that the system is calculated to raise upon to description of men *viz.* the Zamindars, the miseries of another infinitely more numerous, useful and defenceless; that the Zamindars being declared in act and name lords paramount of the soil, their object and helpless vassals, the ryots, trained up to hereditary submission, will bear insolènt dread whatever their imposing tyranny may inflict".

It is worth to note here John Shore's view, "that time would be required to settle what under the circumstances was really meant by the proprietory right conferred. Due to the circumstances prevalent at that time. He was in favour of Permanent Settlement, but he further predicted that "if the Zamindars were left to make their own arrangements with the ryot without restriction, the present confusion would never be adjusted. The system, in short had not defined the relation of the new landlord to his tenant, would it not be better to introduce a new system by degrees than to establish it at once beyond the power of revocation.

It has already been pointed out that just after the Permanent Settlement, the landlords found it difficult to collect rent from their tenants. To remedy of the situation, Regulation VII of 1799 known as 'haftam' (the seventh) was passed and the Zamindars were vested with arbitrary powers of distraint in order that they in turn could pay the Government revenue in time. Regulation V of 1812, also known as 'Panjam' (the fifth) armed the Zamindars with extra powers.

Causes behind the change in Land system

The next point, that arose, is what was the urgency of circumstances that ultimately led to change in the land-system and made a road for a series of reforms.

Pressure on the Land

The pressure of population on the land had created the necessity for change in the land system. Before the arrival of the British, the Industries of India, as also of Bihar, was flourishing. But due to the oppressive economic policy of the British, the handicraft, village and cotton industries, mixed cloth manufactures, Indigo and opium industries and the sugar manufacture had been continuously on the decline. So the dependence on the agriculture increased.

During the British rule Indian wealth began to flow out of the country. Not only that, the British policy in India was so adjusted as to meet the needs of industrialized England. They came to secure market for goods produced in their own mills in England and to export raw materials from India to feed their mills. Thus India was turned into a British colony which led to the impoverishment of the country. The Company's Government in India as the instrument of the industrial classes of England imposed heavy duties upon Indian goods finding way to England while British goods were forced on India without payment of any duty. They tried to mitigate the affects of free trade on indigenous industries.

The native industries thus, were given a calculated death blow. The Indian weavers were forced to work in English factories. The decline of the 'cotton industry' in particular, produced disastrous results. Many flourishing villages were soon nearly depopulated and several thousands of people were thrown out of work. Pandit Nehru has rightly said that: "One village industry after another began to collapse and India became an economic appendage of another country. The people engaged in handicrafts lost their means of livelihood, and the pressure on land increased.

In a fundamental sense, agricultural progress is normally a prerequisite for industrial development. But the notion of prestige prevented the Zamindar from taking any interest in land management and improvement. D.N. Dhanagre had quoted Sinha's views, in the *Journal of Peasant Studies*. Whereas population growth and steadily rising demand for cultivable land led to subinfeudation and rackrenting throughout the 19th Century, the extension of cultivation to all arable lands had reached the point of saturation by 1875. Haque maintains that due to over utilisation of land without adequate capital inputs the crop production had begun to decline particularly in the first quarter of the present century. R.C. Dutt as well as Mukherjee have rightly pointed out that slow disintegration of rural industries and absence of new industrial enterprise and employment further accentuated the pressure on land.

The pressure of population on the land was much higher in

Bihar and there was an "admittedly lower level of awareness of their rights on the part of the Bihar Pesantry.

This can be elaborated through the data as given in Table 2.2 :

Table 2.2
Area and Density of Population

Place		*Area in Sq. K.M. (000)*	*Population*	*Density of Population Per Sq.Km.*
India	:	3,287.3	68,51,84,692	216
Bihar	:	0,173.9	6,99,14,734	402

Source : India-1985 (Page 10) India—A Reference Annual Publications Division, Government of India.

The above data clearly indicates that the pressure of population in Bihar was certainly more explosive in comparison to the India as whole.

Indeed, in the early years of the 19th Century, circumstances had completely changed, and economic condition had become definitely against the agriculturists. At first, population increased slowly and but after 1921, it was surprising rapidity in population. The consequences of such a rapid increase in population, unaccompanied by any proportionate increase in industrial employment, were seen in the intense overcrowding on land, multiplication of uneconomic holdings, low individual income and growth of indebtedness on farming scale and rapid regression of all classes on the agricultural ladder".

The social and political appeal of land-reforms in countries like India, where hunger of land is pronounced and the pressure of population on land is excessive, rests clearly on the interpretation of land reform.

Confiscation of Estates and Principalities

The British rule affected not only the artisans and craftsmen but also the princes and estate-owners. The land tenures and revenue measures that Government took during the first half of the Nineteenth century deprived Taluqdars of the estates, which in many cases were held for ages, and the dispossessed landowners became the bitter enemies of the British rule. The main reason behind this decision was that the revenue collection had been oppressive, and was often managed under the system of farming, or through the agency of local Raja's and Taluqdars.

The Permanent Settlement brought changes in the rights and status of both the Zamindars and the ryots. Indeed, the 1793 settlement created proprietary rights in the land for the Zamindars for which they were required to pay a land tax that could not be increased regardless of any eventual rise in population, land values and agricultural prices.

But in practice no mercy was shown to the tiller and the exaction of taxes were on increase day by day (not covering the terms of the Permanent Settlement). The majority of the Zamindars and the army of the rentiers on land became "an oppressive and blood sucking parasitic lot, foisted on the vast masses of peasant proprietors of the country and many of them proved to be a miserable imbecile set brought up in women's apartments and sunk in sloth debauchery."

As far back as 1857, Canning wrote about some Taluqdars of Oudh "The majority are men distinguished neither by birth, good service, no connection with the soil."

The interposition of a buffer in the shape of the Zamindars between the Government and the cultivators of the soil deprived the Government of close contact with and intimate knowledge of rural conditions. But there was no provision for the maintenance of an upto-date record of rights and what to talk of the contact.

At the time of the Permanent Settlement Cornwallis saw the image of the British aristocrat in the Indian Zamindars. But as epigrammatically said, "Lord Cornwallis desired to make English Landlords in Bengal and succeeded only in making Irish landlords."

Some Zamindars became so powerful that they were busy in making several speed breaker to the prosperity of British empire. Several cases of oppressions done by Zamindars on the tillers, also drew the attention of the British Government as well as the common people. No security or safety whatsoever was accorded to the tillers of the soil. *The London Economist* wrote that "the most creditable product of Zamindari have been Rabindar Nath Tagore, the poet, Liaquat Ali Khan, the Prime Minister and Maharaj Kumar of Vizianagram, the cricketer..... the majority have been as vicious as Thakersay's Lord Steyne, as idle as Jane Austen's Mr. Bennet and as druken as Surtees Square". Therefore, it became essential for the Government to make land reforms.

Stagnation in Agricultural Development

It is well-known that the overwhelming majority of the 'absentee-Zamindars' and intermediaries were directly not interested in improving agricultural production. They were not at all enthusiastic in improving the lands, using improved seeds and fertilisers or making use of improved and more efficient tools and implements. They were also not interested in the development of irrigation so essential for augmenting production. They simply used the vast surpluses pumped out from their tenants or sub-tenants for conspicuous consumption or other uses. They did not plough back the surplus into making agriculture more efficient. Not only that, the landowner was usually a money-lender, and this capacity depended more on loan to small cultivators than on increased income from improvement of land.

Thus the village *Sahukar* or the money-lender was the third scourge of rural India. Rural indebtedness increased rapidly during the last quarter of the 19th century and became one of the most acute problems of the countryside. The exorbitant rates of interest charged by the rural creditor led to two major evils : interest charges absorbed a large part of the peasant's income; and the peasant's frequent inability to repay the debt led to the large-scale transfer of land to the non-cultivating money-lenders. The old ryot was thus increasingly transformed into a tenant at-will resulting in the further depression of agriculture as well as the agriculturist.

The Amrit Patrika on 12th June, 1884 observed that the money- lender, the blood-sucking *Sahukar* : is a creature of the land revenue system of the Government. The money-lender was created because the Government rack-rented the ryot, and never gave remissions of revenue during seasons of distress. Some of the Indian leaders also cast the blame for rural indebtedness on the complicated and elaborate system of laws, which in practice helped the money-lender and encouraged him to seize possession of land and thus intensified all the evils of usury. Also most of them firmly contradicted the official assumption that the peasant borrowed for unnecessary expenditures such as marriages, funerals, and other social or religious ceremonies or that, in other words, the peasant was in debt because he was extravagant. It meant that, wealth was held in the form of land, that the accumulation of the capital did not lend to productive investments. Thus, in order to improve the economic condition of the cultivators the change was must.

It is also necessary to point out that the tenant had also little incentive to increase his output, since a longer share in any such increase accrued to the landlord who had incurred no part of its cost. The high share of the produce taken by the land owner left the peasant with a bare subsistence minimum with no margin of investment.

Joseph W. Elder failing to account for cultural variability, had assumed that Indian Zamindars would become like English barons, for variety of reasons have to do with the hierarchic nature of Hindu Society, orientation towards maximising profits rather than maximising production, and status consumption patterns, the Zamindars chose to increase their own and their children's income not so much through irrigations and fertilisers as through exacting additional payments from their tenants.

Dr. Jagannath Mishra has pointed out on the basis of a statement made by K.B. Sahay in the Bihar Legislative Assembly, that while in 1793, the Zamindars were left with 1/10th of the rent (9/10th being payable as revenue), owing to the permanent nature of the Government demand it was the landlord who benefitted from extention of cultivation, "Sayer" income from fisheries, orchards, pasture, etc., benefits from invalid grants (under 100 acres) which they chose to resume, and from the increase in agricultural productivity.

One can easily see the loss of Rs. 14 crores annually incurred by the Government on account of the Permanent Settlement and the manner of management of the Zamindari estates. However, the exact amount of rent that the Zamindars were sucking from the tenancy between 1937 and 1953 is given below:

Table 2.3
Movement of Rent and Revenue in Bihar

Year	*Gross Rental Value of Estates and Tenures (Rs.)*	*Revenue of Estates on Tauzi Roll (Rs.)*		*(4) as a percentage of (2)*
		Demand	*Collection*	
1	2	3	4	5
1937-38	NA	1,40,08,334	1,24,23,995	—
1938-39	NA	1,39,29,119	1,20,53,294	—
1939-40	NA	1,37,93,134	1,21,33,052	—
1940-41	NA	1,37,08,912	1,21,33,408	—
1941-42	12,78,40,755	1,36,54,152	1,23,38,312	9.65
1942-43	12,42,30,184	1,36,50,110	1,23,40,561	9.93
1943-44	12,14,67,663	1,34,48,530	1,25,07,197	10.29
1944-45	13,95,27,316	1,32,16,514	24,31,009	8.90
1945-46	15,94,72,152	1,29,74,720	1,22,21,406	7.66
1946-47	17,18,15,251	1,28,85,131	1,21,47,186	7.06
1947-48	18,04,16,805	1,29,84,593	1,20,83,917	6.60
1948-49	18,33,71,096	1,34,50,405	1,22,37,910	6.78
1949-50	20,96,02,405	1,36,19,500	1,20,74,032	5.76
1950-51	21,29,03,358	1,39,66,130	1,18,78,520	5.57
1951-52	21,28,77,803	1,39,66,130	1,18,78,520	5.57
1952-53	21,98,75,448	1,46,24,771	97,77,202	4.26

By the end of the British rule, they had become a brake on agrarian production. Indian Society needed a breakthrough from this stagnation in agriculture.

Political Consciousness

As political consciousness grew and the kisan awakening became widespread, the ennui and worthlessness of Zamindari System was realised. This ultimately created the situation for land reforms. The Zamindari was one of the most irresponsible and oppressive systems that feeling could be seen in the mind of the masses.

Politically, the Zamindars had been created to serve as a prop to the Colonial Rule on the stability of which depended the stability of their own landed property. They had their own courts for trial of poor peasant and surprisingly for no faults. Thus, under these two-fold systems (British Government and Zamindars) or due Government the peasants felt crushed. Of course the tenants were economically crippled and physically exhausted. As administrators, the Zamindars did not perform any useful creative role except bossing over the tenants and exploiting them for their selfish ends. Needless to say that the Zamindars did not take part in production processes, and even as managers they did not contribute much to agricultural production. The tenants remained sore with them.

"The awakening of Tenants which the grant of political power is occasioning has had the natural and inevitable effect of producing symptoms of unrest in areas where grievances exist or friction has occurred and it is much to be designed that an amicable settlement will be found before relations become more embittered".

Amicable settlement could never be found and relations remained embittered all along. However, by 1930 it was complained by the Kisan leaders that the Zamindars of Bihar collected nearly Rs. 20-21 crore as rent but paid Rs. 1.75 crore as revenue to the Government and pocketed the rest.

Even the Government report tells us that the Zamindars collected 18 crore as rent from the tenants. The misfortune was not limited. They further extracted money or its worth through various illegal impositions.

A Kisan Sabha report on Gaya enumerates 44 kinds of impositions in early thirties, some of them were procured for four or eight annas; milk, ghee, curd etc. were purchased at almost half the rate. Washermen, carpenters, potters, oil pressers, blacksmiths etc. had to give free services to the landlords and to remain at their back and call. It is to be noted that the chamars had to supply shoes and the Koeris vegetables free of cost. The height was that even the Green crops were cut away for feeding landlord's cattles. The rural masses were also subjected to the exploitation of army. A letter from Collector of Bhagalpur to Major Lunas shows how the bullocks were taken away from the rural inhabitants, without payment or any other consideration by the daroga of the Basa."

The privilege of illegal exraction was not only exercised by the Zamindars but also by their Amlas and Agents. In the Darbhanga Raj such cases were very rampant because the Maharaja hardly took any interest himself and everything was left to his amlas and agents. "Every year on the eve of the festival called 'Punyah' a huge fair was organised the expenses of which were incurred by the Kisans of Dharampur. Thus, a large number of taxes were imposed upon the poor tenants, e.g., Bhusavin, (supply husk for the Zamindars cattle), Motoravan (for purchasing car), Hathiyavan (for purchasing Elephant) Boragavan (for planting Zamindars orchard), Patpiravan (where Zamindar's wife conceived), Janumavan (where Zamindars was blessed with an offspring), Holiyavan (on Holi) and many types of Nazrana; salami etc.

Even the general behaviour of the landlord was tortuous and untolerable as indicates the "*Journal of Peasants* 'Vol. II, 1975. Reference is given to the "Revolution of China." It is remarkable that the tenants mounted a protest in 1935 not because they questioned the rent or its rate but because they objected to the behaviour and corruption of the newly instituted rent-collectors".

With the passage of time, it was clear that the Zamindars had proved themselves to as a class of *'doubtful political value'* for the Government. This led to the change in the 'Bengal Tenancy Act of 1885.' The Act was designed to regulate agrarian relations and strengthen the position of the Tenants against the oppressions of the landlord.

Pandit Nehru had rightly observed: "The taluqdars and the Zamindars, the lords of the land, the natural leaders of the people" as they are proud of calling themselves, had been the spoilt children of the British Government. They did nothing at all for their tenancy, such as landlords in other countries have to some little extent, often done, and became complete parasites on the land and the people. Their chief activity lay in the efforts to placate the local officials, without whose favour they could not exist for long, and demanding baselessly a protection of their special interests and privileges. He further says:

> They have not even the virtues of an aristocracy. As a class they are physically and intellectually degenerated and have outlived their day; they will continue only so long as on external power like the British props them up.

Practically, Zamindars became cancerous for British Government as well as the Indians. It was essential to cut its rotten part. After independence, the anti-Zamindar campaign in India was naturally charged with an emotional appeal and subsequently land reform was done.

Class Struggle

The class struggle in rural India had also made the reforms easy. The background of the class unrest is deeply rooted in the social arrangements relating to land. These gigantic and permanent discontent, which prevailed among various sections of the agrarian population, with regard to the British agrarian policies, exploitation and oppression, led to a number of struggles in different parts of the countryside.

The socio-economic dangers could well be imagined when a few important landlords and Zamindars held very large estates and the majority of the small land owners and tenure holders possessed an extremely small area. Such a situation resulted in sinister class struggle owing to the concentration of economic power into a few hands.

These economic exploitations led to the social unrest affecting the relations amongst various classes of proprietors and tenants. The system of revenue farming (the newly created tenures or sub-tenures), as one may term it, attracted the people, especially the money-lenders from urban and suburban areas who had acquired properietory rights in land.

In the absence of alternative avenues for investment, and with high rates of interest in rural areas, there was a flow of capital into the villages, which caused vital socio-economic changes in the agricultural community". Money-lender virtually replaced the Zamindars and the small Zamindars were reduced to the status of mere tenant-at will. The Collector of Shahabad reported that Babu Dhrub Narain Singh (powerful Zamindar of Jagdishpur) had incurred a debt to pay the revenue demand. Even a big Zamindar like Rajah Bikramjeet Singh of Bhojpore, was unable to extricate himself from utter dependence on money-lenders or mahajans.

The origin of the class struggle at the village level in the British India could be traced in the process of changes in the tenure system itself. Thus, the new process led to the concentration of land in the hands of the money-lenders, traders and big landlords. It could be said that these agrarian movements were sparked off by incidents of oppression which were getting particularly harsh as Zamindars progressively got alienated from the village social structure. For example, the Zamindar of Rewa in Gaya District was so brazen that, faced with shortage of cow milk, he sent his man to milk lactating tenant-women. Not only that the sale of daughters were also a source of livelihood of tenants belonging to the higher castes.

The Zamindari system also gave rise to a social formation, generating tensions among different strata, which were in a different shape previously. The Zamindars oppressed the rural masses in various ways. J.R. Hand writes, "on 8th of Oct., 1782 after visiting Shahabad Mr. Broke reported that on 30th June, he visited Arrah but found many villages deserted. No body was there to cultivate land because of the oppression of Raja Bikramjit and Dewan and Ziladars employed by Babu Bhup Narain. He tried to pacify them but the cultivators did not agree. So he dispossessed them of their large possession. After that the farmers were pleased and went back to their farm".

A letter was sent from Tirhut to Sir John Shore . . . . But the present occupant Madho Singh instead of relieving the distress of the ryots has multiplied it. He desolated the country in which once the fields were loaded with fruits. As such the forfeiture of his rights must be passed".

In Darbhanga, "illegal enhancement of rent, oppression by the landlords, and consequent discontent among the tenancy were found to be prevalent in a greater or less degree in nearly all parts of the District. In one village of the Zamindari of the Madhubani Babus, the misconduct and oppressions of the landlords agents had driven the tenants into open revolt. During 1922-23 in Pargana Dharampur of Purnea considerable friction arose between the tenants and Darbhanga Raj over those areas from which Kosi had receded.

Even the settlement officer for South Monghyr had reported that there was always a fierce tussle between the landlords and the tenants on the question of produce rent, the factors chiefly affecting the result being the fighting power of the raiyat, his ability to bribe the amla, and the amount of supervision exercised over the latter by the landlords.

In the large estates of Raja Ganga Prasad Singh Bahadur, the tenants to whom no proper rent receipts were given, were reduced to the verge of despair by confused account which showed them as hopelessly indebted to the landlords.

Insecurity was prevailing in the minds of the tenants throughout Bihar, as indeed elsewhere in India also. References of Darbhanga District is given by Lieutenant Governor, who regrets to note that "the facts brought to light were far from creditable to the management . . ." The letter written by the Collector of Bhagalpur is an important source, that highlights that the proprietors considering their lands greatly overassessed were afraid to venture. Indeed he had no hopes of setting them at the Jummah at 1197 as he found the raiyats had deserted in great numbers".

However, after 1793 desertion of land by the peasants considerably lessened. Perhaps the Zamindars now felt that any oppression on the ryots would bring their own economic ruin.

The process of pauperization and proletarianisation, with mounting indebtedness and slavery had generated anger resulting in unrest in agrarian India. These movements had upset the programme imposed by the Indian National Congress and other parties wedded to the capitalistic path of development. Indian National Congress was apprehensive of this oppressed strata, which being engaged in fighting the British could break the bourgeoisie limits and confiscate without compensation the lands of the landlords and Zamindars making a bid for a social revolution, which would then usher in a non-capitalist path of development. This fear was not baseless. The struggle in Russia, China and some other countries which proceeded on non-capitalist, socialist path of development amply demonstrated the feasibility of such a turn in India, if proper leadership emerged.

This phenomenon continued and increased over time to such an extent that a hundred years after the permanent settlement, the Government had to examine it seriously in order to try to find a remedy. In the manner of the officialdom a 'Note' was prepared and it was observed.

Therefore, the official report of this period is full of remarks decrying these exactions but little was done to stop it. In these circumstances the change was inevitable, of course the above situation forced the return of the independent India to take the land reforms. But the history of the Indian peasantry is rather an unexplored area even today and the land reforms in real sense had to be completed to avoid hundreds of class struggle in Jahanabad, Aurangabad, Nawadah, Gaya, Patna, Sasaram and even some North Bihar districts.

Need to overthrow the old Regime

Being new to the country and affairs, the East India Company was interested in creating a class of persons whose loyalty it could count upon. There were many reasons behind it. At first, the Company was interested in a regular inflow of revenue to enable it to consolidate its position. Its desires were best served if cultivation expanded and agriculture flourished, as agricultural development ensured regular flow of revenue.

The Company, therefore, considered it desirable to create a class of people who would take interest in the development of agriculture and would act as entrepreneurs in the rural sector. Against such a background the Permanent Settlement was introduced and a new class of prprietors and land aristocracy emerged.

In course of time, the Zamindari became hereditary and saleable and the number of Zamindars rose. "A very crucial movements, these landlords had thrown their entire weight on the side of the British imperialists. They had continuously tried to adopt all possible means in order to support the foreign rule."

But with the passage of time, the defects in the system began to manifest themselves. The nationalist Newspapers also played an important role emphasising the painful tale of the tenants at the hand of the landlords. It expressed humanitarian solicitude for the tenants in Zamindari areas and protested against the rackrenting, evictions and the general oppression of the tenants by the Zamindars.

Newspaper *Bengalee* of 9th Dec., 1882 while criticising oppression by powerful Zamindars wrote :

> "Tyranny is hateful in all forms, whether it is the whiteman or the black-man who is the tyrant, whether the oppressor has been born and bred amongst us or whether he comes from the far west."

Som Prakash of 24th July, 1882 disapproved a system of revenue collection under which one person enjoys all the luxury of case and the hard earned wealth of ten thousand persons" asked rhetorically on what ground should one enjoy the fruit of another's labour,' and declared : that the landlords have in course of time become increasingly miserable. The 'Banga Nivasi' of 30th Oct., 1891 in its editorial condemned the inhuman and unspeakable oppression of the ryots by the Zamindars and their gomastas and other underlings. It also criticised the inaction of the educated people in these words :

> "If these countrymen of ours (Zamindars and their agents). dressed in a little brief authority can commit this hideous oppression, how can we reasonably clamour against a slight stretch of authority by a foreign head of a District possessed of unlimited power. If we call the oppression by English a spark, we ought to call the oppression by the Rajas and Zamindars conflagration.

The vital defect of the Permanent Settlement was that it did not make enough provision against arbitrary enhancements of the rents by the Zamindars. Subsequently, Tenancy Acts had to be passed to overcome these defects and to give protection to raiyats. But inspite of these, the oppression by the intermediaries, continued to increase with the growth of agricultural population and the consequent scarcity of land. By the end of the Second World War a climate had already been prepared in the country for the immediate abolition of the intermediaries on land.

It was, therefore, true that no improvement was possible in the standard of living of the people till landlordism was abolished. If India was to prosper and if planned economy had to have any meaning; a balance had to be struck between agriculture and industry, and no such balance could be struck unless landlordism was abolished.

The high-handedness of the Zamindars and the poverty of the actual tillers drew the attention of the Government and political organisations.

A few of the Indian public men also assailed the system of Zamindari. In the early 1870's a powerful attack on the Zamindars was made by Bankim Chandra Chatterjee in his articles on 'Samya' in *the Banga Darshana*. He was followed by young R.C. Dutt. In a long article *the Mahratta* of 17th February 1884, vigorously attacked the system of Zamindari. As discussed below, the Indian Association and many nationalist leaders adopted a pro-ryot attitude during the controversy of the Bengal Rent Bill, later still, Prithwi Chandra Ray held the Zamindari system and the oppression by the Zamindars responsible for the poverty of the people in his two publications. *The Poverty Problems in India*, published in 1895 and *The Causes of Indian Famines*, published in 1901. G.V. Joshi made a detailed criticism of landlordism, both in the Zamindari and the Ryotwari areas, in his essay, *'The Economic Situation in India'*, published in 1890. He pointed out that all over the country sub-leasing of land was increasing and the number of intermediaries and tenants-at-will multiplying, and that the rents were being forced up to ruinous heights by the increasing competition for land, which in turn was the result of increase of population combined with the progressive collapse of non-agricultural industries. High rents and insecurity of tenure in turn destroyed all effective motives on the part of the actual cultivator to improve land. To sum up :

"The Ryot is so placed that he had nothing to gain by any amount of industry or prudence that he might practise, and nothing to lose by any amount of recklessness; he has nothing to hope, and being above all anxious not to be dispossessed of his few acres, he pays any rents rather than starve. A situation more devoid of motives to self-help and self-exertion can hardly be imagined."

In his essay, *Notes on Agriculture in Bombay*, published in 1894, Joshi dealt at length with the growth of landlordism and tenants-at-will, 'owing partly to the extended practice of sub-letting and partly so the consequences of unrelieved indebtedness.' and bemoaned the fact that no proper tenant-right or tenancy laws existed in the Presidency of Bombay, so that there was no provision for the accrual of occupancy rights and the under-tenant has no legal protection against rackrenting or eviction.

Many of the Indian leaders suggested positive steps for the protection of the tenants. The most popular of these were the grant of legislative protection to them against enhancement of rent, rack-renting, eviction, destruction of tenancy rights, etc. and the extension and strengthening of occupancy and other rights. It is of some interest to note that three of the leading national economists, namely, Justice Ranade, G.V. Joshi, and R.C. Dutt, lent full support to the tenancy legislation undertaken by the Government and put in vigorous pleas for further strenghtening of tenant rights. G.V. Joshi also asked the authorities to extend legislative protection to the utterly unprotected under-tenants in the Ryotwari areas of Bombay.

It was quite natural on the part of the independent India's national leaders that they should lose no time in formulating a land policy to succeed the one they had bitterly criticised and attacked during the British rule. So their first and foremost object was to abolish landlordism.

There were other views that went against this landowning parasitic class. The Zamindars and other feudatories were vestiges of the old order and were too closely associated with the previous regime to be able to survive long after that regime had dissappeared, and therefore, the overthrow of this class was only a continuation of the struggle for the overthrow of old regime.

Firstly, it was no use to continue the old, bogus and arbitrary system in this fast changing era of liberalism, democracy, fraternity and co-existence.

Secondly, the number of interests affected by the legislation was comparatively few. Their displacement, therefore, did not present a major social problem.

Thirdly, these superior rights were the creation of political expediency more than of economic necessity.

The abolition, therefore, implied a system of land tenure, which allowed no room for the passing away of the land from the actual tiller of it, into the hands of the individuals and bodies of persons, who had got within themselves the fatal germs of rent receiving and absentee landlordism.

Zamindars class is often charged with helping in the consolidation of the British rule in India, but now when British have quit, the Zamindar class continues to face the charges of anti-national collaboration with the foreigners and acting like fifth columnists in the past. The anti-Zamindar campaign in free India was naturally charged with an emotional appeal evoked by the Zamindars' role in the past. Indeed in the post war years, however land reforms became the 'chant of the times,' not only in India but in most of the under-developed countries of the world. Water C. Neale, in his book writes about the significance of this development as follows : "In the present struggle of former colonial areas to raise their standard of living, it has become axiomatic that land reform is a prerequisite to any advance, while the present tenurial systems are often blamed on the colonial powers. Land reforms has been supported by interests as diverse as scholars, U.N. Committees, American ambassadors, Independence movements, and Marxists revolutionaries. Countries as different as Gautemala, India and Hungary have undertaken to 'redistribute the land and change the system of tenure. The purpose is always to assure the agriculturist security, prosperity and a "fair share". Behind the reforms lie an interpretation of history and an assumption about peasant motivation. Land reform rests partly upon a theory of exploitation, a belief that a small group of landlords has lived parasitically on the labour of the cultivating "masses" and that, as a rule, the landlord has secured his position by force, fraud, special privilege or some other dubious means contrary to public morality. With reform, however the cultivator will have the security and incentive to change his ways and improve his land. With security and his "fair share" the cultivator will strive to achieve prosperity and to enjoy it.

And even if we accept that in the case of Bengal, Bihar and Orissa being its part, Zamindari is an institution of very ancient origin, could it not be said that as an institution it had lost its usefulenss. The system gave birth to a class with leisure, but little of culture. It was out of the fashion, it was outdated. So the need was to overthrow it.

Therefore, the reform of the land system, which was so urgently needed in India, involves the removing of intermediaries between the peasant and the state.

Notes & References

Diwakar, R.R., *Bihar Through the Ages*, Calcutta, 1958, p. 38.

Bihar : Ek Jhalak, Directorate of Statistics and Evaluation, Bihar, Patna, 1980, pp. 1-2.

Choudhary, V.C.P., *The Creaion of Modern Bihar*, Darbhanga, 1964, p. 173.

Van Derpost, *The Economics of Agriculture*, 1937, p. 5.

Hsiao Tung Feli *Peasants life in China*, 1938, pp. 181-82.

Malviya, H.D., *Land Reforms in India*, Economic and Political Research, New Delhi, 1955, p. 69.

Rousseau Jean Jacques, *Social Contract*, 1762

Sinha, N.K., *The Economic History of Bengal*. Vol. II, Calcutta, 1962, p. 19.

Original rent in the Public Register, Minute of Share, 18th June, 1789—*Fifth Report*, Vol. II, p. 4 (App.).

Ghosal, H.R., "Two Mughal Farmans" in *Indian History Congress Proceedings*. Patna, 1950. p. 431.

Revenue Administration of Mir Qasim in Bihar and Bengal (1760-63) J.B. & O.R.S.T. Vol. XXXI, p. 66.

Baden Powell, B.H., *The Land System of British India*, Vol. II Oxford London 1892, p. 48.

Atkinsons Kumaon Gazetteers quoted in Baden Powell, p. 313.

Fifth Report, Vol. I, Intro. p. CLXXXIV.

Hunter, W.W., *The Annals of Rural Bengal*, (App.). Calcutta, 1965, p. 420.

Darbhanga Distt. Gazetteer, 1907, p. 60.

Champaran Distt. Gazetteer, 1907, pp. 124-25.

The Commission that gave right to possession of land, also a written order to an amil for that purpose—Fifth Report, Vol. III, p. 4 (App.)

Fifth Report, Vol. I, Intro, P. CCCII.

James *Selection from the Correspondence of Rev. Chiefs of Bihar*, p. 44.

Guha, Ranjit, *A Rule of Property for Bengal*. Paris, 1963.

Dutta, Romesh C., *Economic History of India*. Vol. I. New Delhi, 1976, p. XXIV.

Ray, S.C., *The Permanent Settlement in Bengal*. Calcutta, 1915, p. 68.

Ray, S.C., (Comp.), *Land Revenue Administration in India*. Calcutta, 1915, pp. 38-39.

Fifth Report, Vol. II, p. 2180 (APA).

Baden Powell, *The land System of British India*. Vol. I. London, 1892, pp. 405-6.

Field, C.D., *Land Holding and the Relation of Landlord and Tenant*. Calcutta 1885, pp. 576-79.

Basu, D.D., *Ruin of Indian Trade and Industries*. Calcutta 1935, p. 38-51. Also see Chapters *Transit and Custom Duties*, 31-66 *"The Export Trade of India"*, 67-76; and *Ruin of Indian Manufactures*, pp. 77-108.

Nehru, Jawaharlal. *Discovery of India*, Calcutta, 1946, p. 356.

See, Agriculture, *Land Reforms and Economic Development*, Preface by O. Lange, also p. 4 of the same book.

Dhanagare, D.N., *Journal of Peasants*, p. 360, Jan., 1975.

Hunter, *The Annals of Rural Bengal Op. cit* 1875, p. 390-91.

Haque, 1939 : 49-55 taken from the Journal of Peasants in the essay of D.N. Dhanagare, p. 360.

Dutt, R.C., *The Economic History of India under Early British Rule* (1759-1837) London, 1956 also see Ram Krishna, *Dynamics of a Rural & Society*, Berlin.

Chaudhary, Binay Bhusan, *Land Market in Eastern India*. 1793-1940, Indian Economic and Social History Review, Vol. XII, No. 1, Jan.-March, 75, p. 33.

Mishra, Jagannath, *Land Reforms in Bihar*, 1974, Patna, p. 30.

For a detailed study of the revenue measures, See Tarachand, N. 7, 338-58. Also see, Chaudhary, S.B., *Civil Rebellion in the India* Calcutta, 1959, p. 8-15.

Fifth Report, I.P. 63, Where there were no Rajas or Taluqdars, the Nawab divided the territory among his amils, and left everything to them.

Mclane, J.R., *Land Revenue and Peasant in South Asia*, New Delhi, 1977 "*Op. cit*", p. 29 and also G. Mishra. "*Op. cit.*", p. 301.

Mangles, R.D., Quoted by P.N. Driver *Problems of Zamindari and Land Tenure Reconstruction in India*, Bombay, 1949.

Jain, A.P., *Abolition of Zamindar in Bihar 1946*, p. 26.

Baden Powell, B.H., *Land System of British India.*

London Economics, quoted by The Times of 14th June, 1952.

Hume, A.O., *Hints on Agricultural Reforms in India* Calcutta, 1870, p. 35.

Reports of U.N.'s Land Reforms Defectes in Agrarian Structure as Obstacles to Economic Development. p. 18.

Report of the Land Reforms Committee, 1946, p. 10.

Economic Development and Cultural Change, Vol. XI, No. 1, Oct., 1962.

Proceedings of the B.L.A., 1950 Vol. II, Part J. p. 24. Speech of the Revenue Minister on 20th Feb., 1950.

Sharma, G.P., *Congress & the Peasant Movement in Bihar.* Bombay, 1985. p.1.

Das, A.N., *Agrarian Unrest and Socio Economic Change.* Delhi, 1980, p. 1-2.

Sen, Sunil, Agrarian Relations in India 1793 to 1947. New Delhi-1972, p. 2.

Government of Bihar & Orissa, Deptartment, file No. 1199/IVI-57R dated 6th Dec., 1921.

Bihar Prantiya Kisan Sabha Ki Report, Nov. 1921 to Nov. 1935 (B.P.K.S.R.) p. 19 estimated by Swami Sahjanand Saraswati.

Bihar Prantiya Kisan Sabha Ki Report Nov. 1929—Nov. 1935; p. 19; estimated by Swami Sahjannad Saraswati.

Letter from Collector of Bhagalpur to Major Lunas, Bhagalpur District Records, Vol. V, p. 80.

Haminghma, Stephen, *Agrarian Relations in North Bihar, Peasant Protest and Darbhanga Raj*, 1919-2011 in Indian Economic and Social History Review V. XXI. No. 1. (1979) p. 32.

Malviya, H.D., *Land Reforms in India*, New Delhi, 1955, pp. 103-4.

Is' Wi-Chi L Hung Shui—Chien, 1936. Cited in *Journal of Peasants*, April, 1975 by Jerzy Tepchit.

Bhatia, B.M., *Famines in India*, (ed.) Bombay, 1967.

Important provisions of the Bengal Tenancy Act of 1885 (with amendments up to 1950) have been given in the Appendix.

Nehru, Jawaharlal, *Autobiography.* 1936, New Delhi, p. 58.

Ojha, Gyaneshwar, *Land Problems & Land Reforms*. New Delhi, 1972, p. 47.

Gupta, Sulekh, *Agrarian Relations and Early British Rule in India*. Bombay, 1963, p. 323.

BOR Prog., 17th Jan. 1793, Letter from Collector, Shahabad to the Board.

BOR Prog., 2nd July, 1793, Letter from Collector, Shahabad to the Board.

Sankrityayan, Rahul, *Naye Bharat Ke Naye Neta*. Allahabad, 1973, p. 140.

Hand, J.R., *Early English Administration in Bihar*, 1781-85. Calcutta 1894, pp. 35-36.

Muzaffarpur old records, dated 9th Nov., 1789, p. 81.

Ghosh, H.P., Bengal, 1750-1800. *The Calcutta Review*. Calcutta. p. 227.

Government of Bihar & Orissa, Department, File No. 1199/IVL-57 R, dated the 6th Dec. 1921.

BDR 1974, Vol. 13, dated 6th June, 1794.

India, Note on Land Transfers and Agricultural indebtedness in India Calcutta, 1895.

Som Prakash, June, 14 (RNP., Beng., June, 19, 1880) *Mavavibhakar*, July 12, (*Ibid*, July 17, 1880) *Burdwan Sansivani*", Nov. 9, (*Ibid*, Nov. 20, 1880) *Bharat Bandha* Nov. 26, (RNPPN, Dec. 12, 1880) *Prayag Samachar*, Dec. (RNPPN, Dec., 14, 1882) *Gramvarta Prakasika*, March 22 (*Ibid*, April 5, 1885, *Banganivasi*, Oct. 25, (*Ibid*, Nov. 2, 1895, *Hindustan*, Aug. 25, (RNPPN, Aug. 31, 1898) and several others.

Bengallee, Jan. 23, 1892.

Rup Beng, July 29, 1882.

Dutt, R.C., *Banga Darshana*, under the article Maharatta 17th Feb. 1884.

Joshi, J.V., *Notes on Agriculture in* pp. 870-94, Bombay, 1894.

Mallet, Graham, *The Economics of Agricultural Land Tenure*, 1960, p. 17.

Neale, Walter, *Economic Changes in Rural India*, Land Tenure and Reforms in Uttar Pradesh 1962, p. 3-4.

Election Manifesto of the Congress Party, 1936.

CHAPTER 3

INDIAN NATIONAL CONGRESS AND THE LAND PROBLEM

During the early years of the inception and activities of the Congress Party, it could not formulate its well thought out policy in respect of land and its gainful utilisation for the people for boosting the economic benefits of the society and nation as a whole. Primarily, the Congress in those days was confined to a small number of western minded intelligentia who were more concerned with the liberties of the people than with the economic problem. Besides, they believed in the theory of petitioning the grievances of the people rather than in any mass movement against the British Raj. The thrust of the discussion is on the attitude of the Congress Party to the land system and the comprehensive changes necessiated by change in the outlook of the people as well as the pressure of colonial economy.

Though the Congress had done very little to sponsor a radical programme of agrarian reforms, yet an attempt was made by its leadership during the war to draw the peasant masses into their organisation.

Congress and the Peasantry

With the coming of Gandhi at the forefront of the national scene after his return from Africa and more specially after his visit to Champaran at the invitation of Rajkumar Shukla, a sturdy peasant agitating against the brutalities of the indigo planters in that area, the situation however changed. Gandhi had embarked on a plan which proved in course of time a milestone not only in the career of Gandhi as a pacifist revolutionary but also in the history of the Congress Party.

Appreciating the achievement of Gandhi in its editorial dated 23rd April, 1917, *Amrit Bazar Patrika* wrote "The part which he has played in this sensational matter is no less than what he did when he started his passive resistance campaign in South Africa ..... God bless Mr. Gandhi and his work. How do we wish, we had only half a dozen Gandhi in India to teach our people self abnegation and selfless patriotism".

Thus, it began slowly but surely a regular attempt to bring the masses within the fold of the Congress by highlighting the grievances against the inhuman and brutal Government policy to squeeze the key and fair activities of the people and to make them the agent of British economic exploitation in India. Indeed, Gandhi's travel in Champaran in course of time spelt out the attitude and the policy of the Congress towards the sufferings of the Indian Peasantry. Not only did Gandhi, making hectic tours of the area, collect their grievances but was also bold enough to show them the path of peaceful agitation against the government so that the indignities and exploitation could be removed. The Champaran experiment was the basis for future Congress policy towards the land system in India.

Thus, the Congress politics of masses began with the advent of Mahatma Gandhi on the horizon of Indian politics.. He understood the importance and implications of extending the mass base of the national movement in course of the Champaran Satyagraha of 1917 in Bihar. Indeed Champaran has the glory to become the first place in India, where he introduced his two great weapons *i.e.,* (1) *"Satyagraha"* and (2) *"Non-violence"*. As he himself writes in his Autobiography: "it is no exaggeration but the literal truth to say that in this meeting with the peasants he was "face to face with God, Ahimsa and Truth".

However, it was aimed at "curing all human ills, the awakening and salvation of downtrodden masses, the eradication of economic inequalities and the purification of society". K.K. Dutta has rightly pointed out that it was primarily a humanitarian crusade which effected emancipation of a large number of peasants from an explitative economic system and a great social injustice. It infused into the minds of the much oppressed peasants of Champaran a spirit of awakening which is a necessary pre-requisitie for a national movement. Gandhiji attached such a great importance to the Champaran struggle that he once said: "Those who should know my method of organising kisan may profitably study the movement in Champaran where satyagraha was tried for the first time in India with the result which whole of India knows. It became a mass movement which remained wholly non-violent from start to finish".

Though the Champaran Movement was carried against the authoritarian attitude of the Indigo planters yet it did not bring to surface the dormant conflict between the landlords and the peasants, but it certainly showed the way towards an organised method by which the oppressed tenants could fight against the Zamindars. So Champaran became the gateway of the mass contact movement which constructed the road for the Bihar to international politics.

Many flowers of patriotism sprang-up from the mud of Bihar who helped Gandhi in Champaran viz. Dr. Rajendra Prasad, Dr. Anugraha Narain Sinha, B. Brij Kishore Prasad etc. They had channelised the organisational work round 1920 that prepared the way for the future effectiveness of the mass movement in the province. Certainly the main manpower for such movements was drawn from the country's vast rural mass. This is not surprising because even though the Weltanschauung of the peasant is limited his involvement with the land question has invariably led him to a militant nationalist position. After all, in the ultimate analysis, the national question is a peasant question. The peasants were drawn to the movement due to their economic grievances and the price rise. Hat (Market) looting was a direct result of price rise. Such incidents occurred in Purnea, North Bhagalpur, North Monghyr and Darbhanga but Muzaffarpur topped the list.

Bihar had so far been a backward area without established

political traditions and not many people had been attending the annual sessions of the Indian National Congress. However, Mahatma Gandhi had built up a local reputation and a network of sub-contractors. No wonder this province 'swung powerfully into all India Politics' in 1919-22. Further, the Congress formed a number of committees at the town level and increased its membership considerably by the time kisan agitation started in 1930.

Not only that, one can easily see the intention of Gandhiji while introducing 'Khadi', (hand spun cotton) in order to make mass contact more broad and effecitve. 'Khadi' enabled the Congress to identify itself with the poorest in the land whose dress it was. It became a symbol of its mass base as also its elite mass rapport. It enabled the Congress to combine the advantage of a cadre and a mass party.

Moreover, under the guidance of Mahatma Gandhi the Congress opposed the association of the traditional and the landed aristocracy with the administration of the country. It also wanted to keep the illiterate multitude out of the ambit of politics.

While it took up the cause of the rural tenants, agrarian problems and peasant unrest attracted the attention of the leaders. Repeatedly, in its annual resolutions, the congress demanded that land revenue be fixed on a permanent basis and protested against the increase in land tax. It championed the cause of the pesantry, even though the peasantry was conspicuous by its absence in the pre-Gandhian Congress. But in any real sense the Congress leadership at the centre did not bother to give importance at once to the peasant problem. It could only arise when the agrarian problems became accentuated in the wake of the economic depression of 1929. It was clear that the Congress would lose her mass base in the national movement unless it took up the burning economic issues.

The other cause which led Congress to think over the peasants is well defined by Walter Hauser: "while the Congress was the only Political spokesman for the Indian masses, if its mass character was to have any meaning the peasant problem must form the core of its programme".

It was for the first time on an all India basis, the Karachi Congress (1931) session formulated an economic programme which called for a complete overhauling of the agrarian structure by providing substantial relief to the lesser peasantry.

Karachi Session of Congress (1931)

While moving the resolutions on the fundamental rights in the open session of the Congress, Gandhiji said about the peasants that they were being crushed to extinction. He suggested, let the money-lenders adopt 8 per cent as maximum rate to afford some relief.

He was also anxious that the displeasures of Zamindars may occur with his approach. A reference to Mahatma Gandhi's speech at Karachi may be included here to know his actual views. He was not willing to lose their (Zamindar's) eager support to Congress in the national movement. "Let the Zamindars and the Maharaja's be assured that the Congress does not seek to destroy all wrong and injustice. Let them make an earnest endeavour to understand the grievances of their tenants and introduce adequate measures of relief before legislation overtakes them".

The resolution was seconded by Mr. Sengupta. He said that it is all very well to say, as it has been said for the last ten years, that the Congress stands for the masses. Now the test has come and the Congress had got to pass the test. He again asserted that "If its programme is right, then do not think of annoynace being caused to some people, however influential, who after all, are but a small fraction of the total population of India. Let us give them the "Real meaning of Swaraj." But like Gandhiji he was also committed to the Zamindar class. As he told that rich people, mill owners and the Zamindars have helped a lot to our Indian National Movement, have come along, and have opened their purse strings for the cause of independence, yet we are judging them wrongly. He pleaded that the Congress committee should be certain that both the rich and the poor people will help it. According to him, it is an unfair charge that the Zamindars would not come to our rescue because we have framed the programme of Swaraj to benefit the 90 per cent of the population of India.

Thus, the Indian National Congress at the Karachi session had spelt out its radical policy and the emergence of the socialist wing inside the Congress, thereafter, influenced the thinking of leftist Congress figures like Nehru, Subash Chandra Bose. After the Satyagraha Movement of 1930 and the Karachi Congress Session as well, it was felt by Gandhiji who had inaugurated the village industries association in October, 1934 that the true India dwelt in the seven and a half lakhs of villages of India and not in the three thousand towns and cities. Therefore, it was Gandhiji's wish that instead of bringing the villages to the Congress hold in the cities, the cities should be taken back to the village and the villagers.

While withdrawing himself from the Congress Presidential Election Sardar Patel issued statements that Congressmen should be (to be) logical and true to their profession and must believe in the possibility of weaning those who are mercilessly exploiting the masses from what is a crime against humanity. He was afraid that when the masses awake to the sense of their terrible condition, they will know how to deal with it. "Their difficulty is my subscribing to the doctrine that all land and wealth belongs to all. Being a farmer myself and having identified myself with the peasantry for years, I know where the shoe pinches. But I know that nothing can be done except through the power of the people." He further, during the course of his tour of the (Bihar) districts made fairly inflammatory speeches against the landlords and aroused the confidence of the peasant. He said at Sitamarhi that the peasants are the backbone of the nation. "What is the need of the Zamindars? In any case what is their strength? If one catches their heads and presses strongly the brain will come out". But with the passage of time like all Congressmen Patel also chose the line of moderates vis-a-vis Zamindars.

Even Swami Vivekanand's view pays much attention to the people. Swami Vivekanand also deeply sympathised with the peasants. *Let New India Arise*, he wrote, "out of the peasant's cottage, holding the plough". Similarly, one can see that Bankim

Chandra Chattopadhyaya's patriotism was imbued with warm sympathy for the toilers and the exploited people. Bankim Chandra wrote the following about the unfair deal for the peasants :

> "His share represents the atom of an atom. What he has got has not altered his condition to the present day. He cannot live entirely by the produce of the land . . . he who produces crops by the sweat of his brow does not come in for a share in the profits. The cultivator alone is not benefited. Nine hundred Ninety nine people out of a thousand have not been benefited".

Above mentioned statements of the leading nationalists, shook the leadership as well as the masses. At this stage the leftist section of the nationalist movement were roused to the urgency of bringing some "immediate relief" to the "suffering millions" of the countryside and saving them. They were not satisfied with this only, rather they wanted to advance the idea of bringing about a radical change in the "Agrarian situation." According to Prof. Gyanchand : "To remove the poverty and misery and ameliorate the conditions of the Indian masses, it was essential to make revolutionary changes in the existing economic and social structure of society and to remove the gross inequalities."

The emergence of Nehru gave a new direction to the Congress to improve the condition of the downtrodden masses. Of course, he (Nehru) was full of socalistic and Marxian ideas. He clearly advocated for it, as he once clarified : "Call it socialism or call it Gandhism, that is exactly what Congress seeks." He was not at all satisfied with the achievement of the Congress (towards the land problems). He found himself as one against the world. It is rightly admitted by him that "The wind is blowing to the villages and to the mud huts where dwell our poverty stricken pesantry, and it is likely to become a hurricane if relief does not come to them soon. All our political problems and discussions are but the background for the outstanding and overwhelming problem of India—The land problem".

The Lucknow session committed two important duties to the care of the All India Congress Committee. One was the final shaping of the Agrarian Programme and the other was the preparation of the election manifesto. But it did not satisfy him. The situation was well defined by Panditji : "the peasantry were a blind, poverty stricken suffering mass, resigned to their miserable fate and sat upon and exploited by all who came in contact with them—the government, landlords, moneylenders, petty officials, police, lawyers, priests".

As Nehru again expressed his views in the presidential address at the Lucknow session (April, 1936) : "The major problem of India today is that of the land, of rural poverty and unemployment and a thoroughly out of date land system". The resolution on the agrarian programme was an apology for an ambitious scheme of social upheaval which he had been ardently hoping to commit the nation to. He proved his views by taking three ardent Socialist into the Working Committee viz—Jayaprakash Narayan, Narendra Dev and Achyut Patvardhan.

But the main difficulty before him was how to come with these socialistic school of thought in the present prevailing circumstances. In his message to the Socialists (Dec. 20, 1936) conference he said that "As you know I am vastly interested in the socialistic approach to all question". But he was worried as to how to interpret it in terms of India, how to win over the hearts of the people with it".

The changing situation and heart touching statement intensified the whole situation and it alerted the Zamindars and their patrons too. So in order to keep away the epidemic of socialism, a virtual censorship was imposed on some innocent books like *'Why Socialism' 'Soviet Sidelight'*, *'Wide Sea Canal'*, *'Challenge of the East'*, *'U.S.S.R. Handbook'*, *'France Today'*, and *'People's Front'*. However, these acts did not change the course of resentment and awakening among the peasantry but rather it led to the worst. Moreover, situation was not remained as in the month of the same year between the Lucknow and Faizpur Congress Session, the Congress decided to contest election to the Provincial Assemblies. The A.I.C.C. Bombay, on August 1936 in its election manifesto also highlighted the Agrarian programme. With the attitude of the Zamindars the disheartened peasantry was in a state of grief and sorrow. But in such rough weather the Faizpur Agrarian Programme (1936) actually sanctioned the idea of socialism and made the road somewhat easy for further improvement. At last, the Congress by and large had accepted the radical programmes of the C.S.P. Nehru's presidential address at Lucknow and Faizpur embodied the radical aspirations of the left, especially of the C.S.P.

Faizpur Agrarian Programme (December 1936)

Since the awakening among the peasantry had been one of the outstanding features of the year, it was needed to give some relief to them. Therefore, at Faizpur, a comprehensive agrarian resolution was adopted for the peasant's cause. The salient features of the resolution are given below:

1. Rent and Revenue to be substantially reduced.
2. Uneconomic holdings to be exempt from taxation.
3. Canal and other dues for irrigation to be abolished.
4. All feudal dues, levies and forced labour to be abolished and all such demands to be made illegal.
5. Crushing burden of rural debt to be removed and a moratorium to be declared until the readjustment of debts.
6. Arrears of rent to be wiped out.
7. There should be statutory provisions for securing a living wage and suitable working conditions for agricultural labourers.
8. Peasants union to be recognised.
9. Fostering industries for relieving rural unemployment.

Thus, the final solution of this problem inevitably involves the removal of British imperialistic exploitation, a thorough change of the land tenure and revenue system and a recognition by the state of its duty to provide work for the rural unemployed masses. The Faizpur Congress was a better success than anticipated. Really, it gave a particular spirit to the Mass contact that became not merely a programme for the future but a *fait accompli* in the organisation of the Faizpur session itself. The Faizpur Congress in its resolution reaffirmed its faith in a radical change in the land tenure system. The main reason of the success of this session lies in its resolution. However, according to Sahajanand Saraswati "the reason of its success is the growing peasants movement in the country, need for catching the peasants' votes in the elections and the influence of Jawaharlal Nehru and other socialists in the working committee of the Congress".

The left wing's proposal to abolish the zamindari system was kept in cold storage for the time being but they were assured that the whole land question would be rediscussed when reports on the agrarian question had been drawn up by the various provincial committees of the Congress.

As a matter of fact the Congress decided to change the land tenure system much before independence. The very idea of organising the session in Faizpur symbolises Gandhi's wish to teach them the lesson of organisation of national Assembly and the knack to keep control on it. So after Faizpur many small places i.e. Haripura, Tripuri and Ramgarh carried the torch of Nationalism and gave manual help to the newly grown plant of mass rural social progress by highlighting their miseries.

The atmosphere at Faizpur, which was rural in character, was naturally charged with ideas of mass contact and such contact were promoted directly in the establishment of primary committees in villages and the Mohallas of towns. With the setting up of these provincial committees, the congress had raised the hopes of the peasants. Certainly, it showed the inclination of Congress towards the masses at the grass root level. But the situation did not remain quiet over the question of candidature in the election. As Anugraha Narayan Sinha admitted most of his party's candidates came from the Zamindar class. In the same year in 1936 while introducing the constitution of B.P.K.S. Sahajanand regarded the agricultural labourers—as peasants and he was not interested in creating a separate organisation of the agriculture labourers —a position identical with that of the A.I.K.S. *The manifesto of Bihar Provincial Kisan Sabha* also aimed at preventing a strife between them. It contained the slogan of 'Land to the tiller'. The Kisan Sabha made its attitude at Gaya session (AIKS) more clear by stating that the Kisan Sabha wants to maintain amicable relations with the Zamindars but at the same time also warned them of any tyranny on their part and assured them that it will consider properly and sympathetically any reasonable problem of theirs.

Prof. N.G. Ranga, the then secretary, presented the accounts and through the annual report it was unfolded how phenomenal and wide an awakening had taken place among the Indian peasentry which was pulsating with new life and vigour. The report presented a bird's eye view of the kisan movement in the provinces and narrated how badly the kisan underwent prosecution with special reference to *Barhaiya Tal and Reora Satyagraha*. It deplored the growing tendency of the Congress towards constitutionalism and hinted at the growing discontent with the opportunities of reconstruction through legislation and rural uplift. If the Kisan Sabha and its workers, did not continue their struggle, the national emancipation movement would have, by this time been in complete stagnation.

Conflict of Ideologies

Hence, the conflict of ideologies begins between the prominent Bihar Congress leaders and the Kisan Sabha which was already formed in 1929. Some Bihar leaders had reservations over the abolition of intermediaries and landlordism because they belonged to that class only. Names of Dr. Rajendra Prasad, Sri Krishna Sinha and Sri Anugraha Narain Sinha came in this line. Though Dr. Rajendra Prasad was a member of the Provincial Kisan Sabha, yet he did not try to go into the depth of their demand. These leaders believed that the agrarian problem could be solved by bringing about a change of hearts of the Zamindars. As Rajendra Prasad said in 1931 : "The Kisan should maintain those relations with their landlords which were in existence. They should not hear anybody who told them to stop payment of rent. They should not create any friction".

The statement of Rajendra Prasad expresses his weakness towards the landlords. Instead of preaching to the landlords he preached to the kisans. The irony of fate is that most of the leaders of Bihar started their career as lawyers whose clients were mostly Zamindars. Obviously, Bihar did not have any big industry. The question of finance was there. Darbhanga, Hathwa, Amawan, Bnaili, Dumeraon etc. were the patrons and financiers of the Congress leaders. Sachchidanand Sinha revealed in his works that: "Among them the biggest landlord of Bihar, the Maharajadhiraj of Darbhanga had been one of its foremost financiers". Quite naturally, therefore, in several annual sessions in its formative years, the Congress had passed resolutions asking for the extension of the Permanent Settlement beyond Eastern India. Needless to say that in the beginning the Zamindars dominated the Congress scene in Bihar and most of the Congress leadership stuck to its pro- Zamindari policy. So it was very difficult for the congressmen to adopt an anti-Zamindari attitude. Even at this stage the Congress leadership was in the hands of dedicated Gandhians who did not take up the matter in a decisive way. Their main aim, at first, was to give people swaraj because without swaraj one cannot think of social liberty, equality and justice.

Another reason behind their slackness was the feeling that any drastic step in land tenure might have led to the launching of a class war in the province. They were loath to start agrarian movements like no rent campaigns, and when such movements were started, many Bihar leaders opposed them. Zamindars were occasionally reapproached by the BPCC for their misdeeds, but the emphasis was always on a reconciliation of differences rather than their exploitation to achieve redress. Under above circumstances, the peasants of Bihar had no way out. They turned not to the Congress but to the Kisan Sabha for redressal of their grievances.

Moreover, the Congress leadership was clearly divided into two camps trying to propagate their own views, i.e. Rightwing and Left wing. Walter Hauser has clarified it in this way: "If the Kisan Sabha moved to the left in fulfilling the characteristics which it had developed in the previous years, the Congress party and its ministry amply demonstrated the Right wing characteristics of its dominants and controlling element". Describing the peasants of India attempting to improve their condition as "hordes of Kisans organising themselves", as the leading Rightwing congressmen and Mahatma Gandhi did, "was not an attitude designed to create harmony". Though Sitaramayya has given the national figure, yet the same attitudes were present in Bihar. Therefore, Gandhiji tried his best to moderate the radical intentions of the younger elements or the left wing led by Nehru or Subhash Chandra Bose and stood out as an innovative leader in the political sphere but also as conservative protector of agrarian property, an occasional statement to the contrary not withstanding.

Babu Brajkishore and Rajendra Prasad also exercised the "moderate influence", over the younger section of the Congress camp which wanted to follow the U.P.

Therefore, the Bihar Congress made a modest start to look into the problems of the pesantry and appointed an Enquiry Committee in 1931 for the purposes.

Congress Enquiry Committee

The Enquiry Committee was set up with Rajendra Prasad as Chairman and Sri Krishna Sinha, Abdul Bari, Bipin Bihari Verma, Baldeo Sahay, Prajapati Mishra and Ambika Kant Mishra as members. Along with this, the Congress now undertook the ambitious task of setting up the mass contact committee. This Committee was meant to enquire into the actual strength of the congress in the countryside, and the extent of the membership of its various committees at the thana and the district levels. It further wanted to find out the activities of these committees with regard to peasant problems and to ascertain whether or not the peasants were involved in the local decision making bodies.

But there was a lot of confusion among all. Only some provinces sent their detailed reports; some provinces were not able to complete even their enquiries. Of course, the task was a difficult one. It required theoretical study and practical collection of data., evidences of the villagers, officials, ability and co-operation of the zamindars. Due to the laziness and lack of willingness of party workers as well as the sub-divisional officials the enquiry committees, reports were not submitted within the time limited for it. Bihar did not have revenue officials as it is a permanently settled province and the revenue of each village was paid directly by Zamindars—who held the villages as proprietors, subjects only to the payment of revenue fixed in perpetuily.

The Enquiry Committee issued towards the end of March, 1936, a comprehensive questionnaire requesting the association and individuals concerned to communicate their answers to the secretary at Sadaquat Ashram by the 25th April next at the latest. The real nature of the sincerity and commitment of the Congress to the Kisan cause was revealed by the actual working of the Kisan Enquiry Committee that was set up in the second half of 1936 to look into the grievances and condition of the rural masses.

Indeed, the Congress again played a safe game between the Zamindars and the peasants. From all accounts it is clear that the Committee did not have the patience and interest to go deep into the problems of agrarian discontent which was consequently treated by it very superficially. As the Collector of Arrah said that "the inquiry had led to no concrete result and it was doubtful whether they had any intention of doing anything tangible for the agriculturist".

Firstly, the Committee kept extremely modest behaviour while addressing the agricultural population. Speculations behind this modesty was said to be the coming elections.

Secondly, the Committee's aim was to undo the effects of Sahajanand's recent campaign and to show that the Congress was still a respectable body of men who were not committed to anything such as communism. G.P. Sharma has very well defined the Enquiry Committee's attitude towards the Zamindars as well as the peasantry. While reviewing the whole situation, it was clear that the Committee did not expose its views clearly. In other words Zamindars and peasantry were kept in the dark. The Zamindars had a feeling that the Committee at least won't be harmful to them while Kisans felt that it is their own committee which will take up their causes more promptly. This very act proves that the Committee's approach was favourable. It did not attack the evils of landlordism in public but they attacked the Zamindars locally and sympathised with the Kisans. Therefore, the exploiter thought it was working for their interest only. As several Zamindars told the Collector that the object of the Congress was to waterdown the impact made by the oratory of Swami Sahajanand and to show the Zamindars that although the Congress was out to improve the conditions of the tenants they were not a party to any attack on the Zamindars. So they (Zamindars) became a bit carefree. Most of the Zamindars did not attend the meetings of the Committee but several agents of the big landlords watched the proceedings.

It does not mean that the Committee did not bother for the peasant cause. The Collector of Patna as well as Gaya reported that the Committee told the kisans not to pay the excessive rents and as a result the attitude of the tenants throughout the districts had stiffened. The Committee, for the time being, got the sympathy from both classes (landowner and tenants) but later on its manner of conduct again became an issue of suspicion.

However, Walter Hauser has given his opinion over the Congress's act in this way. "The Congress did open itself to the charge of playing politics with the agrarian question when it suppressed the report of the "Congress Kisan Agrarian Committee". It was said that a report has been written on the basis of enquiry but such a report was neither released by the Enquiry Committee nor was it placed in the hands of the Congress in compliance with the Lucknow resolution. Another mistake on the part of the Committee was that Sahajanand Saraswati was not included in it. The reason behind this is well analyzed by Walter Hauser: "His influence was either considered great, or undesirable, and perhaps both".

Difference-cum-split in Congress and Kisan Sabha

With the above strained background, a gap was naturally enlarged between the Congress and the Kisan Sabha. Pandit Nehru emphasised their relations like this : "In the twentieth century especially after the First World War, too streams—which may be conveniently called bourgeois liberal nationalism and peasant nationalism—came together". At this stage it is needed to observe the difference of opinion between the two (Congress and the Kisan Sabha) which ultimately led to the split.

The formation of the Kisan Sabha in 1929 itself gives the proof of the differences between them. Sahajanand himself agreed that "the difference between the B.P.C.C. and the Kisan Sabha, of course, dates almost from the founding of the latter organisation". Indeed, the Congress was at fault by not associating any of the Kisan representatives in conducting the two enquiries (1931 and 1936). This very Act became an issue for the sabhaites. But one should also not forget Sri Krishna Sinha's inclusion (who was Secretary of the Kisan Sabha) in the Kisan Enquiry Committee, thus giving representation to the Kisan Sabha.

Another allegation levelled against the Enquiry Committee members was that they had some link with the Zamindar class, but this charge is baseless. It is a well-known fact that even if Sahajanand happened to be appointed to (supreme of Kisan Sabha) the Committee, the situation would have been the same, because he also hailed from a Jujhautia Brahman and small zamindar family from Ghazipur District in the United Provinces.

The relations further strained over the Congress policy of distributing tickets to various candidate for District Board and Provincial Assembly (1937). Not to talk of the Kisan Sabha leaders, even those Congressmen who had made great sacrifices in the national struggle were ignored, and their place was taken by several Zamindars and their hangers on. The criteria of candidature was caste and wealth. It also became the matter of criticism. But according to Rajendra Prasad, one important consideration in the selection of the Congress candidates was whether the prospective candidate could cover his own election expenses. In addition, he commented, local circumstances compelled the nomination of candidates who were adequately representative of the prominent class groups. In many instances locally influential men who were hostile to the national movement, became absorbed into the Bihar Congress and filed their own nomination as candidates. It was the demand of the time. Moreover, it was necessary to send our people more and more.

But despite considerable tension and occasional eruptions of conflict, an open cleavage within the Bihar Congress did not develop until after the January, 1937 elections to the Provincial Legislative Assembly. D.A. Low has also added that: "a clash between Kisan Sabha and the Congress was inevitable over the ideals but the Congress maintained the facade of unity of reasons of election in 1937". But here S. Haningham clarified the intention of both nicely. As he says : "prior to the elections mainstream Congressmen and kisan activists were bound together in a relationship of mutual need. For the Kisan Sabha it was the time to increase its membership as they had only a small minority within the Bihar Congress and as well as the Provincial Congress Committee. They had some hold on Patna District and for some time Gaya District too. However, they formed substantial minorities in Champaran, Muzaffarpur, Darbhanga and Monghyr District Committees. Kisan activists needed to delay confrontation with their opponents. Meanwhile they sought to increase their leverage by rallying mass support". Therefore, Congress leaders wanted to take advantage of the Kisan Sabha's immense popularity in strengthening their own position in the legislature but were careful that Sabha candidates be given ticket in as small a number of constituencies as possible.

The reason behind it was that giving ticket on a large scale to the sabhaites would have meant that the Congress leadership would be digging their own grave. So due to the Congress attitude Sahajanand resigned from the Congress Working Committee before election in 1937.

During the election year 1937, the Congress had the opportunity to spread the message of the nationalist movement to the remotest part of the country. Not only that; the election campaign also induced the Congress to organise units in those localities which had so far been left uncovered; thus increasing its organisational base. Nehru's whirlwind tour to the two notable centres of kisan agitation in Patna and Gaya Districts and the popular enthusiasm it aroused, became a legend. Same was the report of the Government. Nehru was reported to have attracted large crowds and he "harped as usual on the poverty of the masses. Rajendra Prasad has also affirmed it that tours of leaders like Sri Jawahar Lal Nehru and Sri Govind Ballabh Pant in Bihar added to the enthusiasm of people."

However, Nehru explained that the voting for the Congress was only a step towards the attainement of Panchayat Raj. Local candidates "were inclined to point extravagant pictures of the golden age which would ensue upon their being elected at the polls". Arvind N. Das has defined in his works the Congress hope of a 'Ramrajya' at some date in future, where the wrongs would be right, and" not a single person should be starving. But the Congress leaders should not forget that Ramrajya was possible only in 'Treta-Yuga' with one dignified leader 'Ram' while this is 'Kali-yuga', with a lot of confused leaders. So it was to imagine the concept of Ramrajya is like growing peanuts in the sky.

The differences between the Congress and the Kisan Sabha grew more bitter after the Assembly election of 1937. The Bihar Congress achieved a thumping majority in the election. Again controversy developed over the formation of the government. The Sabhaites called on the Congress to boycott the Legislature and to press forward with a programme of mass protests but most of the Congressmen did not agree with their point of view. Instead, the Congress assumed office.

However, when the Congress finally decided to form the Government, the Kisan Sabha did not in any way seek to undermine it. On the contrary, the Sabha decided to make use of it, as far as possible, for promoting the peasants cause. It tried to convince the Government of the urgency of the peasant question by organising big peasant rallies. The Kisan leaders for instance asked the peasants throughout Bihar to muster strength before the Legislative Assembly on 23rd August, 1937 the opening day of the Assembly. This demonstration by the peasant's was considered to be historical—as about twenty thousand peasants gathered near the Assembly shouting the slogans "Give us water, we are thirsty, give us bread, we are hungry; remit all agricultural loans, down with Zamindars and save us from oppression". Again on November 26, 1937 a mass demonstration of peasants was staged in Patna, demanding 'Zamindari Abolition, an immediate 50 per cent reduction in rents, a moratorium pending the cancellation of the debt, equitable tenancy laws and higher prices for sugarcane'. The Zamindars observed that some change in agrarian policy was inevitable by the newly formed ministry. In order to cash their sympathy they approached the ministry and offered their help and co-operation in instituting tenancy laws to ameliorate the lot of the kisans and suggested negotiations. In this way a situation emerged to pave the way for the "Congress-Zamindar agreement". On the eve of tenancy legislation in December, 1937 the compromise was necessary. Rajendra Prasad alongwith Maulana Azad took a lot of interest. At this stage Rajendra Prasad clearly described the views of both Ministry and the Kisan Sabha : "we felt that both parties would have to climb down to arrive at a settlement and the Congress should act as a neutral party in the negotiation. But it did not bring any fruitful results. The question of the representation of Kisans was there, and also it seemed quite difficult for the Zamindars as well as the Kisans to do mutual agreement with the Congress".

Once the Congress came into power it did everything to discredit and cripple the Kisan Sabha. They (sabhaites) were charged as a traitor and not as a sympathiser during the election. Not only that, the Congressmen were told not to attend the Kisan Sabha meetings. Even the ballot boxes of Ramnandan Mishra and Yamuna Karjee were removed from the booth by the observer and the presiding officer (manipulated by Congress). Kisans were beaten up and were not allowed to cast their votes. So in reaction Ramnandan Mishra decided to quit the Congress.

The Sabhaites wanted to introduce all the tenancy reforms immediately, while Congress was not in any hurry. As Hamingham has included in his works : "The Bihar Congress remained what McDonald has described as 'multi-interest party' dedicated to the preservation of stability and social harmony. It, therefore, initiated policies designed to improve the position of the tenancy without substantially affecting the position of the small Zamindars. The Kisan Sabha (left wing) responded by claiming that the ministry was betraying both the general

Congress policy and the specific promises made during the election campaign".

Naturally, the radicals and the leftists who had expected too much from the Congress ministry were sorely disappointed. They gave a call for the abolition of Zamindari without compensation and there were threats of violent actions. Of course, kisan movement carried on with agitation for the eradication of abuses connected with Bakasht land. Many incidents of violence occured during this period. For instance "in South Bihar in the Gaya and Patna Districts and in the Barhaiya Tal of South Monghyr, peasants and landlords clashed repeatedly".

Tension further sharpened the situation. The Congress Committees of Saran, Champaran and Monghyr opposed projected visits by Swami Sahajanand, the kisan leader, to these districts. Their decision was later approved by the Provincial Congress Working Committee and rectified by the All India Working Committee. There was also some controversy about the use of the red flag in Congress meetings by the Kisan organisations.

The Patna Commissioner also reported to the Government on 27 October, 1937 that the Kisan agitation was "becoming dangerous." To check its activities which threatened peace the Government officer took immediate steps. Hon'ble Chief Minister Sri S.K. Sinha, while presiding at the Patna District conference at Bakhtiarpur on the 4th December, 1937 asked the Kisans not to resort to force for possession of the bakasht land.

But these advices fell on deaf ears. The kisan feelings had been roused very much by the fiery speeches of their leaders at the meetings held at frequent intervals. Moreover, their activities in certain areas were aggravating agrarian unrest at the risk of peace.

Resolution of the Provincial Congress Committee

The Provincial Congress Committee passed the following resolution on the 14th of December, 1937:

"In the opinion of this committee the kind of propaganda that is being carried on in this Province has been responsible for

> producing a poisonous atmosphere and attacks are being made on the principle of 'Non-violence' which is the cherished creed of the congress." It also apprehended that the "situation is going from bad to worse and there is likelihood of the Congress work being hampered."

It also suggested District Congress Committees to keep an eye on the activities of its workers and report them to the Provincial Congress Committee.

At a meeting held on the 14th of December, 1937, the Bihar Provincial Kisan Council considered this Congress ban "to be very unjust". Sahajanand once again highlighted on the manifesto of the Kisan Sabha. "If the Congress wishes to serve at the same time the interests of other classes, it may do so. But it may never do this at the cost of and inspite of the rich, and not only after fully serving the rich". Henceforth, the *danda-cult* got its way in politics, though Sahajanand justified it in the name of "self-defence." While clarifying it he said, "so long its meaning was religious, but now its purpose has became political and economic. From now Sahajanand became famous as 'dandi-Sanyasi.'

Even Jayaparkash Narain (C.S.P. & BPKS Leader) threatened that if the P.C.C. were so unwise as to take action against Congressmen for their Kisan Sabha activities, such Congress Kisan Sabhaites might have to part company with the Congress. Though the Congress Working Committee in its meeting at Bombay in January, 1938 highly deplored the act of Kisan Sabha for creating an atmosphere of violence yet the Haripura Congress sought to restrain divisiveness by recognising the right of peasants to organise themselves into the Kisan Sabha, while warning Congressmen against condoning any propaganda calculated to incite anyone to violence. The Congress, therefore, called upon Provincial Congress Committees to bear the above in mind and in pursuance of it take suitable action wherever necessary.

Kisan Conferences in Various Parts of the Province

By now the differences took a shape of rupture between the Congress and the Kisans (who had the support of the leftists).

The Sabhaites were shocked at the mendacious charges of preaching violence and creating a poisonous atmosphere made repeatedly against responsible leaders of the Kisan Sabha in Bihar and elsewhere without giving them the slightest chance of answering them. As a result, one after another kisan conferences were arranged by their leaders and the Provincial Kisan Conference held at Bachwara more then 20,000 persons demonstrated and speeches were delivered attacking the agrarian policy of the Ministry with particular reference to their agreement with the Zamindars. There was also big Kisan Sabha and a youth conference held at Madhubani from 25th to 27th March, 1938. Now various Kisan Sabhas took the organisational work. Kisan Sabha offices were established here and there viz., Bettiah and Motihari. Sahajanand while addressing the third All India Kisan Conference at Comilla (13th to 15th May) 1938 spoke of economic independence, without which political independence had no meaning. The kisan and mazdoors all over the world were invited to come under the unbrella of Kisan Sabha carrying Red Flag.

"In North Bihar and particularly in Darbhanga the (leftwing) activists kept trying to capture control over the local party organisation. They even set up rival, parallel District Congress Committees in both Darbhanga and Saran." However, in August, 1938, Ramnandan Mishra reported from Darbhanga that—"In the interest of the cause . . . we must get out of the party struggle at least for a year. Kisan problems require our immediate attention. Situation is very critical and serious, how can we leave the kisans, who are being assaulted, murdered, abused and their crops and property looted. Even yesterday one of my workers was attempted to be murdered". Jadunadan Sharma, Sheo Shankar Bharti, and Malaya Krishna Brahmachari at Gaya and in part of Patna and Monghyr took prominent lead to activise the Sabha. Inspite of Sahajanand's tour of Santhal Pargana the kisan movement did not secure firm ground there. Again kisan demonstrations were organised under the guidance of Sahajanand in the District headquarters on 8th August, 1938 and the demonstration at the provincial level took place at Patna on the 15th of August, 1938. Further, on 1st September, 1938 a kisan demonstration was staged on the eve of "All India Kisan Day." Consequently, the District Kisan Conferences were held at Masaurhi (16th to 17th November 1938) in the Patna district and on 19 to 20th November 1938, at Lakhisarai, Monghyr. Saran district was also toured by Sahajanand Saraswati to intensify the struggle of the peasantry.

The tension between the Congress and the Kisan Sabha continued when Sardar Patel questioned the right of peasants to form class organisation at all and Gandhiji suggested that "kisan sabhaites who sought to win majorities in Congress Committees were bound to win opposition to their activities." So at the Delhi meeting of the All India Congress Committee (September 1938), a resolution directed at the Bihar Kisan Sabha charged some Congressmen with violence, arson and murder and asked the Congress Committees to take action against them. When the resolution was passed the leftists walked out, whereupon Gandhiji is said to have invited them to leave the Congress. As a result, N.G. Ranga (All India Kisan Sabha) decided to launch a peasants struggle while remaining in the party until driven by the Rightist whereas Sahajanand did not accept the resolution.

Malayakrishna thought that the Congress alienated the Kisan Sabha. Thus, there was polarisation of classes in agrarian areas. But this view was not wholly true because the Congress organisations tried their best, and were still trying, to effect a compromise but with no success.

From late 1938 onwards, this storm of charges and counter-charges made the situation more critical, with the kisan activists concentrating on leading the peasantry on mass protest against their landlords and against the pro-landlord policies of the Bihar Congress and the provincial administration.

Bihar Provincial Kisan Conference, Waini (Darbhanga)

Under these grim circumstances "the Annual Conference of the Bihar Provincial Kisan Sabha held at Waini in Darbhanga on 3rd & 4th December, 1938 resolved to use satyagraha as the chief weapon of struggle in defence of the peasants' interests". There were naturally some "extreme speeches" in the conference. Rahul

Sankratyayan advocated "Satyagraha in every district." Henceforth, the Kisan movement was engaged in frequent direct action.

Thus, the struggle for the restoration of the Bakasht land forcibly occupied by the Zamindars from the tenant on one pretext or the other, took place in the Districts of Darbhanga, Saran, Champaran, Arrah, Patna, Gaya, Monghyr and Bhagalpur. Among them one can see the hightened peasant consciousness in Barhaiya Tal (Monghyr district), Reora (Patna district) and Majhiyama in Gaya, where the intensity and organisation of the Kisan movement were well planned.

Before those incidents on the issue of Bakasht land, in the Padri (or Parri) circle in south east Darbhanga, the situation became very tense. In June, 1936 the local officials of the Darbhanga Raj broke up a large kisan meeting by driving an elephant into the crowd. Using this incident as a rallying cry, kisan workers continued their efforts to have the peasant's grievances redressed. In 1939, in response to continuing agitation Sri Krishna Sinha had to visit Pardi. Naturally, the Chief Manager of Darbhanga Raj, G.P. Danby made personal investigation and reported in May 1938 that "The Tenancy are generally in a deplorable condition . . . If we do not give immediate consideration to the tenants, so distressed will they become that I cannot imagine their future. There has been considerable agitations and I am ashamed to say that it is due to some extent to the neglect and lack of sympathy shown to tenants . . . I believe the tenants are still loyal to the Raj and would become as good as any other if now and in the future, due consideration were given to them. While Karynanand Sharma started satyagraha in Barhaiya Tal, Jadunandan Sharma started it by cutting the crops in the disputed land at Reora, while Rahul Sankratyayan took the lead in Amwari in Chapra.

Thus, the Kisan movement affected practically all the permanently settled areas in Bihar except those which belonged to the tribal areas with different forms of land tenure. But one thing that is remarkable was that these land struggles were not carried on against the big Zamindars but against the small and middle Zamindars. In such cases the scope for opperession was carried by the agents of the Zamindars rather than the Zamindars themselves. The attacks were directed not so much against the Zamindars as against their amlas. Whereas in case of the small and middle Zamindaries, the properietors were more under fire, because their lands were not permanently settled.

But the situation at Barhaiya Tal in Monghyr district became worse due to the long drawn agitation of the kisans. S.K. Sinha who became the 1st chief minister later on, along with Nand Kumar Singh, interfered and both had talks with the tenants as well as the Zamindars, and brought about rapprochement between the Zamindars and the tenants in the presence of Karynanand Sharma, but the rapprochement did not last long. Karynanand Sharma was blamed for the whole episode. Later the Monghyr District Political Conference under the presidentship of Sarojini Naidu spoke highly in favour of kisans but did not blame the Zamindars at all. Now a committee consisting of N.K. Singh (later president of B.P.C.C.), Shyama Prasad Singh (later chairman of the Bihar Legislative Assembly and Mahanth Siyaram Das was formed to enquire into the whole situation. Over its report Rajendra Prasad visited Barhaiya and in order to ease the situation he offered an award which is known as "Rajendra Babu's Award." The conditions of the award was that the Zamindars must settle atleast that much area of their Bakasht lands with the tenants as they used to settle with them before the agitations of 1936. A list of tenants alongwith the area of land which used to be settled with them by the Zamindars was drawn up. But this did not resolve the complaint of the tenants. However, the struggle continued till 1939. The Bihar Congress Ministry initiated ameliorative measures designed to defuse kisan protest. The measures included legislation allowing reduction of rents in view of the low prices prevailing and the legislation concerning newly made Bakasht lands. The Bakasht Restoration Bill provided, under certain conditions, for the return to the tenants lands which had been sold off during the period from 1929 to 1936, if in return the tenants paid, within a period of five years, half the auction price of the holding as well as the legal costs. The amount of land to be returned varied in proportion to the amount that had been sold off.

Table 3.1
Formula for Restoration of the Bakasht Lands, 1938

Area sold of	*Quantity Restorable*
Less than 6 acress	All to be restored
More than 6 but less than 15 acres	Half to be restored
More than 15 but less than 30 acres	One-third to be restored
more than 30 acres	One-quarter to be restored

Source : Indian Nation, 31 July, 1938.

By September, 1939 the struggle was clearly on the wane. Protests recurred in subsequent months but not with the same intensity. With the outbreak of the Second World War, the kisan workers (who were not in jail) got distracted from the Bakasht issues over the question of what attitude to take towards the war. In December, 1939 despite the commencement of the harvesting season, the agrarian situation remained quite. And in January 1940, the situation of the countryside was officially estimated to be unusually quite. Therefore, the Bakasht struggle which had caused grave anxiety had come to an end.

CONSTRUCTIVE MEASURES OF THE BIHAR CONGRESS MINISTRY: FIRST PHASE OF AGRARIAN REFORMS

Bihar Tenancy (Amendment) Act

The Congress Working Committee authorised congressmen to accept office by its resolution of the 7th July, 1937. Accordingly, the Bihar Congress Government took office on the 20th July, 1937. The most important legislative measure to the credit of the Ministry was the Bihar Tenancy (Amendment) Act, which was intended to afford relief to the tenancy. They organised a meeting in the State capital (Patna) on 13 September, 1937 and they even thought of "Civil Disobedience and Passive Resistance". In the meantime, an agreement was reached between the Zamindars and Maulana Abul Kalam Azad, both of whom were eager to mitigate the rigours of a chronic social malady. At first, Bihar Money Lender's Act was passed to give relief to the debtors. In all these measures intended to ameliorate the condition of masses the guiding principles had been those which were laid down in the *Congress Election Manifesto* and *Faizpur Resoltuion* and the Government had done their best to bring relief to the masses.

The new Tenancy Act provided the following measures of relief to the tenants :—

1. The Bihar Tenancy (Amendment) Act, 1927.
2. The Chotanagpur Tenancy (Amendment) Act, 1928.
3. The Bihar Tenancy (Amendment) Act, 1928.
4. The Champaran Agrarian (Amendment) Act, 1928.
5. The Bihar Restoration of Bakasht Land and Reduction of Arrears of Rent Act.

An important provision of the Bihar Tenancy (Amendment) Bill was approved by the Select Committee and finally passed as an Act in December, 1937 related to distribution of holdings of the occupancy raiyats for purposes of sale, partition/ inheritance.

The relevant provisions under section 315-A reads as follows :—

(1) when an occupancy holding had been the subject of a partition by order of a court:

(a) The division of the said holding made in pursuance of such order shall be binding on the landlord.

(b) If the rent of the holding is distributed by agreement between the parties, and the landlords do not accept this distribution, the landlords or any of the parties to the partition may make an application to the Collector to distribute the rent of the holding.

(c) If the parties to the partition are unable to distribute the rent of holding by agreement, any of them may apply to the Collector to distribute the rent of the holding.

(2) When an occupancy holding has been the subject of partition, otherwise than by an order of a court :—

(*a*) The division of the said holding made in accordance with such partition shall be binding on the landlord.

(*b*) If notice in writing of the partition and distribution of the rent had been served on the landlord in the prescribed manner, such distribution of the rent shall by binding on the landlord. Provided that, the landlord may if he objects to such distribution, make an application.

Thus, the Act cancelled all enhancement of rents made during the years 1911-36. Rents were reduced by 25 per cent generally in proportion to the fall in prices in the same period. There was a provision for the total or partial remission of rents where the soil had deteriorated, in consequence of sand deposits or other causes. Section 67 relating to interest was modified by inserting the following provisions:

(1) "67(1) clause 9 : An arrear of rent shall bear simple interest at the rate of 61/4 per annum.

(2) Such interest shall be payable in the case of a money rent, from the expiry of that quarter of the agricultural year in which the installment falls due, and in the case of rent payable in kind from the end of the agricultural year in which the payment falls due, and shall in either case be payable up to the date of payment or of the institution of the suit which ever is earlier.[111]

The Bihar Tenancy (Amendment) Act 1937 also provided for the abolition of all abwabs and illegal exactions which were levelled by the Zamindars in addition to the normal legal rent. It also banned Section 75 in the 1885 Tenancy Act. Now any such extortion on the part of the Zamindar was made punishable.

The provision relating to the settlement of rent is found in Section 17 under 112A (i) of the *Bihar Tenancy (Amendment) Act.*

In order to meet the demand for conversion of *Bhoali* into *nagdi*, Section 40 already existed in Bihar Tenancy Act, but now with the passage of time certain provisions were added to Section 40 of the Tenancy Act.

With these somewhat changed provisions, discussions were held in Legislative Assembly. Many views were given about its possible effects on the occupancy raiyats. Attempts were made to obtain for permanent tenure holders the facility for the distribution of rent in the event of two tenants sharing the plots of one landlord. Commenting on it, Shafi Mohammad Hafeez (a member) said that the position of tenure holders including Permanent Mukarridays and those who held land fixed rates of rent stood altogether on a different footing from that of occupancy tenants. While the former were not given the facility of rent distribution and of splitting up of holdings, for the tenure holders there was no provision over rent reduction.

Jamuna Prasad Sinha also spoke on the question of tenure holders but Baldev Sahay a Congressman and Advocate General of Bihar, very clearly pointed out during the Assembly debate that the tenure holders were not a class of tenants for whom the relief was meant.

However, some of the clauses of the *Bihar Tenancy (Amendment) Act*, 1937 could not satisfy a section of the people. Hon'ble Sri S.K. Sinha informed the house that on 28th July the Bihar Tenancy (Amendment) Bill, 1938 (Bill No. 8 of 1938) as reported by Select Committee (on recommittal) be taken into considertion. Dr. Ganesh Dutta Singh thanked the Government for admitting the matter. It was repealed by the Bihar Tenancy (Amendment) Act of 1938.

The Bihar Tenancy Amendment Act (1938) repealed those sections of the Bihar Tenancy Act which dealt with right of the landlords to take out certificate for recovery of arrears of rent, abolished landlords' transfer fees and defined the rights of the tenants in trees, plantations and Jalkar in their holdings. In this way the Act of 1938 went further and abolished the system of kind rents, prohibited rent enhancement during the next 15 years, withdrew the Zamindars right to claim damages against rent arrears to 6.25% and conferred hereditory right on such tenants as had occupied lands for 12 years and provided against their eviction.

Special tenancy legislations in the shape of *the Champaran Agrarian Amendment Act* and the *Chotanagpur Tenancy Amendment Act* were passed with a view to meeting the local needs of those areas. The former cancelled enhancement made in the list of Champaran by landlords after releasing their tenants from the obligation to grow indigo, and the latter was intended to mitigate the hardships of the tenantry on account of the operation of some of the provisions of Chotanagpur Tenancy Act of 1908 which gave them certain facilities, and conceded to them the right of transfer, though to a limited extent.

Further, the Bakasht problem attracted a good deal of attention of all congressmen and it was debated at great length in both the Houses of the Provincial Assembly. The Bihar Restoration of Bakasht Land and Reduction of Arrears of Rent Act sought to effect restoration of lands of the kisans which were sold during the period of depression for arrears of the rent and were purchased by landlords for grossly inadequate prices.

The reduction of arrears was opposed by the representatives of the Zamindars Sir Ganesh Dutt Singh came up with the plea that any reduction in rent or arrears would not prevent the tenant from getting into the bad habit of not paying rents. In his view, the reduction would lead to the non-payment of rent. When the Bill was passed it provided not only for reducing the amount of arrears of rent by half but also for its payment in five instalments in five years.

Agricultural Income Tax

Another great measure taken by the Ministry was the Agricultural Income Tax which had been perplexing the Congress Ministry for quite sometime. To begin with, the very idea of taxing agricultural income was opposed by the big Zamindars and their spokesmen such as Sir Ganesh Dutt Singh, C.P.N. Singh, Tazammul Hussain etc. They asked why should only agricultural income be taxed. Why not the Government service holder, and military men who gets excessive salaries, be taxed? Government justification for its imposition was that this amount will be spent on education, Irrigation etc. However, Jamuna Karjee, the Kisan Sabha spokesman, favoured the progressive taxation.

The leaders of the Congress, however, kept pretending that the tenants had been able to reap the advantage of the new law

(The Bihar Tenancy Amendment Act—Act 8 of 1937—and the Bihar Restoration of Bakasht Lands and Reduction of Arrears of Rent Act—Act 9 of 1938) almost immediately. Inspite of this the Kisan Sabha as well as the officials admitted marked increase in the number of rent suits in Monghyr district: *(a)* due to the landlords fear(sic) of anticipated proceedings for reduction of arrears of rent. These events led both of the parties (Landlords and kisans) to consolidate their position and organisation. Their activity (Kisan Sabha) was so intensive that the kisan-cum-socialist group captured the district and town Congress Committees. The slogan of "kaise lagay Malguzari, Lathi Hamara Zindabad" (How will you collect rent, long live our lathis) became the order of the day. They even did not care for the presence of the Gorkha troops called by the Government. The Gaya district alone restored the dispossessed tenants about 90% of their holdings on an original 1500 bighas through a compromise negotiated by the District Collector between the Zamindar and the Kisan Sabha representatives. After such events in 1938, the relation between Congress and Kisan Sabha stood on the verge of explosion.

However, the Second World War intervened and the relations between the Congress and Sabha were left in a state of 'animated suspension' till 1945-46. In this period Kisan Sabha finally got attracted towards the Forward Bloc of Subhash Chandra Bose and again to the Communist Party of India. After such events, the relations between the two never revived.

Extreme view of the Leftist : The Socialist and the Forward Bloc

To the leftists group belong none but the Congress Socialist Party, the Forward Bloc, the Kisan Sabha and the Communists and Radical Democrats; all trying to win over the masses with their programme under the banner of Congress.

It is remarkable that after large scale Socialist participation in Kisan Sabha, the dominant reaction of the Socialist were not so critical of the Congress leadership as before. Though they were not satisfied with the programme and policies of it yet they never opposed the leadership which, time and again, provided some measures to the masses. Congress Socialist Party expressed its total faith on Congress leadership as regards the success of the national movement. They even supported Gandhiji as against Subash Chandra Bose at Tripuri and again at Ramgarh Session of the Congress. Sahajanand's efforts during this period was to maintain the balance of power. Sometimes he felt close to C.S.P. and sometimes to Forward Bloc or C.P.I. but never with the parent Congress Party. By weakening the Congress he thought of a united left as an alternative to the Congress.

The Congress Socialist Party leaders did not agree to it. They (specially Achraya Narendra Dev) also had reservation on the formation of the Kisan Sabha and its Red flag replacing the tricolor. But they could not put their point (on the issue of flag) strongly because of the support by some comrades earlier. Sahajannad left Consolidation Committee with N.G. Ranga as the representative of Kisan Sabha.

The left Consolidation Committee did not bring any positive result to the unity effort after its two or three meetings. Frustrated by it, Sahajanand reported that the "Socialists never participated in it, though he had requested Jayaprakash Narain (leading Socialist leader) and others and they promised too but they relapsed into silence. They criticised their Socialist friends for their lethargic behaviour telling them that "they wanted to turn the Kisan Sabha into the tail of the Congress." They were more interested in making speeches and finding fault than working sincerely.

But Jayaprakash Narain charged the Kisan Sabha that its nature was of mutual discord, endless bickering and party politics . . . etc. At this stage Socialists edged closer to the position of the official Congress leadership. Moreover, at the Ramgarh Congress (1940), the Sabha for all practical purposes was on the verge of split and it happened in 1941, at Dumaraon Session.

Ultimately, Sahajanand decided to join the Forward Bloc in an attempt to find a forum for consistent and militant anti-imperialism. As he himself realised : "My experience during these years have convinced me that the Communists are more prompt and interested in the welfare of the kisans than the Socialists."

After having separated himself from the CSP, Sahajannand found shortlived hope in his alignment with Bose in the Forward Bloc. He had confidence in Bose's leadership and the Bloc as an instrument of unified action. Justifying his move he (Sahajanand) wrote to Mr. P.C. Joshi : "We cannot do without some such bloc or platform. If we still hesitate in this most timely, opportune and wise move and fail to support Mr. Bose, the future of the country is doomed atleast for sometime, I am confident".

Hence, the two (Sahajanand and Bose) combined and Sahajanand gave the call for 'direct action', but their alliance did not last long.

After the Palasa session of AIKS, Sahajanand was jailed. There he came in contact with some founder Communist members of the party. Later Sri Karynanad Sharma, took the lead and Uma Shankar Shukla, Indradeep Sinha, Rajkumar Purbey, Bhogendra Jha, Yogendra Sharma and many others at the district level controlled the Kisan Sabha organisational machinery as it was already passing into the hands of the C.P.I. leaders. Though even till as late as 1940-41 Sahajanand was under the illusion that Communists do not count in the Kisan Sabha. It also gave support to the "Peoples War of Soviet Russia against Germany." With this background Sahajanand was released. Even before his release the AIKS adopted the 'peoples' war line. Now he further changed his line of action and advised restraint to the peasants. With Subhash's dramatic escape, Sahajanand's short lived alliance with Bose came to an end. The situation further changed in the Bihta session of AIKS in May, 1942 when Ranga and his followers left the Sabha and decided to revive the Kisan Congress. Now there remained the CPI and the Sabhaites.

In jail, Sahajanand was highly impressed with the programme of the Communist Party. They surrounded him and he imbibed heavily of their ideology and he read the classic writings of Marxism, as also Engels, Lenin and others. Swamiji became immersed in theoretical speculation to the point of producing a large volume on the relationship of the peasant and revolution as he saw it in India. Many of the peasant activists were attracted toward it and on 19 Oct., 1939 from the Bihar branch of C.P.I.,

Rahul Sankratyayan, a noted leader spoke in the ninth BPKS Conference. Sahajanand gave a new policy on the agrarian agitation in the Province. He says Zamindari dies hard and it goes on kicking, we have to defeat it and end it with all our might but let us wait therefore for some time." Today the Government also must be anxious that its energy is not wasted in local strifes and it has to find a way out of them. Let us tell all concerned that for the present we do not want to wage any kisan struggle unnecessarily : Let us at the same time assure the kisans to have patience and wait . . . Let one more chance be given to them (the Zamindars) and if they fail even after that we shall go on our own way.

Really, it was a new and different Sahajanand, not that militant and active one. But as Walter has judged, this transformation neither benefited him nor the movement he had founded. On such reduction of his position, one bewildered kisan asked has the 'dandi sanyasi' lost his danda? He became disenchanted with the Communists policies even and in 1945 he left them to seek new political alignments. But this time he failed as he had alienated not only political associates in these years but also his mass support.

It may be said that he chose to ride on different horses (Socialists, Forwards Bloc and Communists) with the same speed under the same banner (of Congress) at the same time which was quite impossible and the fall was inevitable. He was left alone and helpless. As Walter wrote: "He had misjudged the sentiments of India and Bihar".

Second Phase of Agrarian Reforms : Election Manifesto of 1945

In the *Election Manifesto of the Congress* issued in 1945 on the eve of last general election great stress was laid on the reform of the 'Land System' which was regarded as one of the urgent need of the country. It was further considered that in order to effect substantial reform in the land system, it was essential to remove all intermediaries between the peasant and the State, and that the rights of such intermediaries should be acquired on payment of equitable compensation.

In pursuance, therefore, of the pledge given to the electorate, on behalf of the Congress in the election manifesto a resolution urging the State Government to take immediate steps for the abolition of Zamindari System in Bihar was adopted by the Bihar Legislative Assembly.

After the assumption of office by the Congress Ministry in 1946, the Bihar Tenancy (Amendment) Acts, 1946, 1947, 1948 and 1950 were passed. The uniform object of these amendments had been to bend the provision of the Bihar Tenancy Act of 1885 in favour of the peasants. The Amendment Act of 1946 inserted a new Section 178 C, which provided that where rent in respect of an occupancy holdings was payable in kind by division of produce, the landlord was not entitled to a share in the straw or *Bhoosa* as rent out of the produce of that holding. These provisions were made applicable to any suit or appeals pending for recovery of arrears of rent on the date the Act came into force. The Amendment Act XIV of 1946, amended Section 40 of the Bihar Tenancy Act of 1885 relating to the commutation of rent payable in kind by an occupancy raiyat. It provided that the officer should determine the commuted rent, having regard to the average value of rent actually received by the landlord during the five years before, the first day of Aswin, 1347, Fasli.

The Amending Act XXII of 1947 amended several sections of the Bihar Tenancy Act of 1885. The main changes introduced in the Act were: *firstly,* one new Section (21-A) that was inserted regarding the settlement of the Bakasht lands. The Bakasht land meant any land other than the proprietors private lands as defined in Section 120 of the Bihar Tenancy Act, 1885, which was for the time being in the cultivating possession of a proprietor. *Secondly,* it provided that every person whether he was a settled raiyat of a village or not was entitled to the right of occupancy in all lands held by him as raiyat. But the raiyat did not have such rights in any Bakasht land settled with him by a proprietor whose total holding did not exceed 40 acres, unless the settlement was made by a registered document. Certain restrictions were placed on the proprietors in settling his Bakasht land: For example, he had to give preference to a resident of the village, could not charge rent more than the prevailing rate, could not charge salami or premium, etc. In the event of his accepting any monetary considerations the Act provided for illegal exactions.

Provisions have been made, giving the occupancy raiyats rights for manufacturing bricks and tiles, excavating tanks and sinking wells and constructing buildings for the use of educational and charitable institutions and other public purposes on their own raiyati lands.

Provisions also included that the consent of landlord would not be necessary for planting trees, etc. In Bhaoli land, the landlord and the raiyat have equal share in fruits and trees.

Section 29 of the Bihar Tenancy Act contained certain conditions which practically nullified the restrictions regarding enhancement of rents; they were, therefore, omitted.

Provisions for enhancement of rent on the ground that the rent was below the prevailing rate for lands of similar description and with similar conditions in the same village or neighbouring villages has been omitted.

Section 52(B) has been added providing that where a landlord dispossesses a tenant from the holding or part thereof, he shall not be entitled to any rent in respect of the holding or part thereof for the period of such dispossession.

Where rent is remitted by Postal Money Order, it has been provided that the postal acknowledgement will be taken as an acquittance for the amount of rent remitted in the same manner and the same extent as if the amount of rent has been received by the landlord.

In order to ensure that the tenants get valid rent receipts, provisions has been made in Section 59 making it obligatory on the part of the landlord to issue receipts only from the Collector's office which will keep a record of issue of such books after they had been numbered and sealed in the Collector's office. The landlord have to give a return showing the number of receipts in each volume used in granting receipts for payment of rent in each village during the agricultural year.

If a landlord contravenes this provision of law, he shall be liable to fine not exceeding Rs. 500 which will be imposed after a summary enquiry by the Collector.

Section 69 has been amended so that if a landlord applied for the division of his produce, the application has to be filed within the prescribed period, whereas no such limit has been prescribed in case of application by the tenants.

Section 88 of the Act which provided that the division of a tenure would not be binding on the landlord without his consent has been omitted. Another Section (88 A) has been introduced by which a division of any tenure of holding or distribution of rent has been made binding on the landlord. If by registered post, a notice of such division or distribution, containing the prescribed particulars, is given to the landlord, the landlord may file an objection to the Collector praying for fair and equitable distribution of rent within three months of the date of service of the notice. If the parties to the transfer are unable to divide the tenure or holding or to distribute the rent payable in respect thereof by agreement, any of them may apply to the Collector for the division of tenure or holding or distribution of rent.

Provision regarding distraint of crops for realisation of arrears rent have been omitted.

The tenant has been given the right to file written statement without leave of the court, provision has also been made for the payment of decretal amount of arrear rent in instalments.

A tenant cannot be turned out of his homestead, even if the holding is sold for arrears of rent.

Section 178(B) of the Act has been amended so that before the produce is divided between the landlord and the tenant the cost of harvesting may be deducted.

Bihar Tenancy (Amendment) Act, 1950 was passed with the object of giving to Tenants unrestricted rights in the trees standing on their holding on the analogy of the rights enjoyed by the Tenants of the Chotanagpur division.

Thus, the Bihar Tenancy Act of 1885 was torn to shreds, it was the ghost of its former self. Though the same Act was in vogue, it was a new Act more in accordance with the current tempers and scales.

On the eve of India's independence, the Zamindari System was tottering, likely to crumble of its own weight. Certainly all credit goes to the Government to move the Bihar Abolition of Zamindari Bill in the Assembly in 1947, which gave the highest priority to the 'Abolition of Zamindari System', a long due demand of the masses.

Thus, the Congress Ministry took definite steps to safeguard the rights of the raiyats and improve their economic conditions.

Notes & References

Amrit Bazar Patrika, 23rd April, 1817.

Diwakar, R.R., *Bihar Through the Ages*, 1958, p. 658.

Gandhi, M.K., *An Autobiography*, Ahmedabad, (reprint of 1863), p. 304.

Diwakar, R.R., *Bihar Through the Ages*, Calcutta, 1958, p. 665.

Datta, K.K., *Mahatma Gandhiji in Bihar*, Patna-(n.d.) p. 72.

Tendulkar, D.C., *Gandhiji in Champaran*, Delhi, 1960, pp. 114-115.

Ranga, N.G., and Saraswati, Sahajanand; "Agrarian Revolts" in A.R. Desai (ed.) *Peasant Struggle in India*, p. 55

Dutta, K.K., *Gandhiji in Bihar*, p. 34.

Sharma, G.P., *Congress and the Peasant Movement in Bihar*, Bombay, 1985, p. 70.

Johnson, Chalmens, *Peasant Nationalism and Communist Party*, Stanford, 1962.

Lin Piao (ed.), *Quotations from Chairman Mao Tse-Tung*, Peking, 1970.

D.I.G. Police to Chief Secretary, Government of B.L.O., Jan. 20, 1921, Polo spl. file 21, 1921.

Reports of the special session as well as the regular session held between the period in Bombay and Delhi—shows Bihar poor represenation.

Gupta, M.P., *The Indian National Congress*. Delhi, 1985, p. 92.

Seal, Anil, *The Emergence of Indian Nationalism*, London, 1968, p. 274.

I.N.C. 1888, Resolution of XIV; 1889, Resolution VI; 1893, Resolution 1893, Resolution X; 1904, Resolution II, 1900.

Report of the 45th Session at the Indian National Congress held at Karachi in 1931, p. 4.

Hauser, Walter, *The Bihar Provincial Kisan Sabha and the Congress*. Chicago 1961, p. 109.

Report of the General Secretaries 45th Indian National Congress, published by R.K. Sidhwa and Dr. Tarachand J. Lalwani.

History of the Indian National Congress, Vol. II, 1936-47. Sitaramayya, P., Bombay p. 28.

Shiv Kumar, *Peasantry and the Indian National Movement*, 1919-33, *Op.cit.*, p. 21, also see Swami Vivekanand, Collected Works Vol. VII, . 309.

Gyanchand, *Socialist Tranformation of Indian Economy*, New Delhi, 1965.
Cited in Malviya, H.D., *The Land Reforms in India*, New Delhi, All India Congress Committee.
Nehru, Jawahar Lal, *An Autobiography*, Calcutta, 1962, p. 48.
Quoted in Tarachand, *History of Freedom Movement in India*, Vol. IV, p. 218.
"Congress Election Manifesto" August 23, 1936, Bombay.
Indian National Congress Resolution on Economic Policy and Programme, 49th Congress session at Lucknow, April 12-14, 1936, p. 6.
Saraswati, Sahajanand, *Mera Jeevan Sangarsh*, Patna, 1952, pp. 69-70.
The Communist, February, 1937, p. 37.
Tomlinson, *Indian National Congress and the Raj*, London, 1976. pp. 80-85.
Manifesto of B.P.K.S., "Government of Bihar, Home Political Department (Special), File No. 68/1936.
"All India Kisan Conference, Gaya", Government of Bihar, Home Political Department (Special), File No. 217/1939.
Chaudhary, Valmiki, *Dr. Rajendra Prasad Correspondence and Select Documents*, Vol. III (January to July), New Delhi, 1980.
Rajendra Prasad's letter to Ram Dayalu Sinha, Dec. 7, 1937, Rajendra Prasad's papers file No. 111/37 NMML.
Home Political File No. 34/1931.
Sinha, Sachchidanand, *Some Eminent Bihari Contemporaries*, Patna, 1944, p. 37.
Indian National Congress Resolution on Economic Policy and Programme, New Delhi, 1954.
Das, Arvind N., *Agrarian Unrest and Socio-Economic Change*, New Delhi, 1980.
Dhanagre, D.N., *Peasant Movements in India*, New Delhi, 1983, p. 226.
Agrarian Situation in Bihar or Orissa, Kisan Sabha, file no. 34/1931, BSCRO, Patna.
Rajendra Prasad papers, file no. IX/36 NMML.
Congress Bulletin Report of the General Secretaries, AICC. Allahabad, A.L.J. Press Allahabad.
Fortnightly Report of the Patna Commissioner for the period ending 11th April, 1936, *The Searchlight*, 1st April, 1936, Vide Appendix XVIII.
Home Political File No. 6/1936 (Part III-B).
A letter from Collector Arrah to the Commissioner, Patna division, Home special file no. 6/1936.

Home special file *Op.cit.*, letter from the Magistrate to the Commissioner of Patna, 10th July, 1936.

Sahajanand: Mera Jeevan Sangarsha, *Op.cit.*, P. 339.

Hauser, *Op.cit.*, pp. 3536; Searchlight, Dec. 29, 1922.

Low, D.A., *Congress and the Raj*, (1917-47) p. 305.

Rajendra Prasad, *Autobiography*, Bombay 1957, pp. 427-30; Report of the Violence Enquiry Committee, f. p. 6, 1939-40, AICCP, NML, [hereafter violence report] Ramanand Singh to J.L. Nehru, 10 Nov. 1936, Ps, 1936, AICCP, NML, GB, FR(2) Nov. 1936, FR(2) Dec. 1936, FR(1) Feb. 1937, HP Files 18/11/1936, 18/12/1936, NAI, *Op.cit* Tomlinson, National Congress and Raj, pp. 79, 83.

Heningham, Stephen, Peasents Movement in Colonial India, Canbena—1982, p. 147.

B.L.A. Debates, 1938, pp. 1310-21.

Brecher estimates his total audience of 10 million, see Brehcer, p. 227.

Government of Bihar, *Note on the Kisan Movement in Bihar*, p. 5.

Prasad, Rajendra, *Atmakatha*, pp. 465-66.

Government of Bihar, *Note on the Kisan Sabha*, p. 5.

Wasi, S.M., *Bihar in 1937-38*, Supd., Government Printing, Bihar, Patna, 1941, p. 3.

Das, A.N., *Agrarian Movement in Bengal and Bihar*, 1919-39, Oxford, *Op.cit.*, p. 364.

Singh (ed.) the Bihar code. P. III

Janata, October 27, 1938, p. 8.

Janata, August 11, 1938, editorial. pp. 5-6.

Mc C Donald, Unity on Trial, pp. 307-311, Sahajanand's statement of September 1937, f.G. 98, 1937-38, AICCP, NML; GB FR(1) Sept. 1937 to GOI, HPF 18/9/1937, NAI.

Chaudhary, R.K., *Government of India Act and the Congress.* (1935-39) 'History of Indian National Congress in Bihar (1885) K.P. Jaiswal Research Institute, Patna, 1985, p. 457.

GBDFR(2) March 1936, HPf 18/3/1936; GBFR(I) July 1936, HPf 18/7/1936; GBFR(I) Dec. 1937, HPf 18/12/1937 all in the NAI, Indian Nation, 10 April and 5 Aug. 1938.

Wasi, S.M., *Op.cit*, Patna, (1941) p. 3. Also see S. Hanningham, "Peasant Movement in Colonial India, 1917-42, Canberra, 1982, p. 149.

Fortnightly Report of the Patna Commissioner for the period ending 27th Dec. 1937.

Saraswati, Sahajannad, *Mera Jeewan Sangharsh, Op.cit*, (My life struggle), pp. 509-11.

Indian National Congress Report of the General Secretary, Jan. 1937, Feb. 1938, pp. 31-32.

Mitra, N.N. (ed.), *The Indian Annual Register*, January-June, 1939, (Calcutta : The Annual Register Office, 1938) 349.

All India Kisan Sabha, All India Kisan Committee Meeting at Vithalnagar (Bihar) 1938, p. 3.

Report on Political events in Bihar for the second half of January, 1938.

Krishna Chandra Mukherji, General Secretary, Bihar CSP, Darbhanga Branch to J.P. Narayan, Aug. 5, 1938 CSP, f 23, 1937-38, JPNP, NML; GBFR (2) June 1938, FR (1) Aug. 1938, FR (1) Sept. 1938, HP files, 18/6/1938, 18/8/1938, 18/9/1938, NAI.

Ramnandan Misra to Dear Comrade (presumably J.P. Narayan), Laheriasarai, Aug. 17, 1938, Agriculturalists Union, f. 149, 1930, JPNP, NML.

Report of the General Secretaries 'AICC.' New Delhi, September 1938.

Janata, December 1937, pp. 21-23.

Home special, confidential file no. 29 (vii) 1939 containing a note on p. 9, Para. 1.

Bihar Landholder's Association Papers, S.N. Sinha Library, Patna; Indian Nation, 2 April, 27 July, 31 July, 1938. Hauser, Bihar Kisan Sabha, pp. 127-30, Note by M.G. Hallet dated 26 Sept. 1938 enclosed with Hallet to Brabourne, 27 Sept. 1938, MSSEURF 125/45, IOL.

GBFR, Land Revenue Administration Report for 1939-40, pp. 12-13, and for 1940-41 pp. 11-12.

GBFR, (1) Dec. 1939, HPG 18/12/1939; GBFR (1) Jan. 1940, HPG 18/1/1940, NAI, In the ensuing months there were some minor disturbances, but in late May the administration reported that 'Purely agrarian agitation has almost ceased : See GB Fortnightly Reports for February, March, and May 1940, HP files 18/12/1940, 18/5/1940, NaI.

Letter from the Magistrate of Patna to the Commissioner, Patna Div., 26th September, 1937.

Bihar Government and its work, Government of Bihar Review of past 18 Months by information officers.

Roy, Ajit Gopal, *et.al., The Bihar Local Acts, 1993-1963,* Vol. III. p. 61-64.

Bihar Tenancy Act, 1885, Section 178C. pp. 144-45.

R.S.C.B.T., Section 9.

Bihar Legislative Assembly Debates, 1938, p. 135.

Bihar Ligislative Assembly Debates 1938.

Bihar Tenancy Act, 1885, Sec. 178 C, pp. 144-45.
Bihar Tenancy Act, 1885, Sec. 178 C, pp. 144-45.
Bihar Restoration of Bakasht Lands and Reduction of Arrears of Rent, Act, 1938, Sec. 2-3, in Ram Ratan Singh (ed.) The Bihar Code, p. 103.
Bihar Legislative Assembly Debates, 1937, pp. 164-174-5.
Prasad, Rajendra, *Autobiography, Op.cit.*, p. 459. Also see proceedings B.L.A. 1939 Vol. II, Part-I, *Op.cit*, pp. 1055-1132.
Bihar Report on the Administration of Civil Justice in the Province of Bihar during the year 1938, 1939, p. 5.
Times of India, Bombay, 17 Aug. 1938.
Britt, G.T., Report of the Administration of the Police in the Province of Bihar.
Bihar Legislative Assembly Progress 1928, Vol. III, Part-3 pp. 3721-22.
Das, A.N., *Agrarian Unrest and Socio-Economic Change in Bihar*, 1900-1980, New Delhi, 1980, p. 160.
The Congress Socialists, Bombay, 12 March 1938, p. 87.
Home special file no. 33 (c) 1938
Limaye, Madhu, *Evolution of Socialist Party*, Hyderabad, 1952.
Ranga, N.G., *Kisans and Communists*, Bombay, 1949, pp. 6-7.
Sahajanand, *Kranti A Samyukta Morcha*, Patna 1943.
Saraswati, Sahajanand, Presidential address, Ninth Session of the Bihar P.K.S. conference sherghati Gaya, 4th and 5th April, 1942, pp. 28-29.
Extracts from the Congress Election Manifesto, 1946.
Bihar 1946-51: A Brief Review. Director of Public Relations, Bihar.
Annual Report of the Land Revenue in Bihar, 1946, p. 5.
Bihar Tenancy Act, 1885, published by the Law Department, Government of Bihar, 1957 (Act VIII of 1885).
Bihar Tenancy Act, 1885, Land Development Report, 1975, pp. 21-27.

CHAPTER 4

AGRARIAN MOVEMENTS DURING 1937-52

Peasant revolts and agrarian tensions are not certainly unknown but it was rather well-known in India during the British Raj. It dates back to the first intrusion by the British into the agrarian relations in India through the acquisition of Diwani rights of Bengal, Bihar, Orissa by the East India Company in 1765. In fact, the strength and extent of such movements have been greatly underestimated.

The *Great Fakir* and later the *Sanyasi* rebellion that broke out during 1722-1789 was India's first agrarian or national revolt after the British had subjugated the land.

In Bihar, there had been isolated cases of peasant uprisings like the *Santhal* Insurrection of 1885-86, *Munda* uprising of 1899-1991 and *Indigo* Riots of 1867, 1877 and 1907, but it was only after the First World War (1914-18) that peasant unrest took a less sporadic, more sustained and continuing form.

However, these early rebels against foreign rule revealed, "the role of the struggle for agrarian reforms as the main axis of the movement for national liberation.

Awakening of the Peasant

The establishment of British Colonial rule in India was accompanied by an unmitigated disaster for Indian culture. The rate of accumulation of wealth fell quite low owing to the ruthless plunder carried by the officials of the East India Company and their agents in the name of collecting revenue. The neglect of administration and irrigation and the systematic destruction of indigenous industries, series of famines, ravaged and depopulated the country, driving the peasantry in various places against the landlords, planters, money lenders and the British ruler who stood behind them all. But these movements were not so organised and widespread. As Neilson Charlesworth describes: "the movements, typically against land revenue payment on landlord exaction, were always sporadic or localised. They lacked the power or technical means to destroy the Raj, or even boycott of land revenue. Moreover, the agrarian movements since the third decade of the twentieth century are quantitatively (in terms of time span), if not qualitatively, different from the earlier movements about which information and analysis is available. Further, peasants and their leaders had enough experience of the armed power of the British Indian State, since their earlier violent, nineteenth century revolts including the massive revolt of 1857, had been successfully crushed by the armed might of the British and they knew, therefore, the high cost that would have to be paid if a peasantry armed with lathis and axes and bows and arrows and spears challenged the modern weaponry of the British Empire. At this stage, the expediency and calculation of the costs organically propelled the peasant movement towards use of non-violent or non-insurrectionary forms of resistance and struggle.

In fact, some revolts which are said to be the 'peasant revolts' were not at all peasantry-based in nature and widespread in form. In true sense, it was not organised by the real 'peasants unit'. For example : The revolt of 1857 which was undoubtedly the most widespread peasant revolt of the nineteenth century was led by dispossessed rulers, Taluqdars and Zamindars. In the famous Indigo revolt or Blue Mutiny 1859, the leadership came from Zamindars or Zamindari based intellectuals, money lenders, substantial peasants, headmen of villages, Calcutta educated mukhtars or attorneys and journalists and missionaries (Kling, 84-86). At Champaran in 1917, besides Gandhiji, it was the rich peasants and local money lenders like Raj Kumar Shukla, Sant Raut and Khendar Prasad Rai and traders, village mukhtars, school teachers and a number of the urban intelligentia like

Rajendra Prasad who provided the leadership. Similarily, in Kheda or Bardoli Movement (Gujrat) the leadership was in the hands of the upper class and members of the urban intelligentia. Though the Communist leadership of Telangna Movement (1946-51) managed to mobilise the poor peasantry among contemporary peasant struggles, but in its early stages it was initiated by none other but the well to do peasants and landlords. Also in Tebhaga Movement in Bengal 1946-47 (under the banner of Communist party and Kisan Sabha) the leadership was in the hands of urban middle class or well-to-do rural families. It is also to be noted that during the Kisan Sabha movement that developed in various parts of the country in the 1930's and 40's, the leadership was primarily in the hands of the radicalised sections of the urban intelligentia, and the upper layers of rural society, such as small landlords and well to do peasants, and this was true for Bihar where the Kisan Sabha of Sahajanand, though supposedly an organisation of peasants, was led by sub-feudals, village level landlords, chiefly from the Bhumihar caste. The target of this movement was not all kinds of landlordism, but only the feudalism from above, the revenue collecting Zamindari rights created by the permanent settlement. The Kisan Sabha failed to reflect the full antifeudal aspirations of the peasantry and besides alienating the backward caste peasantry set itself firmly against granting land rights to the dalits, or agricultural labourers.

As far as its region of action is concerned, it is also clear that the peasant rebels arose mainly out of particular local grievances and was confined to a local group of peasant association. These peasant organisations which already existed were far from adequate for building up a sustained movement. However, the movement pertaining to the Bengal Tenancy Bill was also fairly widespread but here the organisational base was very weak.

The intensity of the movement reduced later on, when the agrarian protest campaigns came to play a valuable supporting role in undermining of British rule. Of course, the first three decades of the 19th century were characterised by a series of peasant uprisings.

Forms of peasantry

Prior to finding out the seeds of the peasant unrest and courses of resentment, the survey and analysis of the different forms of the peasantry have been focussed. On the basis of the inadequacies of legal and native terminologies the peasantry were divided into three categories—rich, middle and poor.

Rich peasants possessed more than 20 acres of land, maintained atleast two pairs of plough bullocks or more and carried out their cultivation primarily with the help of agricultural labourers or share croppers. They lent their ploughs or ploughmen to poor peasants on hire. They were in a position to save sufficient surplus foodgrains after meeting their own needs. Not only that, they could add to the acreage of their land by purchasing the lands of needy Zamindars or middle and poor peasants.

Middle peasants were those who owned land from 3.5 to 20 acres, atleast one pair of plough oxen or more and employed quite a few agricultural labourers for cultivation. They also had some land for occasional share cropping and also lent their plough to others on hire. That means most of the middle peasants coincided with occupancy raiyats. As the survey settlement report shows, in the Maksudpur estate (Gaya belt) as well as in Saran, the average holding of an occupancy tenant was more than 3.5 acres. Thus, the middle peasants were those who were not only able to meet their needs of subsistence but also save some surplus.

The poor peasants were those who owned less than 3.5 acres, maintained one plough or no plough oxen at all. Indeed such peasants accounted for the majority of the peasant population. It is quite necessary to point out that none of these categories of peasants, in the permanently settled areas, were legal owners of land, although they actually possessed it. They (peasants) had to pay rents in cash to the Zamindars and due to the economic depression effected by a sudden fall in the prices of agricultrual products, their situation deteriorated. These resentments forced almost all sections of the peasantry to participate in the occasional agitations, for the abolition of the Zamindari System; what to talk of the poor peasant, even the middle peasants reduced to the condition of the poorest stratum of peasantry, as a result of the economic crisis, joined in the agitations. Later on, their lands were seized by the Zamindars by force and turned into bakasht or self-cultivated land.

The poor peasants supplemented their income by share cropping in which case 50% of the produce went to the rich peasants or the small landlord who gave his land for share cropping. They were used to take lands annually on lease for which they had to pay very high rents in cash or kind. The irony of the situation was that in both cases (*batai* or *lease* cultivation), they did not keep the written record so that the peasant could not go to court against the arbitration of the Zamindars. Often unable to earn their livelihood, the poor peasants had to borro more and more. Since they were illeterate, they found themselves completely at the mercy of the exacting Mahajans, who in many cases were the same landlords and rich peasants, who gave land on *batai* or *lease* to the poor peasants.

Below poor peasants were the agricultural labourers who mostly worked as ploughmen and belonged to the lowest sections of society consisting of Chamars, Dusadha, Mushar, etc. who were later known as Harijans. Occupationally, they were called harwaha or Halwaha, who carried cultivation from generation to generation. In the Maithili speaking areas of North Bihar, these ploughmen and agricultural labourers were called *bahias*. The *bahias* were actually bonded labourers whose fate were tied with their masters. The census report 1912 shows that the field workers were more than one-fifth of the total rural population in the permanently settled districts of Bihar. However, this number increased in the census of 1931 which accounted for a little more than one-third of the rural population. It is the fault of the census authorities that they did not divide the rural population into the similar categories. But one thing is clear from the details as given by G.P. Sharma : that the poor peasants who were marginally agricultural labourers and peasants together accounted for the overwhelming majority of the agriculturists.

The census of 1931 mentions the following figures for Bihar:

Rural Population

Non-Cultivating proprietors	—	1,99,966
Cultivating owners	—	3,75,126
Tenant cultivators	—	88,42,429
Agricultural labourers	—	39,70,963

The above data of the census shows that the tenant cultivation alongwith agricultural labourers represented 70% of the total rural population. Thus, it is apparent that cultivating owners, minority of the rural population, feathered their own nest by exactions from the majority of the population consisting of the tenant cultivators and the agricultural labourers.

Peasant Reaction

Analysing the peasants reaction, A.N. Das says : "while this sort of semi-feudalism became the characterising aspect of Bihar's agrarian social structure, the slow but inevitable process of commercialisation broke down the politically isolated village whose peasantry had for long periods stoically borne up with exploitation and oppression. Combined with the worsening economic condition, it led Bihar towards instability, disequilibrium and unrest. Further, the socio- political placidity which had been caused by the economic stagnation was broken by the changes in the economy of the state and Bihar became witness to an era of agrarian tensions, unrest and movements.

Causes Behind the Unrest

There were many causes inherent in the socio-political and economic base of India in general and Bihar in particular that led to peasent unrest. During the thirties, one of the most burning question which called for immediate attention of the government was the tenancy problem. Though several Tenancy Amendment Acts were passed after the original Bengal Tenancy Act of 1885, yet they did not bring about the desired relief to the peasants.

World Economic Depression

When the world economic depression of late 1929 engulfed the entire capitalist world, India was not spared with its ravages and among the hardest hit sections of the Indian population was the peasanty. Consequently, in the early thirties, the economic situation of rural India presented an extremely gloomy picture of poverty, unemployment, pauperisation, misery and starvation and utter despondency. Some of the causes of unrest have been examined below:

Problem of Rent/Rackrenting

The great depression made the burden of rent on the peasantry unbearable. Hence, Bihar was the scene of widespread agitation on the question of rent remission, rent reduction or cancellation of rent. Of course, the high rents and rackrenting affected the tenant immensely. It is apparently made clear that the high rents were the result of both private agreement as well as illegal enhancement. Under the above agreement, the tenants were bound to pay whatever may be required or demanded by the Zamindars. The agreement was followed till the rising trend in prices after the First World War. But due to the depression, with the fall in the prices, the tenants were unable to fulfill the same demand and consequently, they started taking arrears.

The landlords did not bother about the problem but rather deliberately ignored the tenant's inability while collecting the higher rents. Another error was that the fixity of rent rates could not be ensured. In the absence of the fixed rate of rents, the Zamindars of Bihar enhanced them illegally. Though the settlement authorities were against the higher rent payment and objected to it, yet the landlords were inclined to collect the same amounts. It led to sinking them in heavy arrears. The official report of Monghyr points out that the Zamindars of Monghyr indulged in enhancement of rates of rent and had merely increased the rent on the plea that the area of cultivation had been increased, while in reality, the said increase was unreal. Tenant's positions was so pitiable that in some areas landlords did not even give receipt of the rent payment. Tenants were helpless to take any action against the oppression of the landlords in the court in the absence of any receipt of rents. Even the settlement officials were silent spectators to the excesses done by the Zamindars and if they happened to raise their voice to such enhancement the landlords challenged their decision in the Civil Courts either in the title suit or in the rent suit, and many of these suits were decided against the tenants, ex-parte, without a complete investigation into the facts or by a compromise. The rent was so high that the kisans of Gaya, Patna and South Monghyr had to pay rents of about Rs. 8-10. to Rs. 15-16 per bigha,[38] while the average yield was only Rs. 20 per bigha. Even the official reports admit that in the five villages of old Saran district the rent exceeded Rs. 10 per acre. Same was the condition in the 26 villages of Chapra Thana and 15 villages of Sonepur Thana. It was also a known fact that the tenants were forced to take arrears. The landlords even charged interest on the arrears. Obviously, those illegal exactions or *abwab* played a major part in high rents.

Produce Rent System

A more fundamental factor that was responsible for the rise of peasant movement in Bihar, was the produce rent system. This system was more prevalent in Gaya, Patna and to a lesser degree in Shahabad and South Monghyr. The produce rents of these districts are indicated in the table 4.1.

Table 4.1

Districts	*Percentage of area held on produce rent*
Gaya	67.9
Patna	44
South Monghyr	32
Shahabad	21

Source : E.L. Tanner, Survey and Settlement Operations in the District of Gaya 1911-18 (Patna 1919), Chapter XI.

The table shows that the maximum incidence of produce-rent was in Gaya followed by Patna, South Monghyr and

Shahabad. Most of these districts were scene of serious agitation conducted by the Kisan Sabha of the province.

The produce-rent was known by different names such as batai, bhaoli, kankat, mankhap, manhunda, danbandhi, chauraha, etc. But there have been too major systems of produce rent danabandi and batai found in Gaya, Patna, South Monghyr and Shahabad. Other systems were also found. Batai was a type of share-cropping based on mutual agreement between the proprietors and the share cropper. Under this system, the crop was divided on the threshing floor after harvest. Bhaoli was another form of share cropping, wherein the Zamindars' share was fixed on a permanent basis and recorded in the survey settlement. In accordance with this system, the tenant had to pay half of the produce to the landlord but in actual practice the Zamindar's share was much higher. The produce was divided into 15/16 share of which 9 went to the Zamindars and only 6 or 7 to the tenants. Numerous such illegal collections were associated with Bhaoli in Patna district. and elsewhere. The *kankat* produce rent system meant division of the produce in equal shares after apprisement. Manhunda, mankhap, danbandhi and chauraha meant fixing a certain quantity of produce per bigha irrespective of the loss or otherwise of the produce. Whatever be the actual produce in many cases, the Zamindars' men forcibly removed their share and what more, straight from the threshing floor.

With the passage of time, the produce rent system lost its basis of mutual goodwill and it allowed the landlords agents to practice the worst form of oppression. The reason behind the oppression was well observed by J. Reid, "The tendency is, however, for the landlords share is as much as 28 seers in a maund, the raiyat's share of the crop is reduced, although he is to undertake the labour of cultivations and all the expenditure in connection with sowing. The heavier incidence of produce rent under the 'danbandhi' system appears to be due to the constant imposition of abwab, known by various names such as *dehiaks, nocha manseri, sonar* etc. and their gradual amalgamation with what is known as the asal rent which is in reality the rent which is legally payable". In some villages of Patna district, the share of the landlords was enhanced from

27 seers to 40 seers and it was seldom less than 22.50 seers in a maund.

The following case of Patna can be seen in the table 4.2 :—

Table 4.2

1282	Asal	20	
	Dahiak	2 .50	Total 22.50
1286	Asal	20	
	Dahiak	2.50	
	Mangan	1.25	
	Nocha	1.75	Total 25
1296	Asal	20	
	Dahiak	2.50	
	Mangan	1.25	
	Nocha	1.25	
	Road area	1.25	
	Amin Karcha	3.25	Total 29.50

Source: Note by J.A. Hubback on the produce rents of Monghyr and Patna District found in course of Survey Settlement Operations in 1908-09.

It is quite clear from the above table that the system of produce-rent was disadvantageous to the tenants because the occupancy tenants paid away rents aggregating nearly to 3/4th of the value of their crops. It has been the case frequently, the occupancy rights of the tenants became merely the servants of the landlords. Hence, there was a campaign for commuting the rent in cash. A study of the case records of the period 1915-33 shows that landlords time and again ruined tenants by systematically, suing them for arrears of produce rents. So commutation of the rents became the demand of the time. As the survey and settlement operation, particularly in South Bihar, indicated the old system of produce rents was breaking down and there was need for commutation of rents into cash.

Commutation of Rents

The commutation of rents (1915-32) into cash during this

transitory phase coincided with the period of exceptionally high prices. Later on, it proved to be not worthy in practice for the welfare of the tenants. As officially discovered, these commutations were made in far excess of the cash rents, irrespective of the old cash rent, paid for similar land in the vicinity. The rents were fixed at the rates ranging from Rs. 15 to Rs. 40 per acre in Patna, Gaya and Monghyr districts. Instead of easing the situation, the new system posed acute problems resulting in peasant agitation for rent reduction. The tenants who applied to the courts for the commutation of their produce rents into cash were sold up by the Civil Courts before final orders were passed in the commutation cases. It must be noted that the length of the commutation proceedings had crippled and exhausted the tenants economically and as a result, they lost their lands. It is pitiable on the part of the tenants that the families of the cultivators retained their lands by paying the high cash rents from sources other than the income from the land.

William observed that "these commutations at high rates were done partly because of the defects in the produce rent system, partly due to the procedure adopted in commuting them and partly owing to the high prices during the twenties of the present century." In this way, the court procedure conferred great powers on the landlords and provided a strong incentive for demanding an increased share of the produce.

Fall in Prices

Another major cause that took tenants on the path of agitation was the fall in the prices. Of course, the fall in the prices of the staple crops during the World-wide Great Depression caused greater hardship to the peasants. The prices started an upward trend since 1885 (exception being 1911, 1913, 1917-18) and remained steady till 1927. But misfortune came with the depression when it dropped sharply and reached the bottom in 1933, which was equivalent to the price level of 1912. Also, due to the depression, the tenants found it difficult to pay rents on time to the Zamindars on account of sudden fall in prices of rice, wheat, maize. Thus, they fell in arrears and the only way to recover the arrears of the rent was to make the tenants part with their lands. Although they felt that in times of depression changing peasants from the cultivation of their land would not be of much use.

It created annoyance and uneasiness that ultimately led to a large number of rent suits being instituted in various districts. The table 4.3 shows the magnitude of suits in various districts.

Table 4.3
Magnitude of Suits Instituted in Districts

Districts	*Number of cases*
Muzaffarpur	32,369
Saran	26,699
Darbhanga	26,608
Purnea21,255	
Shahabad	19,178
Patna	18,743
Bhagalpur	18,662
Monghyr	17,396
Gaya	10,475

Source : Report on the Administration of Civil Justice in the Province of Bihar and Orissa during the year 1933 (Patna, 1939)

But gradually the number of the rent suits increased during the period 1929-33 as is indicated in the table 4.4.

Table 4.4

Years	*Money Suits*	*Rent Suits*	*Title Suits*	*Total No.*	*Total Value (Rupees)*
1929	52,514	123,458	21,414	197,386	6,64,94,470
1930	52,581	122,355	19,355	193,966	5,73,02,406
1931	53,196	122,116	16,588	191,900	4,42,32,266
1932	54,659	121,926	25,275	191,860	6,19,57,896
1933	54,149	149,036	15,386	218,786	4,90,78,980

Source : Report on the Administration of Civil Justice in the Province of Bihar and Orissa during the year 1933 (Patna, 1934) p. 4.

Rural Indebtedness

Rural indebtedness was generally widespread all over India but the Bihar peasant was most heavily burdened in particular.

The details can be seen from the following comparative figures:

Table 4.5

Province	*Population (in lakhs)*	*Debt. (Rs. in crores)*
Bengal	501	100
United Provinces	484	124
Madras	464	105
Bihar	376	155
Punjab	235	81
Central Provinces	115	36

It was an irony of fate that if the debt of Bihar landlords is deleted, the Bihar raiyats had to pay 155 crores as debt and Bihar had then the strength of 376 lakh of kisans. This meant that every kisan of Bihar had to pay a debt of rupees 60[59] although it works out at Rs. 41 per head. It was quite impossible for the tenants to pay the rent. Therefore, the pressure for the rents and arrears from the Zamindars sank them into deep and rather chronic indebtedness. According to an official handbook, "indebtedness, often amounting to insolvency, is the normal condition of a majority of Indian farmers". The report of the United Provinces Banking Enquiry Committee also reveals that, "everything is against him (the peasant). Because he is a cultivator, he must borrow to secure his crop, because his holding is small and has to support more persons than it can feed, he must increase his borrowing to keep those persons alive while the crop is in the ground. His caste and religion compelled him to borrow a third time to meet the cost of customary ceremony. As the debt grows, the repayment of it becomes more difficult until at last some calamity comes upon him, repayment becomes impossible and he sinks into a state of chronic indebtedness from which death alone can release him".

Though all over Bihar the peasants suffered from heavy indebtedness yet its incidence and rates of interest varied from district to district. In Darbhanga and Saran peasants in order to support themselves, borrowed heavily from Mahajans. In Saran, the gross average value of produce was Rs 32 per cent and the gross average cost of cultivation was Rs. 14 per acre. The peasant was thus left with Rs. 18 as an average. Even when the prices rose high in the years following the First World War, the incidence of indebtedness, although unevenly spread over the districts of northern Bihar as in Purnea, was recorded at Rs. 95,000 and in Muzaffarpur it was under Rs. 500,000.

Regarding the rates of interest, three types of rates were prevalent. Ordinary Mahajani interest varied from 6% to 24% per annum, the Sawai interest amounted to 25% per annum and the athrohaoni to 50% per annum. Among it, Mahajan interest was common all over Bihar and the amount of interest, if unpaid, was converted to compound interest and after a time the total of the capital and the compound interest were entered in a mortgage deed. Hence, this practice eventually led to the passing of the mortagaged lands into the hands of the Mahajans.

The main cause behind indebtedness of the peasants, was the absence of credit facilities provided by the State and similar agencies. This is evident from the reply given to the questionnaire issued by the Bihar and Orissa Banking Enquiry Committee (1929-30) about the Co-operative Societies that were running in some villages. These Co-operative Societies were again dominated by the Zamindars such as Shyam Nandan Sahay and other rational people. Another evident error was that out of 84,804 villages in Bihar and Orissa (according to the Census of 1921), only 7,826 had agricultural societies with lending facilities. It appears that only enterprising people, especially landlord and their agents, succeded in getting loans from the Co-operative Societies. So due to non-availability of loans from the Co-operative, the agriculturists had to depend on the village or town money-lenders.

Thus, it is clear that in Bihar and Orissa the problem of rural indebtedness was most acute. It was 153 crores, out of which 24 crores was that of landlords, 129 crores was that of ordinary tenants and 2 crores that of others. The period well symbolises this proverb that "the Indian Peasant is born in debt, lives in debt and dies in debt".

Illegal Imposition

Several illegal impositions made the filed fertile for the productivity of the agitational plant. It is a well-known fact that the peasants were subject to the rule of two Governments *(a)* The rule of the British Government, and *(b)* that of the Zamindars and his agents. Between the two (British Government & Zamindar) one can imagine that the position of the tenants was like the vehicle having two brakes.

The landlords and their agents were not at all contended with the extortion of high rents from the tenants and they wanted as much as can be sucked from the poor peasants.

Under the Jajmani system, the artisanal castes (the carpenter, potter, oil presser, blacksmith etc.), who were also connected with cultivation and in any case happened to live on the land of the Zamindars had to give free services to the landlord, whenever or wherever required or supply them with products at an exceedingly low price. Not only that, the Zamindar agents called amalas used to frame various kinds of false charges and levy penalties. For example, if the kisans happened to go for the Kisan Sabha meetings they were punished. The kisans did not dare to speak a word against those atrocities fearing harassment and punishment. Really, they became deaf and dumb. Several kinds of impositions under the bhoali rent—*nocha, mangan, dahiak salami, Road* cess and amins's kharcha were in vogue. Moreover, the kisans had to pay *talbana* to the police of the Raj, *Tahir* to the rent Collector (Jeth raiyat/patwari) and *salami* to the Tehsildar.

On the excuse of maintaining schools and hospitals, the tenants had to pay two paise extra per rupee probably of the total amount of fixed rent. Illegal impositions were also made, in the case of cash rents; ordinary batta or loss suffered in weighing/measuring was charged at the rate of one anna in every ruppe. The Company's batta was charged at the rate of 1.5 anna in every rupee, *Tahir* or *scribal* fee was charged at the rate of 0.5 in every rupee. Even *Hujatana* (recompense of difficulties caused by argumentativeness) was charged at the rate of one anna for each *kalam* or entry.

If any tenant failed to fulfil these illegal extortions, the

Zamindars carried several zulums (oppression) on them i.e, by taking their plough share from the plough, by confiscations and perishing the crops by deputing the Dusadh as a muscle men who were not allowed to even move out. Not only that tenants were punished to sit in the scorching sun and received beating, abuses etc. Therefore, the above scenario of agitation was inevitable.

Forced Labour

The question of *begar* or forced labour also made the situation tense and it added to the fuel of revenge. Tenants were compelled to work in the landlords *Khudkhasht* or Bakasht field without either paying them wages or at a very low rate of payment. The kisans at first had to plough the land of the Zamindar and then they looked after their own land. Now the question arises to which caste of tenant begar was carried out. After the study it is found that in some areas high caste people were obliged to work for the Zamindards whereas in some areas generally the low caste tenantry was forced to work. But in the domestic work, mostly lower caste people were engaged by rotation. Thus in most cases, it was the low caste tenants who received bad treatment; for example in Bihar Sharif the owner of the Dharampur Estate came down heavily upon a tenant. When Sarangi Mahto (a kisan) asked for the receipt of the arrears of rent paid to the Zamindar, he was badly beaten up with fists and feet. Same was the fate of Ramdhani Mahto who tried to intervene and advised peace. A goala raiyat Niranjan Raut, who belonged to Manjhoulia village in District Saran, was bashed up for not having supplied ghee and other edibles to the Zamindar. Same story was happened in Arrah where Jang Bahadur Singh a local Zamindar harassed his koeri tenants. Zamindars were that much torturous, inhuman and cruel in their dealing with the tenants that they even did not want to spend money to perform the last rites of the dead bodies of their tenants (murdered by them), instead they washed away the dead bodies in rivers. Recently a T.V. serial "Muzrim Hazir" based on the novel of Vimal Mitra well picturised their real character.

Under-developed Economy

Under-developed economy also led Bihar on the verge of agitations. It is obvious that on account of lack of industrialisation and real urbanisation based on industry and commerce, the overwhelming majority of the people had to fall back upon land, the only source of livelihood. During the half century from 1858 to 1911 attempts were made for the economic betterment of other states whereas in Bihar very little was done in this direction.

With the formation of the province in 1912, the government came forward to encourage industrial development in a number of ways. As a result, Bihar had few factories, the most important being the Tata Steel Factory at Jamshedpur which employed the largest number of workers, i.e, nearly 23,331, But among them labourers of permanently settled areas were very few, rest were the tribals. In the Sugar factories, only the seasonal work for four months was done and it did not provide the worker of the rural areas of the permanently settled districts full time employment and the number of workers was only 16,479. Though Jamalpur in Monghyr district had some railway workshops, rice and jute mills, which offered full time job to the non-tribal people, their number was very small i.e., 118,443 while the rural population of Bihar was over 380 millions in 1931. As Henningham has pointed out, from the late ninetenth century the shortage of land in north Bihar had become increasingly acute. So in the absence of cultivable land, life became grim for the majority of kisans. The industries in Bihar (though few in number) did not burden the cause of the peasantry rather they were mainly centres of consumption based on the earning from the countryside. Even the tenants had to feed and meet the needs of the absentee landlord living in these towns. For want of cash peasant had to sell their produce on uneconomic prices and they had to depend on the rapacious moneylenders, that ultimately led Bihar to the highest rural indebtedness.

Another factor was the lack of townships. Even the largest city of Bihar, Patna, had hardly any big factory worth the name. Even the towns were not better than ordinary villages. Thus, the underdeveloped economy undermined the Zamindars at first and then the British Government.

Nature of Tenure

In Bihar, there were multiplicity of tenures (which were a result of sub-infeudation and difficulties of rent collection, absentee landlordism) and raiyats tenures and tenures of under raiyats. These various forms of tenures led to the agitation on different issues.

Eviction And Bakasht Problem

The raiyats with occupancy rights faced this problem in the most acute form during the period. Of course, the problem existed even earlier, as is evident from khanapuri stage in Shahabad. Bakasht land means any land, as defined in section 120 of Bihar Tenancy Act, 1885, which a proprietor or tenure holder claims to be cultivating with his own stock or by his own servants or by hired labour. The proprietors private land was defined in Section 120 of the Bihar Tenancy Act thus : "land which is proved to have been cultivated as *(khamar) Zirat, Khudkasht, Sir, nij (nijjot) or Khamat*".

After some time they thought of setting these lands with occupancy tenants in return for rents, which was wanted without loosing time. But the situation changed with the outbreak of First World War and the years that followed till the economic depression of 1928-30. Firstly, due to the depression and sky rocketing prices of the staple crops such as rice, wheat and maize in the late twenties, it did not prove to be worth as well as advantageous to the Zamindars while raising the rents. *Secondly*, they were afraid that if a tenant was allowed to stay for more than twelve years as specified in the Bengal Tenancy Act, 1885, the tenant would then have to be recorded as an occupancy raiyat in the survey settlment.

Hence, they invented innumerable excuses to evict these tenants from the lands. Thus in the years preceding the depression, the Zamindars substantially added to their self-cultivated landed possessions by driving out weaker tenants, by making arrangements for the direct cultivation of these land so that they could add to their income. These lands came to be known as Bakasht or the land which came to be merged with the self cultivated land of the Zamindars.

Further, when depression set in due to the sudden fall in the prices of the crops, rice, wheat, maize an unusually high number of tenants holdings were sold up as a result of rent arrears suit. Often the purchaser of the holding was the landlord who was glad by this means to convert what had been ryoti land into Bakasht land.

It is also noticeable that with the price rise the incidence of eviction became frequent as in the case of Barhaiya. However, the different categories of peasants never forgot the harassment, and loss of legal rights to their lands. Even more resentful were those tenants who had actually been displaced from their holdings, which had been passed down to them through several generations to make way for another occupancy tenant or for a share cropper or short term tenant. These resentments were articulated into a recurrent demand for the restoration of ryoti rights in the Bakasht lands to tenants who had lost them during the period of the depression.

Calamities

Several man-made as well as natural calamities shook the whole of Bihar. After the world wide depression in 1929-30, the prices of staple food-grains which had shown a steady rise after the First World War suddenly dropped. In 1929-35, a fall by 60 to 70% was common in many districts of Bengal and Bihar. But even in this worst situation with little income, they had to pay rents and for this they had to borrow more and more.

Worldwide economic depression was followed by the earthquake of 15th January, 1934. It resulted in the major devastation in the town of Monghyr, Darbhanga, Muzaffarpur. In the rural areas in north Bihar, most of the houses were collapsed and deep fissures affected their lands badly. Its effect was so great that it drew the attention of the whole of India and its prominent leaders toured the effected areas. But nature again became cruel to Bihar as the ravaging flood of 1935 made the situation more dreadsome. It damaged the crops, animals, houses and what not?

But stone hearted landlords still did not melt. Instead of giving relief measures to these earthquake and flood victims, they were anxious for their own rents and were not ready to forego it (the rents) for the time being. Hence, the peasants were charged with resentment and anger resulting into a series of agitations which Bihar witnessed.

After going through the causes of the agrarian unrest, it is now needed to examine the various agitations which prevailed in Bihar at that time.

To trace the course of the agitation, the speech of Hare Krishna Konar may be included here : "when these people (Kisans) will be in a position to stand on their own feet, throw away burdens from their heads, stand with their heads up after shaking off the political influences of the representatives of the landlords and the rural rich, then and then only it can be felt that revolution has taken its birth in the soil of India".

The dream of Konar came true in Indian context in general and Bihar in particular. During 1936-39, Bihar experienced important kisan movements which made the Bihar Pradesh Kisan Sabha very prominent.

Gaya, Patna, Monghyr, Shahabad, Darbhanga, Champaran and Saran witnessed many struggles. However, the movement was the strongest in Reora and Manjihiawan (Gaya), Chapra in Shahabad and Padri Circle (or Parri), Dekuli and Raghopur and Laukaha thana in the Madhubani subdivision in Darbhanga district and Barhaiya Tal in Monghyr.

Bakasht Struggle in Darbhanga District

The movement first started in Padri (or parri) circle in South-east Darbhanga where the peasants demand was the return of ryoti rights in newly bakasht lands. "In the padri circle the discontented peasantry engaged in what the circle, manager later described as a violent explosion of . . . . agitation, in course of which rent collection 'almost stopped' and the "Loot of Raj" crops standing in Zirat and Dahnal i.e. (flood affected) lands was a daily feature." However, the situation became cool after interference of S.K. Sinha the then Chief Minister. He requested G.P. Danby (Chief Manager of Darbhanga Raj) to look into the matter. Danby tried to help the padri peasantry by lowering the rents and cancelling rent

Map showing the rate of intensity of Bakasht Struggle in the different districts of Bihar

arrears. But as Chief Manager of Darbhanga Raj, he supervised the determined effort to ensure that all Bakasht holdings were settled on occupancy tennure. Therefore, the effort to settle holdings on occupancy tenures diminished the good done by rent remission and arrears cancellation. It opened a new gate for a small minority of money-lending kisans, who could only afford to pay the high salami rates being imposed and could succeed to influence the local amlas in their favour. As the circle manager reported, 35 percent of the tenantry had become landless.

The veteran Kisan Sabha leader Ramnandan Mishra pictures the things in this way : "By starting land settlement the Raj is forcing us to organise Bakasht struggle. In several plots of land I found standing sugar cane crop but the land has been settled with another person, for instance in the village sihma a plot has been settled with Tribeni Raut, where still stands the crop of the tenant who has been cultivating for long." Once agitation began over newly Bakasht lands, the poor peasants were also inspired to claim possession of lands that had been held as Bakasht by landlords over long period. They appealed to provision of the Bengal Tenancy Act of 1885 which endowed share croppers continuously for a long period of twelve years or longer with occupancy rights in the holdings. But this provision had never benefitted raiyats due to lack of power, or due to ignorance and low morale. Moreover, under the banner of Kisan Sabhas, poor peasants began to compaign for their long due rights in long term Bakasht land.

In order to defuse the kisan protest in 1928, the Bihar Congress Ministry (Zamindars while assuring in consultation with their interest) initiated some ameliorative measures. Out of it comes the legislation concerning newly Bakasht lands. The Bakasht Restoration Bill provided under certain conditions for the return to the tenants of lands which had been sold up in the period from 1929 to 1936, if in return the tenant paid within a period of five years, half the auction price of the holding as well as the legal costs. The status and the position of the Bill is indicated in the table 4.6.

Table 4.6
Formula for the Restoration of the Bakasht lands, 1928

Area Sold up	Quantitiy Restorable
Less than 6 Acres	All to be restored
More than 6 but less than 15 acres	Half to be restored
More than 15 but less than 30 acres	A third to be restored
More than 30 acres	A quarter to be restored

Source : *Indian Nation*, 31 July, 1938.

However, the Bakasht Restoration Bill did not prove to be as fruitful as it appeared. Rather it gave the Zamindars additional time to find ways to avoid its provisions. It was reported that having learnt of the legislation the land-holders of Bhagalpur settled every inch of restorable bakasht lands benami on an acceptance of *salami*. Another difficulty was the tenant's inability to pay the legal costs and half of the auction price for the bakasht lands. One of the strong lacuna that goes against the peasant cause was inability to bring convincing documentation before the courts. It is well revealed by the author of the provincial year book for 1938-39 which is given here. "The cultivators often find it difficult to prove his claim even when it is just because the conditions under which the Bakasht land is let out by the landlords make it impossible for him to produce documents. In the absence of reliable oral evidence on their side, the courts have in the past been compelled to decide cases mainly on documentry evidence. Thus in the absence of documents and evidence, the landlords were benefitted, and tenants were put to heavy loss.

In such situation, the peasantry had no other alternative but direct action. Again the problem arose in Panaul area in Darbhanga. There, share croppers and short-term tenants, began to claim rights to bakasht lands, but the failure on the part of tenants was that they could not prove that they had tilled the land successfully for a period of twelve years or more, as the disputed land had been let out every year by the Darbhanga Raj.

Similar was the nature of discontent in Radhanagar. Though the tenants feared reprisals from their landlords, yet their grievances were aggravated by the Kisan Sabha. Hence, what to talk of Radhanagar, the whole of North Bihar in 1939 saw the intensification of bakasht protest, which culminated in the employment of satyagrah. Though in principle, they pretended to apply non-violence in direct action, yet in practice actually violent crisis occurred. Thus in Radhanagar village, the struggle incorporated numerous law suits, the social boycott of the landlords by their tenants, and the use of physical force. Similarly, struggles were witnessed at Dekuli and Raghopur. But like Reora (Gaya, South Bihar) the settlement was not easy in the case of North Bihar. As the Bihar Government reports revealed, neither the local kisan workers nor the Zamindars were co-operating with officially supported efforts to arrange a compromise settlement. However, the report disapproved the kisan workers "hell bent on satyagraha". At Dekuli in Behera thana of Darbhanga on 16th March, 1939 tension started between the two on the issue of a cart load of rice. The tenants obstructed the cart load rice of the local Zamindars. As a result, quarrel started and one of the Zamindar was assaulted. In retaliation the local Zamindars and their supporters fired on the tenants and wounded nine of them. The tenants not only resisted but they also divided the bakasht land of their owners among themselves. Therefore, in the ploughing season the situation became so serious that the administration had to report that the kisan movement... appears to be working to a crisis. It further pointed out that the agrarian situation continues to deteriorate and reports of attempts or threat to seize bakasht land were there in nearly every district of Bihar. Lastly, at Dekuli attempts to settlement failed, and tension increased. But at Raghopur the dispute was settled on terms that were very favourable to the tenants.

The same story was repeated in the Pandoul area of Darbhanga in July. Here agitations began when some Darbhanga Raj amlas tried to plough disputed holding with a tractor. The local tenants bombarded the tractor driver with a volley of stones and attacked the Raj amlas. So by the middle of July, according to a Kisan Sabha publicity officer, the agrarian situation was getting more serious day by day.

This was a alarm for the landlords and they took several measures in this field i.e. most of the lands have been ploughed and settled by the landlords but attempts have been made to replough the lands and uproot the seedlings. In order to give a severe blow to the movement, the police arrested around 200 kisans agitators in Darbhanga by late July. The large number of arrest thinned the youth population in the villages. When amlas of the Darbhanga Raj came to plough same disputed holdings in the pandoul on 6th August 1939, the main protesters were only women, old men and the children. By sitting in front of the plough bullock, they stopped ploughing and left only after they had been beaten and jostled by the Raj amlas. Thus, Darbhanga became the hot bed of Kisan Sabha activity over the Bakasht issue during 1939. Hence, the Kisan Sabha tried to capture even the Congress party machinery. As the official report indicates : Attempts to seize the land or obstruct cultivation.... have been almost daily occurances and numerous clashes have occured. There has been a large number of prosecution and a number of principal leaders . . . . have been arrested. The agitation was intensified by the provincial Kisan Sabha meeting which was held at Sakari close by on 7th and 8th . . . . volunteers are now being imported from elsewhere to continue the attack. Which is intended to be enlarged into a general attack upon the Bakasht lands of the Darbhanga state. It has been necessary to keep Magistrates and armed police continuously on the spot and a large number of arrests have been made. It is clear that this agitation is going to be made a provincial issue as the attack is upon the principal landlords of the province".

However, the situation became quiet except for a clash in the Laukaha thana in the Madhubani sub-division of Darbhanga district. In Laukaha amlas opened fire, killing two and injuring several others.

By September, 1939 the protest recurred in subsequent months, but not with same intensity. Further in November 1939 there was one notable 'landlord—peasant clash' causing death to a member of the Peasant party. Same was the situation all over North Bihar and even in the harvesting season in December no serious incident occured but ordinary disputes between landlords and tenants were reported. In this way in Jan 1940 the villages were "unusually quiet." Thus, the Bakasht campaign which at one stage had caused grave anxiety in official ranks, had come an end.

Bakasht Struggle in Monghyr

In June, 1936 the struggle started in Monghyr and continued till the middle of 1939. The struggle held in Barhiaya Tal, a low lying stretch of arable land in southern Monghyr district. G.P. Sharma has rightly observed that the Tal area was one of the hotbeds of the kisan movement, as the Kisan conferences were held in October, 1936 in Monghyr, Feb., 1937 in Shaikhpura, October, 1938 and Nov., 1938 in Lakhisarai and February, 1939 in pali in Tal area.

The struggle arose on the question of refusal to do *begari* in Barhaiya Tal area and due to other hardships imposed on them by the Zamindars. Under the leadership of Karynanand Sharma, thousands of raiyats proceded to the collectorate of Monghyr on 6th April, 1936 and filed a written petition and discussed their grievances with the Collector. Karyanand Sharma also presented a memorandum with thousands of signatures. Sahjanand Saraswati also recorded this event.

The main cause behind the demonstration and resentment as reported by the Commissioner of Bhagalpur to Brett was that the pitch of rents in this part was considerably above the average for South Monghyr. On the raiyats' repraisal, the officials found that their grievances were genuine and at this stage they were unable to pay arrears of the rent. Hence, section 144/Cr.P.c had been issued on three of the *amlas* of Ulao's estate against their barbarism and cruelty. This made landlords more despotic and in reaction they took back every inch of land given to raiyats.

The speeches of Congress-cum-kisan leaders produced some ferment among the tenants of Pali Mahramchek, Kothwa, Fadarpur, Bhanpur and Kamarpur in Barahaiya Tal area. Seeing the gravity of the situation Shri Krishna Sinha (who later became the C.M. of Bihar) alongwith Nand Kumar Singh visited Pali in the presence of Karyananad Sharma and enquired into the matter. They also met Zamindars and collected information from them. Subsequently, both paid another visit to Barahaiya and brought about rapprochement between the Zamindar and the tenants in the presence of Karyanand Sharma.

But this rapprochement proved to be short-lived. Shortly

after the compromise during the harvesting season of 1936, there occured several incidents of uprooting of crops by tenants in the Zamindars Bakasht lands in some villages of Sheikhpura police station and at Kamarpur in the Tal area. The violent speech of Karyananad Sharma add fuel to the fire in the two days District Kisan conference held at Sheikhpura in February, 1937. He openly instigated them to 'sit over the chest of the Zamindar.' However, Sahajanand kept patience and gave mild speeches. On March 1, 1937 in Gangor and Gadbadia, under the Sheikhpura police station, the crops of the Zamindars were looted. It was followed by similar acts of loot on March 2 and on subsequent dates in some of the Tals and others villages. The Zamindars of the Tal in Barbigha police station were the first victims of the kisan fury. As a result, numerous cases were filed against the kisans and even 60 to 70 of them were arrested including Karyanand Sharma.

Sarojini Naidu in her presidential address in the Monghyr District Political Conference of Congress also highlighted the highhandedness of the Kisans. Hence, a committee (with Nand Kumar Singh, Shyam Prasad Singh and Mahanth Siya Ram Das) was formed to enquiry into the earlier incidents.

The Committee's report was presented to Rajendra Prasad who had come over to Barhaiya to have discussions with tenants and Zamindars in order to give a solution. The solution is known as 'Rajendra Babu's Awards'. The most important para in the award was that the Zamindars were told to settle at least that much of their Bakasht lands with Tal tenants as they used to settle with them before the agitation of 1936. Both parties accepted this award. Accordingly, its working started. Thus a compromise was worked out by Rajendra Prasad. S.K. Sinha became in-charge with three members of committee to prepare a list of tenants along with the area of land, which used to be settled with them. Such a list was prepared in April 1937 in respect of villages Mehramchak, Kothwa, Fadarpur and of a part of village Pali.

But the award did not make any change. During the sowing season of 1937, complaints were received from some tenants that the Zamindars were not prepared to honour the accord and settle lands with them according to the list. After going through the enquiry, it was found that three or four Zamindars were at fault; but this was an incomplete finding as the number was definitely larger.

The trouble subsided again when Rajendra Prasad visited the area of struggle and was given the wrong impression that there was no serious trouble during the harvesting season of 1937-38. In the meantime Karayanand Sharma distributed handbills to the agricultural labourers in all those areas from where the Barhaiya Zamindar imported their labourers "asking them not to work as labourers in the Tal area". It was an indirect coercion.

However in 1938, the tenants submitted a memorandum to the Chief Minister praying him to look into their miseries and suggesting that if some measures were not taken to safeguard their maintenance, an extreme step would be taken as the last resort. The agrarian trouble started with the advent of *Rabi* sowing season. By powerful speeches of Karyanand Sharma and Sahajanand at Kusumbha Tal and other places, satyagrah was started. It was led by men, women and children of villages Mahramchak, Kothwa, Fadarpur, Pali, Sarora, Bhanpur, Hamirpur, Akerpur, Turkaijni and Repura. The amlas were not allowed to plough the Bakasht lands and minor clashes occured here and there as some lands were forcibly cultivated by the tenants.

The data in the table 4.7 indicates the details of Zamindars and the lands in dispute:

The Barhaiya Tal agitation was confined to the eight villages only, consisting of 616 families with a population of 4500. The area covered about 15,000 bighas of bakasht land. Lastly, the situation was controlled only after the posting of hundred constables in the Tal areas. However, the Government claimed that satyagraha was a total failure in Tal, as almost all the lands in the Tal areas were under cultivation, and Karyananad Sharma was the only person who spoke about satyagraha for the sake of propaganda both in the press and on the platform. Such situation did not remain and continue for long.

By 15th October, 1938 the satyagraha had spread to all the

Table 4.7

Name of Villages	*No. of Houses*	*Approximate population*	*Total Area of Mahal*	*Occupancy of inhabitants*	*Bakasht*
1. Kothwa	40	300	700	50	650
2. Mahramchak	35	250	1000	25	975
3. Fadarpur	36	250	375	75	300
4. Akarpur	30	200	500	—	500
5. Bhanpur	90	600	1600	140	1460
6. Saroa	60	400	1400	125	1275
7. Pali	200	1500	8484	84	8400
8. Kamarpur	125	1000	700	206	500
Total	**615**	**4500**	**14759**	**699**	**14060**

Source : Agrarian Trouble in Barhaiya Tal Area, Government of Bihar, Home Political Department, File No. 42 (II), 1938.

villages. Consequently, the Zamindars turned violent and did not spare even women.

Arbitration of the Government

The kisan activities were further intensified by January, 1939. Thousand of complaints were filed by the Zamindars for the mischiefs and damages done by the kisans on the standing crops. They had even employed about sixty mafia (men wielding lathis) from diara areas to guard the standing crops as it was expected that the kisans would offer satyagraha on the extensive scale than before. At this stage, the District Magistrate of Monghyr, B.K. Gokhale considered to hold a conference of the tenants representatives and the Zamindars of Barhaiya Tal for the appointment of an *arbitration committee* to settle once for all the Barhaiya Tal dispute between the parties. The agreement was signed by both the parties on January, 1921.

Mobilization of Kisan to face Terrorism

In the village Pali, all the concerned people alongwith the officials, five members of Arbitration Committee (N.K. Singh, S.P. Singh, Dwarika Babu, Bachcha Babu and Chunkeshwer Das and

Karyanand Sharma) tried to give final shape to the agreement but it was in vain as the villagers in large numbers kept on shouting, cursing, yelling and rushing headlong to the Bakasht lands of the Zamindars either to prevent the Zamindars from harvesting the crops or to seize the crops themselves. The Committee, however, remained ineffective because the tenants did not co-operate and turn up for evidence. Since the Committee was not agreed over the collective demand for the restoration of 60 to 100% of the Bakasht land in possession of the Zamindars for distribution to the tenants on a per capita basis, the villagers were mobilised by Karyanand Sharma to offer Satyagraha around the Committee and the S.D.O. camp. On 16th February, 1939 about five to six hundred men, women and children with about hundred cattleheads and a number of goats came and surrounded the camp, and kept the members of the Committee and officials confined in tents denouncing the Committee. Karayanand demanded food for these people and fodder for their cattle. It was a new turn in the movement and the Collector described this demand of the tenants as Communistic. It was one of the earliest experiments in gherao. The satyagrahies were asked not to return to their villages before any arrangements were made for food and fodder. Even then the tenants were asked by Karyanand Sharma to uproot the green gram which was standing on the Zamindars field near the river. But the tenants were forced to flee away by the Zamindars armed men. Karyanand tried to cross the river in a boat but the S.D.O. and five constables did not allow him to go. Thereafter, he was brought safely by S.D.O from the attacks of the armmen of the Zamindars to the camp. Luckily, the violent clash did not occur.

By the end of April, 1939, however, the award was given. Out of the terms of the award, 800 bighas of lands were to go to the peasants of eight villages. This was really not substantial for nearly 3500 persons for about 500 families. It did not satisfy to Karyanand Sharma and refused to accept the judgement of the Arbitration Committee. Moreover, the harvested crops was to be distributed between the Kisans and Zamindars by the Committee.

Accordingly, the Magistrate started distribution on the

morning of 23rd May, 1939. But rowdyism was created by the kisans of Pali and Sarora on the threshing floor under the leadership of Jwala Prasad. These villagers armed with lathies and Bhalas (spears), threatened that neither we would take the share of crops nor the Zamindars would be allowed to take away their own share. The magistrate tried to ease the situation but things did not change. In the end, he took security bonds from the Zamindars and ordered them to remove the crops to Barhaiya as there was possibility of looting the *khalihan* (threshing floor) at different centres. When nearly three-fourth of the crop had been removed, the two sub-leaders named Sidheshwar Singh and Singheshwer Singh met the Magistrate and appraised him with the contents of Karyanand Sharma's letter repenting that the kisans had committed a great mistake by refusing to accept the crops according to the award. Later on, the musclemen dispersed, and the Satyagrahis also melted away and most of them took refuge in village Pali.

In 1946, Bakasht struggle occured in Mohirat, Jangal bigha, sedra, where the kisans got back their rightful claims of 150 bigha of land. The Chief Minister ordered that all land was being tilled by the Zamindars themselves, should be returned to them. Similar struggles were seen time and again throughout the period.

While concluding the narration of the struggle in Monghyr, ideology, consciousness, organisation and forms of struggle moved towards mass politics, i.e. more and more on class lines during 1936-39. It is fact that the low castes such as Dhanuks, Dharis, Kahars, Kurmis and Banias, middle and marginal peasants confronted the Brahmin or Bhumihar Community in the Tal village.

Bakasht Struggle in Gaya District

In South Bihar, Gaya was the most active district in the Bakasht struggle. A police report shows that the anti-Zamindar campaign led to several instances of violence, where in some cases Zamindars or their agents were murdered. There were also instances of peasant deaths in the alteraction resulting from the Bakasht question.

Hence, in South Bihar, places like Reora and Mahigama in

the Gaya district became the bed of explosives under the Kisan movement. It is noted that the struggle of the peasants in Reora took place because the land occupied by the raiyat was sold in arrears claiming of rent; therefore, the Kisans of Reora resorted to satyagraha for 1,000 bigha, dispossession from which was threatened. Hence, Yadunandan Sharma initiated the campaign. He was arrested and sent to jail.

In February, 1939 the kisan movement received a fillip, when the District Magistrate, after investigating a dispute that had been simmering for several months, made a settlement which awarded four-fifths of the disputed land to the tenants. The District Magistrate negotiated with Yadunandan Sharma while he was in jail and reached an agreement for leaving 850 bighas to the kisans. Sharma and his colleagues were released. The kisans of Reora decided to take collective farming of the land. But the settlement subsequently created dissension among the peasants, because the Bhumihar tenants resented Jadunandan Sharma's socialist distribution of the land, where equal shares were given to the raiyats, whether of high or low castes. Same was the situation of low castes in Majhigama. Heningham has admitted and also affirmed by Brett is that, "Activity in Gaya was most intensive where the kisan-cum-socialist groups (had) largely captured the District and Town Congress Committees."

Struggle in Patna District

The agrarian movement was also very strong in the Patna district. Here the centres of tension were Majhauli in the Danapur sub-division, Bihta and Mokama Tal etc. There was a serious land dispute between the tenants and the Zamindars of Majahuli. The efforts of the Patna Collector to settle it proved fruitless and the tenants took a bold stand under the guidance of Sahajanand. Towards the end of October, 1939 there was a fracas, in the course of which a number of women who were doing satyagraha on Zamindars field were roughly handled and a male raiyat was seriously injured and subsequently died. The leaders among the tenants were arrested. But still the tenants continued to struggle.

Struggle in Saran District

In Saran district, discontentment was found in similar quantity. At Annawari, the struggle led by Rahul Sankratyayan was arrested while cutting sugarcane from a kisans land, he was beaten up by Zamindars gangsters and awarded six months jail on the false charge of theft.

Struggle in Shahabad District

In Shahabad district, Darihat, Jituara, Anti villages took lead in the struggle against the enhancement of rent which was taken place 12 or 13 years ago due to lack of irrigation facilities and realisation of rents for arrears.

Struggle in Champaran District

In Champaran district, the Bakasht agitation was confined to a few villages only under Adapur and Dhaka police stations. It led to some rioting in Dhaka and ultimately, compromises were arrived at between the two parties in the light of the new legislation.

The Sathi farm struggle was also sparked off in Champaran since the assumption of the first Congress Ministry. The Congress government appointed B.B. Verma, an important Congress leader and land holder of Champaran as the first Indian Manager of the Bettiah Raj which was under the Court of Wards. He remained on the post for two terms. In his second term (1946 to 1950) he settled large areas of land with his kith and kin. Among them, the important person with whom substantial quantity of land was settled were the then Excise Commissioner of Bihar, Ram Prasad Sahi and his brother Ram Rekha Prasad Sahi who got about 350 acres of the sathi farm land surrendered to the Bettiah Raj when the planters left.

The settlement with the Sahis was made on 18 November, 1946 ignoring the claims of the local people, some of whom were in actual possession of the land. The Sahis were the outsiders belonging to Saran district. Local peasants resisted the occupation of the land by the Sathis and therefore, the agitation took a serious turn.

The Bihar Congress appointed one Prajapati Mishra, but his

offer of award (45 acres of the land would be surrendered by the Sahi to be settled) with local peasant did not succeed. However, he was charged with having taken the different part of the Bettiah Raj in his own name.

Later on, Ram Manohar Lohia and Sardar Patel intervened and looked into the settlement of land with the Sahis and Prajapati Mishra who found a number of irregularities. Hence, on Patel's recommendation, the All India Congress Committee urged the Bihar Government to cancel the settlement with the Sahis and Mishra.

At last, the Government of Bihar enacted a legislation entitled the Sathi Land Restoration Act of 1950, but it could not be implemented as it was declared null and void by the Supreme Court on the ground that it was discriminatory. Other similar cases were left out on one ground or the other. Through the fifties and sixties, the Sathi farms struggle remained almost the sole flame of organised peasant resistance in Bihar.

In the 19th century in Chotanagpur, the most visible source of socio-economic friction was the persistant drive of the landlords to convert the significants chanda payments, its land rents where this had been done before. These rents calculated per unit of land and according to the soil quality they were not automatically adjusted to the changes in the cost of living, which rose all over India especially towards the end of the century. Therefore, any enhancement of the rents under the conditions of Chotanagpur became at once a power contest between the landlords and his tenants. These strained relations between landlords and tenants are reported from all over the districts of the Chotanagpur division.

Similar was the position of the landlord and tenant relationship throughout Bhagalpur, Muzaffarpur, Purnea etc.

While summing up, the observation of A.N. Das may be included to show the main reasons behind the tenants physical as well as mental tortures. He revealed that, "There was systematic attempts by the Zamindars in 1947-49 to demoralise the tenantry by physically assaulting kisans and their leaders". So the landlords consciousness hightened. As proved by the 'searchlight' Report : "A Zamindar Youth League was organised" to find ways and means to save themselves and devise their means of existence and sustenance. Thus attempts were made to take forcible possession of Bakasht and other lands occupied by the tenants that is testified by the clashes which occurred at Bigha (Begusarai), Ramgarhwa (Champaran), Barhaiya (Monghyr), Ballipur (Darbhanga), Pathua (Monghyr), Madhepura (Darbhanga), Mahumi (Bihar Sharif), Sasaram (Gaya), Darigaon (Arrah), Alwarpur (Patna), Nabiganj (Gaya), Kursela (Purnea) and many other places. Many tenants were killed and seriously injured. A few Zamindars and their retainers also suffered.

Disgusted by them, landlords threatened to have the tenants' villages bombed from the air. Police were deputed to maintain law and order, even though several peasants died at their hands too. (as they were internally wellwisher of the estates). Later on K.B. Sahay, the then Revenue minister intervened in favour of abolition of landlordism and only after a great drama he could succeed. It would be wrong to think that the peasantry was involved in general agitation or localised land struggles formed a homogenous social groups. Survey settlement reports distinguished between the different legal categories of the peasantry.

Differentiation of Peasantry

A great emphasis on the differentiation of peasentry has been given by different groups of social thinkers. Recently, Gail Omved and Chetna Guha have also jointly given the statement that peasant question is a class question. Certainly the class character of the peasantry including the issue of its role in the revolutionary process, the question of who are its enemies and what are its internal differentiation is one of the burning question. Minty emphasised on the internal differentiation of the peasantry, that has since been a subject of many debates, scholars have raised the question of which peasant is more peasant-like than others.

According to Shanin, the methodological discussions have emphasised the difficulty of defining the peasantry as a type and it has been suggested that one should think of the peasantry as a process. But Marx found the peasantry as a class. Accordingly, the worker-peasant alliance was a lynchpin of the revolutionary process in any society of incomplete bourgeois development. Lenin, Mao and later Communists sharply distingnished sections among the peasantry which they sometimes found as different classes, they had no doubt that the vast majority of the peasants as petty producers were a crucial part of the democratic revolution.

The fact is that while the landless Poor-Middle-Rich distinctions have been part of the vocabulary of all third world revolutions, it is equally true that they have never been seen as a division into fundamental and opposing classes. The worker peasant alliance remained at the forefront of strategy and legitimation of the revolutionary process. However, their (rich, middle, poor) basic line of action was anti-landlordism and anti-imperialistic interest.

But many social scientists and even left activists are making the peasantry fundamentally differentiated by definition. For instance, when middle and rich peasants are grouped together as beneficiaries of development, and poor peasant and the landless are said to be its victims, the seeming persuasiveness of this distinction often prevents us from asking what its class basis is ? Sharp differences in the socio-economic conditions of the peasant further interposed a barrier in the uniform growth of consciousness among the various sections of the peasantry. Thus, neither the landowners nor landless even now form differentiated categories. In terms of the quantity of land owned and according to the nature of control exercised over them, all these groups are highly differentiated and stratified. Lack of group unity and class solidarity among the poor peasants and share croppers thus put severe check on the sustained peasant organisation and movements.

If there is hierarchy of inequality in land holding or income we can draw a line (or two) anywhere or come up with two or more categories which will clearly have differentiated resources and some different tendency or behaviour. But are these classes in the Marxist sense? Of course their interest revolves around the economic interest and for this, they had to work jointly. Poor peasants may engage in some hiring out, and middle and rich peasants may hire in labourers. CPI (ML) has characterised the peasantry as being engaged in 'Petty Commodity Production' which brings us to the capitalistic development today as such it renders the peasant producer dependent on the market for sale and increasingly expensive inputs, which exploits her/him through/via the terms of trade. This exploitation covers a wide range of peasant holdings, that is why, we find very poor peasants along with middle and richer ones in peasant movements; this ties the interest of agricultural labourers and peasants together because they find common enemies of the labour to depend on. Another factor was the inequalities and contradictions of caste, gender, economic character among rural toiling majority. There are contradictions among the people and opposed class enemies; the object of revolutionary strategy should be not to sharpen them but to overcome in the direction of bringing forward the interest of the most oppressed sections in the process of common struggle against the main exploiting force.

Between 1948 and 1951 the organised peasant movement had to carry on under difficult conditions. The Kisan Sabha was subjected to severe repression, the activity of its central bodies was suppressed, a large number of its leaders were thrown into jail and the local organisations had to carry on their activities in semi-underground conditions. However, the peasant struggle was not crushed. Even today it sometimes echoes in Aurangabad, Jahanabad, Gaya, Biharsharif, Sasaram, Patna, Arrah, and sometimes in Monghyr, Darbhanga, Madhubani, Muzaffarpur. Still its bell is ringing all over the rural belt of Bihar leading to the unending violence.

Thus, after going through the various agrarian unrest, the form of peasantry and the question of peasant differentiation, the road links towards the Abolition of Zamindari system in Bihar.

Notes & References

Kumar, Shiv, *Peasantry and the Indian National Congress* (1919-33). Meerut, 1980, p. 19.

Nanda, B.R., (ed.), *Socialism in India*. Delhi 1972, p. 190, 2nd Ed.

Das, A.N., *Agrarian Unrest and Socio-Economic Change*. New Delhi, 1980, p. 57.

Mukherjee, R., *Land Problems of India*, Calcutta 1933, p. 288.

Census of India, 1921, Calcutta. 1924, Vol. I, pt. I, p. 14.

Dutta, K.K., Neil Charlesworth, *The Middle Peasants Thesis and the*

Roots of Rural Agitation in India, 1914-47. Journal of Peasants, p. 259.

Beames, John, *Memories of a Bengal Civilian.* London, 1961, p. 269-60.

Mukherjee, Mridula, *Peasant Resistance and Peasant Consciousness, in Colonial India.* Economic and Political Weekly, Oct. 8, 1988, p. 2109.

Kling, Blair B., *The Blue Mutiny (1859-61)* Penssylvania-1966. p. 84-86.

Hanningham, Stephen, *Peasants Movement in Colonial India,* Canberra 1982, p. 46-50, also see Sumit Sarkar's "Modern India and Popular Movements and Middle Class Leadership". Delhi-1983. p. 183-84.

Das A.N., *Problem of Unity in the Agrarian Struggle, a case of* Bihar. Economic and Political Weekly, May 7, 1988, p. 942.

Chaudhary, Binay Bhusan, *Agrarian Movements in Bengal and Bihar,* 1919-39. Ed. by A.R. Desai, Oxford University Press, Delhi, 1979, p. 338.

Sharma, G.P., *Congress and the Peasant Movement in Bihar,* Bombay, 1985, p. 3.

Final Report of the Survey and Settlement Operation in the Maksudpur Estate in the District of Gaya 1900-1904. Calcutta, 1907, p. 25.

Sen, Sunil, *Agrarian Relations in India.* New Delhi, 1972, p. 2.

Choudhary B.B., *Agrarian Movement in Bengal and Bihar,* 1919-39, in A.R. Desai's (ed.) Peasants struggle in India. *Op.cit.* p. 346.

Census of India, 1921, Bihar and Orissa Part III, Tables XXI p. 200.

Report of the Bihar Provincial Kisan Sabha, Nov. 1929 to Nov. 1955, p. 2.

Gupta, Rakesh, *Bihar Peasantry and the Kisan Sabha,* 1936-47. New Delhi, 1982, p. 59-60.

Williams, R.A.E., *Final Report on the Rent Settlement Operations* 1937-41, pp. 53-54.

Murphy, R.W., *The Final Report on the Survey and Settlement Operations in the Distt. of Monghyr* (South) 1905-12, Supd. Ranchi, p. 79.

Bihar Provincial Kisan Sabha Report p. 17.

Note by J.A. Hubback on the Produce Rents of Monghyr and Patna Districts found in course of the Survey and Settlement Operations in 1908-1909" in P.W. Murphy, Op.cit, Appendix-W.

Sharma, Ram Chandra, *Gaya Zile Ki Kisan Samasya,* Janta, June, 9, 1939, pp. 13-14.

Bihar Provincial Kisan Sabha Report p. 27.

Williams, R.A.E., Final Report on the Rent Settlement Operation under

Section 112, Bihar Tenancy Act in eleven sub-divisions of Patna, Gaya, Shahabad and Monghyr. Patna, 1943.

Based on the judgment of P.W. Murphy, Commissioner dated 13th Oct. 1931, in case Nos. 400 and 413 of 1931 of village M Lodipur, Karasawan alies Aiman Bigha, Paragana, Sahda Tauzi No. 62901/1, 6290/2, extracted from the judgment of P.W. Murphy. Dec. 2, 1930 in case Nos. 556, 557 and 558 of 1938 of village M. Mohanpur Panherisa Tauze No. 16542 and 16543, extracted from the judgment of J.R. Daine, CIF, additional member of the Board of Revenue dated April 1, 1932, in case No. 4 of 1932 of village Lodipur Karasawan aliea Aiman Bigha Tauzi No. 62490, Pargana Sanda, extracted from the judgment of the Hon'ble M.J.A. Hubback, CSI, member dated 10 March, 1937, in case no. 236 and 242 of 1933 of estate Kurni Chak, Pargana Gayapur, Tauzi nos, 9694 etc. Patna.

Home Special Confidential file No. 29—(VII) 1939 Para-I.

Bihar Provincial Kisan Sabha Report, p. 50.

Annonymous, *Bihar Kisan Sabha Comes of Age. Congress Socialist* Vol. III (New series), No. 4, Jan. 22, 1938, p. 51.

Quoted in Shelvankar, *Problem of India* Penguin, 1940.

Final Report on the Survey and Settlement Operations (Revision) in the District of Saran 1915-21, p. 101.

Saran Survey and Settlement Operations Report 1915-21, p. 58.

P. 375 of the Final Report of Survey and Settlement Operation in the Purnea District quoted in *Ibid.*, p. 101.

Champaran District Gazetters 1907, p. 98.

Bihar and Orissa Banking Enquiry Committee, Patna (n.d.) p. 90.

Bihar Provincial Kisan Sabha Report, p. 23.

Bihar Provincial Kisan Sabha Report, p. 23.

Heningham, Stephen, Agrarians in North Bihar peasant Darbhanga Raj, 1919-20 *in Indian Economic and Social History Review*, Vol. XVI no. (1979) . p. 94.

Sankratyayan, Rahul, *Amwari Ke Pirit Kisan, Janta,* Jan. 26, 1939, pp. 11, 12, 20.

Janata No. 15, January, 27, 1939, p. 9.

Home Special file no. 6, 1936 (para III B)

T.V. Serial, *"Muzrim Hazir"*, (still going on based on the novel of Vimal Mitra).

Diwakar, R.R., *Bihar Through the Ages,* Bombay 1958, p. 774.

Janata, editorial, p. 5-6

Hubback, J.A., *Op.cit.*, p. 52., "The chief dispute during the Khanapani seasons of 1910-11 and 1911-12 were those between landlords claiming land as Bakasht and tenants claiming occupancy rights."

Bihar Bakasht Disputes Settlement Act, 1947, in the Bihar Code, Bihar Act, 1936 to 1953, Vol. IV, (Patna 1955), p. 222.

Bihar Tenancy Act, 1885, Patna 1975, p. 109.

Home special confidential file no. 29 (VII) 1939, para I.

Hauser, W. *Bihar Provincial Kisan Sabha, Op.cit* 1929-42, A Study of an Indian Peasant Movement (An unpublished Ph.D. Thesis, University of Chicago 1961) p. 23.

Konar, Hare Krishna, *Agrarian Problems of India*, Calcutta, 1977, p. 104.

Saraswati, Sahajanand, *Mera Jeewan Sangharsh*, Bihar, Patna, 1952, p. 511.

Padri, AR F(1939-40) f. 16D1, Padri, G. 1941-42 RDA : See also S. Henningham *"Op.cit."*, p. 156.

Inspection report, special officer to Chief Manager, 31 Oct. 1938, f. 642, C. Padri, G. 1938-39, RDA.

Conference proceedings, 13 May, 1937 and Jan. 1938, f. 10FG 1937-38; Conference minutes, 4,5 May 1938, f. 10D3, G 1938-39, RDA.

Misra, Ramanandan, 'Condition of Tenant'. For Danby's response to Misra's charges, See Indian Nation 16 July, 1939.

H.K. Prasad to Rajendra Prasad, 30 June, 1938, f. IA 1938 (microfilm 8), pp. NML, See also Hauser, *"Op.cit"* pp. 129-30.

Indian Nation, 1 July, 1938, Note by Hallett cited in note 47 above.

Krishnan, H.R., *Report on Enquiry*, 29 Aug. 1939.

Roy, *North Bihar Village*, p. 306.

GB FR(1) March HP f 18/3/1938, NAI.

GB FR(2) April 1939, HP f 18/4/1939; GB FR(1) May 1939, HP f 18/5/1939; GB FRS (1) and (2) June 1939, HP f 18/6/1939 NAI.

Russell, R., note dated 13 July, 1939.

Krishnan, H.R., *'Account of the Bakasht Struggle'*, Report on Enquiry, 29 Aug. 1939.

GB FR(1) July 1939 11 P f 18/7/1939 See also Indian Nation, 6, 16 July.,

G.B. Land Revenue Administration Report for 1939-40, pp. 12-13, and for 1940-41, p. 11-12.

GB FR (10 Dec. 1939, HP f 18/12/1939; GB FR (1) Jan. 1940, HP f 18/1/1940, NAI, In the ensuing months there were some minor disturbances but in late May the administration reported that 'Purely agrarian agitation has almost ceased'. See GB Fortnightly Reports for February, March & May 1940, HP files 18/12/1940, 18/5/1940 NAI.

Agrarian trouble in Barahiaya Tal area Monghyr, Government of Bihar, Home Political Department (special). File No. 42 (III) 138.

Home special, confidential file no. 29 (VII) containing a note on Barhaiya Tal prepared by Radha Raman Ghosh, S.D.O. Monghyr, p. 9. para. 3.
Kisan Sabha, Government of Bihar, Home Political Department File No. 6 (a) 1936.
Extracted from the confidential diary of the Superintendent of Police, Monghyr, dated, April 17, 1936, *Ibid*.
Home Special, confidential, File No. 29 (VII) 1939. Containing a note on Barhaiya Tal, p. 9. para. 3.
Home special confidential, file No. 29 (VIII) page, para 8.
Gokhale, B.K., Commissioner of Monghyr to J.L. Merriman, Commissioner of Bhagalpur, Ibid.
Agrarian Trouble in Barhaiya Tal area, Government of Bihar, Home Political Department, File No. 42 (III) 1938.
Letter of the Collector of Monghyr dated, Jan 4, 1939 to Russelles, Chief Secretary to the Government of Bihar, Government of Bihar Home Political Department (Special File No. 29 (ii) 1939.
Letter of the Collector of Monghyr dated 11/12 Feb. 1939 to Ressells, Chief Secretary, *Ibid*.
Home Special Confidential file No. 29 VII *Ibid*., para 13.
Home Special Confidential file No. 29 (VII) *Op.cit*., p. 9, para 13.
Rasul, A., *History of the All India Kisan Sabha*, Calcutta 1974, p. 50.
Brett., C.T., "Report of Administration of the Police in the Province of Bihar for the year 1938" Patna, Supd. Govt. printed 1939 p. 1.
Hauser, *Op.cit*., p. 132, GB FR (1) Feb 1939, HP f 18/5/1939 NAI GB FR (1) May 1939, HP f. 18/5/1939 NAI.
A note on the Kisan Movement in India.
Fortnightly Report of the Patna Commissioner for the period ending 13 Nov. 1936.
Dutta, K.K., *Freedom Movement in Bihar, Patna* 1957 p. 274.
Mishra, Girish, *Agrarian Problems of Permanent Settlement*, A case Study of Champaran, New Delhi, 1978, p. 297.
Indian Nation, 1969
Proceedings of Government of Bihar, Revenue Dept. (Land Revenue) Dec., 1947, Nos. 225-31. B.
B.L.A. Debates 24-25 May 1950.
All India Reporter, Supreme Court 1983, p. 220, also see Sinha *Sathi Ke Kisano Ka Aitihasik Sangharsa*.
Report on Land Revenue Administration of the Province of Bihar, For the year 1948-49 Supdt. Printing Press, Bihar 1951 p. 5.

Searchlight, 19 Jan. 1947.
Ibid., 12 May, 1947, News flashed that, "Ears and Nose of the Diwan of Muzaffarpur chopped off". Same method was applied in Purnea towards the cruel Zamindars and their amlas.
Searchlight, 6 Oct. 1947.
Ibid., 20 March, 1947, also see Hunkar 26 March, 1947.
Omvedt, Gail, Gala Chetna, *Economic and Political weekly*, July 2, 1988.
Mintz, W. Sidney, Note on the definition of the peasantry, Journal of Peasant Studies, Vol. I No. I, 1973.
Theodar, Shanin, *Nature and Logic of the Peasant Economy*. Journal of Peasant Studies Vol. I, No. I 1973.
Karna, M.N., *Agrarian Structure in Bihar: A Historical Overview*, Shillong, p. 39.
Kotovsky, Grigory, *Agrarian Reforms in India*, Delhi, 1964, p. 39-40.

CHAPTER 5

ABOLITION OF ZAMINDARI SYSTEMS

The agrarian movements towards the land reforms was the prime issues that led to the Abolition of Zamindari System in the State of Bihar.

Land reforms may be described under the following main heads :

1. 'Abolition of intermediaries',
2. Tenancy reforms, and
3. 'Reclamation and Cultivation of the Bihar wasteland.'

In post 1942, while Gandhiji was in jail (Aga Khan) one day Miraben asked him: "How will the land be distributed after Swaraj?" Gandhiji replied, "Land will be owned by the State, I pursue the reins of Government will be in the hands of those who have faith in this ideal. A majority of Zamindars will give up their land willingly. Those who will not do so, will have to do so under legislation."

In fact, the dream of Gandhiji proved true on the eve of India's Independence when the Zamindari system was tottering into shreds.

The history of the Zamindari oppression and the exploitation of the peasantry is the tale of woes and sorrow. The Permanent Settlement and Zamindari System, the living heritage of the British rule, had crippled the state and interposed a post of intermediary between the state and the actual tiller of the soil. Tenancy had become a very common feature of the agrarian economy. The intermediaries were not always cultivating their home farmlands. Therefore, the owners sank to the level of tenants. The National Sample Survey (8th round) stated that about 24% of the area operated by rural households was held on lease. The percentage varies from 11 to 26 as shown in the table 5.1 :

Table 5.1

Zone	*Area leased in as % of operated area*
North Zone	11
Central Zone	19
South Zone	22
East Zone	20
West Zone	22
North west Zone	26
All India	20

This sorry state of affairs which facilitated the rise of a foreign power has been geographically described by Ghulam Hussain. Therefore, it became essential for the Government to make land reforms.

In its broadsense, land reforms included the whole range of agrarian reforms, but in its restricted sense it applied to the changes in the tenancy, tenures, redistribution of land ownership and regulation of land utilization.

Post-war land reforms measures in Bihar were passed as All India Land Reform Policy which primarily aimed at:—

1. Removing such impediments to agricultural production as arose from the character of agrarian structure.
2. To create condition for evolving an agrarian economy with the high level of efficiency and production. With concentrated ownership of land, abolition of the prevalent intermediary system between the state and the tiller of the soil, to crush the domination of the landlords and to distribute land to the landless peasants and agricultural labourers.

Tenancy implied a divorce between ownership and cultivation, and to that extent constituted a less desirable form of farming than owner cultivation. The Tenancy System was a powerful obstacle to economic development.

Thus, when the second Congress Ministry came into power, it took definite measures to replace the Zamindari System by Raiyatwari System in order to improve the economic condition of the cultivators. The determined mood of Congress was reflected in the substantial reforms in tenancy just after its assumption of power. The first popular Ministry had raised great expectations at the time of its installation. There were kisan agitations. There was even a mammoth kisan march (already discussed in chapter 3) to the capital of the State. Naturally, the powers would not remain indifferent to the burning issue of the day. During the period of Second World War the programme of agrarian reforms remained suspended. But by the time war ended it came to be realised that tenancy problems were so complicated that there was no easy solution. The laws that were passed in Bihar giving relief to the tenants touched only the fringe of the problem. The whole idea of Tenancy Legislation was to grant fixity of tenure, to determine fair rent and ensure the right of transfer of holdings to the tenants without any hindrance. As a result, many Tenancy Amendments were done to give a quietus, to the kisan unrest.

Various Bihar Tenancy Amendment Acts have been discussed in chapter 3. But these Tenancy measures, did not or could not solve the agrarian problems. While reviewing the tenancy legislation upto 1938-39, Nanavati and Anjaria observed:

> "Thus tenancy legislation was only a palliative under the prevailing condition of tenurial relationships, not a cure. The agrarian problem was too intricate to be solved by tenancy legislation alone. It demanded an overhaul of the system of land tenures and tenancies and the development of the more efficient system of land management."

The necessity was, therefore, felt for a change in the tenurial system itself and this was possible only by abolishing the Zamindari system. In the post war years, land reforms became the chant of the times, not only in India but in most of the under-developed countries of the world.

The Bihar Tenancy Act, 1885 classified the tenants into the following classes :

1. Raiyats holding at fixed rate.
2. Occupancy raiyats.
3. Non-occupancy raiyats, and
4. Under raiytas.

Figure-I
Hierarchy of Interests in Land:

The State of Bihar
(The Super Landlord)

The Zamindar (legally a "proprietor", but acting as an intermediary of the state in the collection of rent from tenants).	the Tenure holder (acting as an intermediary of the state in the collection of rent from tenants).
The occupancy Raiyats (a rent paying holder of land having the right of occupancy on the land held by him.)	The Non-occupancy Raiyat (a rent paying holder of land not having the right of occupancy on land temporarily in his possession.

The Under Raiyat

(a rent paying holder of land having temporary possession of a holding under a raiyat).

The Mazdoor

(a wage labourer having no right in hand)

The figure shows that prior to the Bihar Land Reforms Act, there had grown up in Bihar an intricately stratified system of relationship of people to land. In the permanent settlement areas of the state especially, there were numerous kinds of landholdings. At the apex of the hierarchy was the state. Below the state were the Zamindars, tenure holders and under tenure holders (those who had rent collecting powers). The base were the peasants with limited right to land and the landless labourers, wage labourers, with no rights to land.

Apart from these broad types of the tenants, there were some special types of raiyats all over the districts of Bihar, viz. Bargaiyats with Khuntkatti rights, Mundari Khunti Kattidars Hal Hasila, Bhaoli, Khurposh, Bargait, Shikmis etc.

1. The rights and obligations of raiyats holding at fixed rates were identical with those of the holders of a permanent tenure. So for all purposes, they were like holders and their interest were adequately safe- guarded.
2. Occupancy raiyats :—The Act defines an occupancy raiyat as follows :—

   (i) A person who for a period of 12 years, whether wholly or partly, before or after the commencement of this Act, has continuously held, as a Raiyat, the land situated in any village, becomes, on the expiration of that period, settled raiyat of that village.

   (ii) A person shall be deemed, for the purpose of this section tò have continuously held land in a village notwithstanding that a particular land held by him has been different at different times, and his heir shall be deemed for the purposes of this Section, to have held any land as a raiyat. The Act obliterated the distinction made by the 1859 Act between *Khudkahsht* and *Paikasht* raiyats.

   (iii) An occupancy raiyat was entitled to use lands in any manner which did not materially impair the value of the land or render it unfit for the purpose of tenancy when the rent of the land was paid partly or wholly in kind, the landlord or raiyat were entitled to equal shares in the timber. In that case, the landlord was entitled to 9/2 1/2 and raiyat to 11/20th in the flowers, fruits and other products of all trees and bamboos growing on such land. The raiyat was entitled to plant any tree or bamboo without landlord's consent but neither the landlord nor the raiyat was entitled to cut down an appropriate tree or bamboos without the consent of the other.

An occupancy raiyat was required to pay rent to the

landlord on his holding at fair and equitable rates. The rate was payable in cash or kind or partly in cash and partly in kind. The landlord was not entitled to charge more than 1/4th of the produce in rent. The system of produce rent was not in vogue in the districts of Santhal Parganas. Generally, an occupancy raiyat enjoys the privileges of fair rent, fixity of tenure and free transfer, he has the right to improve the land without enhancement of rent, and his cattle, tools, grains, etc. are exempted by law from attachment for the distraint of rent.

Section 6 of the Act has restricted the right of a landlord to enhance the rent paid by an occupancy raiyat was fair and equitable until contrary was proved, and provisions were made to restrict any unreasonable and illegal enhancement of rent. Rent could be enhanced by a suit on grounds of rise in prices, (stable food crop) or improvement made in the land by the landlord or on grounds of increase in productivity etc.

According to Section 10 of the Act, the landlord cannot evict an occupancy raiyat from his holding except in execution of a decree for eviction on the grounds *(a)* that the raiyat has used the land in a manner to render it unfit for the purpose of tenancy, or *(b)* that he has broken a condition consistent with the provision of this Act.

The rights of the occupancy raiyats in their holdings are permanent and heritable. However, the position relating to transferability of land in Santhal Parganas and in Chotanagpur division was different.

In Santhal Pargana, no transfer by a raiyat of his right holding by sale, gift, will, lease or any other contract or agreement is valid. This restriction on transfer exists in the district in order to protect the lands of aboriginals from passing into the hands of money-lenders or others. A non-aboriginal raiyat is, however, permitted to transfer, by complete usufructuary mortgage (locally known as Bhugut Bandh) for a period not exceeding six years upto the extent at 1/4th of their paddy, and first class bariland to another raiyat of the District a grain gola, a registered Co-operative Society or Land Mortagage Banks. In certain circumstances (e.g. sickness, loss of plough and cattle etc.), the raiyat may make over his land temporarily for cultivation to another raiyat of the District.

Similarly, in Chotanagpur division some relaxation are permissible so far as the raiyat's right to transfer is concerned. For example, an aboriginal raiyat may transfer with the Deputy Commissioner's sanction his holding to another aboriginal resident of the same thana, a raiyat may enter into Bhugut Bandha mortagage of his holding for a period not exceeding 7 years usually, and so on.

Position in rest of Bihar relating to transferability of aboriginals lands and lands of members of Scheduled Castes and backward classes :—Protection is afforded to the lands of the tenants who are members of scheduled tribes, scheduled castes and backward classes by imposing restrictions on transfer of their lands in the whole of Bihar. A raiyat of this class may sub-lease his land to or enter into complete usufructuary mortage with regard there to, with another raiyat of the same class without the Collectors sanction. Chapter VII-A of the Bihar Tenancy Act, 1885 is relevant in this connection.

Non-Occupancy Raiyat

A non-occupancy raiyat may be defined as one who has no occupancy right in the lands he cultivates. Such raiyats are liable to be evicted from the land—*(a)* if they failed to pay any arrears of rent, *(b)* if they used the land in the manner rendering it unfit for the purpose of tenancy, *(c)* if they contravened an agreement between them and the landlords, and *(d)* if the Term of registered lease expired. The rights of the non-occupancy raiyats are neighter heritable nor transferable.

Condition of enhancement of rent

The Tenancy Act of 1885, for the first time, tried to regulate the rent to be paid by the non-occupancy raiyats. It provided that when a non-occupancy raiyat was admitted to the occupation of land, he would pay such rent as might be agreed by him to the landlord. The rent of a non-occupancy raiyat could not be enhanced except through a registered agreement or through the court.

Under Raiyat

Tenants holding land immediately are called under raiyat. They are entitled to the occupancy right if they proved the continuous possession of the land in question for 12 years. The rights of under raiyats are neither hereditary nor transferable. In the case of homestead, if an under raiyat occupied it for 12 years continuously, it gave him a permanent and heritable right. Such under raiyats could be evicted from their land if *(a)* they failed to pay the rent, *(b)* they misused the land to render it unfit for cultivation, and *(c)* the raiyat whose under raiyats they happened to be, wants the land for himself to cultivate. As a matter of custom, an under raiyat paid a much higher rate of rent than the raiyat under whom he held the land. The rent to be paid by the under raiyat is generally fixed at the time of admission. A limit is imposed on the landlord for the recovery of money rent from an under raiyat. From an under raiyat, landlord cannot realize exceeding the rent he himself paid by more than 50 per cent. The rent is payable under raiyat under a registered lease on agreement, and 25 per cent in any other case.

Sub-letting of land was prohibited under a Tenancy Law in the districts of Santhal Pargana. There were thus no under raiyats in that district.

Bargaiyats with Khunt Katti Right

A raiyat having Khunt Katti rights held a subsistency title to or occupied land reclaimed from a jungle by the original founders of the villages or their descendants in the male line. A raiyat having Khunt Katti rights possessed all the privileges of an occupancy raiyat.

The rent payable by such a raiyat was not subject to any written contract made at the time of commencement of his tenancy, but it was liable to enhancement if his tenancy of such land had been created more than 20 years before passing of the Chotanagpur Act, 1908. Further, when an order was made for enhancement of the rent payable by such raiyat, the enhanced rate fixed by such order could not exceed one-half of the rent payable by an occupancy raiyat for land of a similar description and with similar advantages in the same village.

Mundari Khunt Karttidars

Mundari Khunt Karttidars meant a Mundari who belonged to the Munda tribe (in the Chotanagpur division) had acquired jungle land for the purpose of bringing suitable portions of such land under cultivation. This type of tenancy was not tranferable by gift or sale etc. However, under certain circumstances an usufructuary mortagage or lease was permissible.

The rent of a Mundari Kutti Karttidars could not be enhanced unless it was created before a period of 20 years, i.e. from the date of presentation of the petition for enhancement. In other cases the rent could be increased but only by an order of the Deputy Commissioner.

Hal hasila—This type of tenants, commonly found in Bhagalpur District, cultivated land according to an agreement, and by virtue of same agreement paid rent according to the actual maturity of the crops. The rent varied from year to year.

Bhaoli—These tenants found mostly in the Districts of Gaya, paid rent in the form of grain, either by weighing at the threshing form (also called agor-batai) or by appraising the standing crop commonly known as danabandi. In the latter case, the tenants made over as many maunds of grain as were estimated would be the shake in the field as it stood. Under this system the crop was regarded by the two concerning parties as their joint property.

Khurposh—This is different from Khurpash. The Khurposh is a local term for the sub-tenants who worked with hoes, usually such tenants held small plots of land on crops share basis and possessed very inferior rights in the land among sub-tenants.

Bargait—This is a class of sub-tenants that cultivated land on share basis. They are also called *Adhiyadars*.

Shikmis—These are also sub-tenants working on similar terms and conditions as the Bargaits. However, in the District of Gaya, a shikmi is a money paying tenant.

A detailed list of local names and legal terminology of tenures and tenancies according to the nature of right in land has been prepared by the Census of India. Such local names run into hundreds have mainly been established through local customs in various parts of the state.

Homestead Lands

Occupancy raiyats and non-occupancy raiyats already enjoyed adequate protection against eviction from their homestead lands. Where the homestead forms part of the raiyats agricultural holdings, the same incidence covers his homestead also. Elsewhere, the incidence is regulated by local customs or wages. The Bihar Privileged Persons Homestead Tenancy Act, enacted in February, 1948 confers right of permanent tenancy in their homestead on all persons (other than proprietors, tenure holders, under tenure holders and mahajans) who, besides, their homestead, hold either no land or hold any such land not exceeding one acre in the area, such persons are treated in the Act as 'privileged tenants'. The confernment of permanent tenancy on such persons, is of course, subject to payment of such rent as is agreed upon between them and their landlords, provided it is not unfair and equitable rent as is fixed therefore by the collector on application or of his own motion. The Act empowers the Collector to restore possession of a privileged tenant over the homestead from which the latter is evicted by his landlord unlawfully.

Land in Direct Possession

The following categories of the land were in direct possession of the Landlords :—

- *(a)* Landlords Private Lands,
- *(b)* Raiyati Lands in temporary possessions of landlords, and
- *(c)* Village Waste Land.

The landlords private lands known as zirat, sir, nij-jote, kamat etc. were those which were proved to have been cultivated by the landlords themselves, with their own stock or by their own servant or their hired labour for 12 continuous years, immediately before passing of the Bihar Tenancy Act of 1885, or which were recognised by village usage of such lands. No rights of occupancy accrued where any such land was held under a lease for a term of years or under a lease from year to year. When the landlord's intermediary interest got vested in the state under the Bihar Land Reforms Act, 1950 these lands became his raiyati lands, subject to payment by him or fair and equitable rent to be assessed on them.

Raiyati Land in Temporary Possession

Lands of this category were known as Bakasht lands. These belonged originally to raiyats, which came into possession of the landlords by sale of the raiyati holdings for arrears of rent, surrender, abandonment or the like. Village raiyats have preferential claim to settlement of lands of this category. A settled raiyat of the village gets occupancy rights in such lands as soon as the same are held by him. In area where the Bihar Tenancy Act, 1885, applies anyone whether a settled raiyat or not, with whom such a land was settled, got a right of occupancy therein when the total areas of such lands in possession of the landlord exceeded 40 acres. Lands of this category, as were used for agricultural or horticultural purposes in Khas possession of the landlord, became his raiyati land on acquisition of his intermediary interest under the Bihar Land Reforms Act, 1950 subject, of course, to payment of such rent as was assessed there on.

Ghairmazrua Khas Lands

The village waste land known as Ghairmazrua Khas, patit etc. remained at the disposal of the landlords who could cultivate it themselves or settle it with others. The new ministry took definite steps to bring the fallow bend land under cultivation. A select committee was formed consisting of 15 members, with Shri K.B. Sahay (Revenue and Forest Minister) as the chairman.

According to Shri K.B. Sahay, "the waste and unproductive land means land which owing to the action of river or natural calamity was lying fallow or which had so deteriorated, owing to a deposit of sand or accumulation of water or growth of forests of any other cause, as to render it unfit for cultivation for the time being unprofitable and shall include land which the Collector by notification declares to be waste and unproductive.

The cultivation of the waste land would have added to the wealth of the province and solved the problems of food also, to a large extent. Thus, these lands had to be reclaimed. This could be done either by lending money to the landlords or the tenants to reclaim. The difficulty was that they might not spent the money on reclaiming the lands.

Thus according to the Bihar Waste Lands (Reclamation, Cultivation and Improvement) Act, 1946 the Government took the lands in its temporary possession, brought them under cultivation and after the lands had been improved and made fit for cultivation, they were restored to the tenants if they belonged to the tenants or to the landlords. Where such lands were converted to their own use for agricultural or horticultural purpose by the landlords, these acquired the status of their Bakasht land and became their raiyati land on acquisition of their Zamindari interest. In the Santhal Parganas, the member of the village community has preferential right to obtaining settlement of such lands. The landlords were not entitled to charge any *salami* (premium), for making such settlement. In the Chotanagpur division the residents of the village were entitled to reclaim village waste lands without the landlords consent but with the previous permission of the Deputy Commissioner of the District. No such right existed in the areas to which the provision of the Bihar Tenancy Act, 1885 applied and the landlords were free to settle lands with whomsoever they chose and realised salami thereafter.

In every village, there were some lands given for the use of village community on the whole. Such lands may be used as Ghairmazrua Aam (common land), Gochar (grazing field), Rasta (Pathways), cremation ground etc. Technically, these lands were belonged to the landlord of the village but he could neither settle them with tenants for cultivating purposes nor could he cultivate them himself. In reality, however, there were widespread reports of the settlement of such lands for individual uses in the wake of the Abolition of Zamindari in the State.

Bihar had 3.2 million acres of cultivable wastelands i.e. little over 7% of the total area. This was included over 7 lakhs acres of bush, forests and bamboo growth, about 8 lakh acres of pasture lands and 5 lakh acres of uplands of poor soil.

There were large tracts of lands in the Chotanagpur and the Kosi area which was lying fallow. The tenants on account of their poverty had not been able to make it cultivable. Therefore, the Government took the lands in its temporary possession, brought them under cultivation and then restored them to the tenants or landlords as the case may be.

The latter had to pay all the revenue and cess for the entire period, that waste land which had been in the possession of the Collectors, and all the recovery was a maximum of 2 to 4 anna per acre for the lands which the Collector held.

The data in the table 5.2 shows the extent of cultivable waste lands in acres in the districts and State of Bihar during 1947 to 1952.

Table 5.2
Area in Acre

District	*1947-48*	*1948-49*	*1949-50*	*1950-51*	*1951-52*
Patna	21,005	26,306	16,309	15,094	8,296
Gaya	154,850	178,988	155,310	164,023	110,119
Shahabad	791,214	74,633	73,335	72,192	55,312
Patna Division	255,069	279,927	244,959	251,905	173,727
Saran	84,751	52711	30,102	36,407	15,915
Champaran	116,534	133,063	103,040	127,830	85,004
Muzaffarpur	74,124	79,921	65,104	64,693	53,681
Darbhanga	89,619	65,864	77,997	59,484	61,918
Tirhut Division	365,068	331,559	276,303	288,415	216,518
Bhagalpur	235,398	62,682	59,685	114,062	90,554
Saharsa	235,653	365,209	188,615	418,452	300,747
Monghyr	253,656	115,348	110,172	112,280	77,431
Patna	417,239	353,455	290,295	307,137	103,654
Santhal Pargana	433,477	323,353	440,941	432,834	304,361
Total	1,393,123	1,220,047	1,089,708	1,384,765	876,727
Ranchi	276,798	228,484	247,346	253,874	199,732
Palamau	230,084	219,693	176,459	174,670	137,698
Hazaribagh	298,998	629,085	428,59	409,231	264,500
Manbhum	245,832	203,703	231,202	227,028	259,862
Dhanbad	60,516	53,826	57,479	69,650	—
Singhbhum	183,339	142,812	137,018	32,193	—
Chotanagpur Division	1,495,567	1,477,664	1,278,103	1,319,290	893,985
Total	3,508,827	3,309,197	2,889,128	3,244,387	2,160,957

The total land reclaimed from 1946 up to the 31st March, 1952 was 142,225 acres out of which 129,565 acres were reclaimed by manual labour with the assistance of land improvement loans and 12,660 acres by the state tractors.

The total amount of loans advanced for reclaiming of waste lands (under the land improvement loans Act) was Rs. 96,36,550 from 1946 to 31st March, 1952.

Two kinds of loans were given to the cultivators for land improvement, and purchase of agricultural machinery under *(i)* the land Improvement Loan Act, and *(ii)* The Agriculturist Loan Act . The cultivators could take loan for meeting their share of subsidy, in the case of subsidised schemes under 'Grow More Food Campaign'. A statement showing the distribution of loan under Land Improvement Loans Act and Agriculturist Loans Act since 1949 is given in the table 5.3 :—

Table 5.3
Land Improvement Loans Act

Year	*Advance during the year*
1946-47	1,31,000
1947-48	4,85,781
1948-49	5,57,499
1949-50	2,37,689
1950-51	5,89,295
1951-52	8,04,286

Zamindari Abolition Enactment

Since long the Congress Party had been wedded to the programme of weeding out the intermediaries. Jawahar Lal Nehru called the Zamindars as the fifth wheel in the coach, not only unnecessary but an actual encumbrance and a burden on the land. On another occasion he remarked, "They have not even the virtues of an aristocracy. As a class they are physically and intellectually degenerated and outlived their day. They will continue so long as an external power like the British Government prop them up."

Even the Congress Election Manifesto, 1946 shows the

direction in which the wind of popular opinion was blowing : "The reform of the land system which is so urgently needed in India, involves the removing of intermediaries between the peasant and the state". Even in November, 1947 the AICC reiterated that all intermediaries between the tiller and the state should be eliminated and replaced all middlemen by non profit making agencies, co-operatives.

While replying to the Famine Enquiry Commission of 1943 and the question No 24, the Bihar Government expressed Gyan Chand's views, "That the tenure system was antiquated and repressive on agriculture."

The Agrarian Reforms Committee of the AICC submitted its report in July, 1949 recommending that the pattern of agrarian economy should be such as would provide opportunity for the development of the farmers personality by eliminating the scope for the exploitation of one class by another. The Committee also envisaged maximum efficiency in production.

The decision to abolish intermediaries was thus not a sudden one, rather, it represented a crystalization of the Congress policy over a number of years since the days of Karachi session and even earlier. The Congress Party had pledged itself to the policy of dispensing with Zamindari system as the feudal relic of an alien rule. However, only after independence, when the Congress Government got power firmly in its hands, the party proceeded in the promised direction. On the eve of the independence, the foundation stone of the Zamindari System was wrecking into pieces.

With the acceptance of office by the Congress Ministry in 1946 in Bihar, highest priority was given to the Abolition of Zamindari System. There was no precedent to go by and decision had to be taken regarding a number of knotty problems viz., the rate and form of compensation, the special case of charitable and religious trust, the conditions under which the various interests of landlords in their estates and tenures would vest in the state.

The Bihar Government had to go into all these questions thoroughly so that their decision might be socially just and fair to all the interest concerned.

Bihar may well take the credit being the first state to enact a law for the Abolition of the Zamindari System. It is in Bihar again, however, that Zamindari obstructionism proved to be at its worst and successfully held up the first abolition of the system by three to four years.

Land Reforms Act, 1950

Within a few years of independence, most Indian States had enacted legislation to abolish intermediaries who collected payments from cultivators and paid land revenue to the Government. They combined the function of what in a European context might be seen as a tax farmer, Feudal chief, landlord and who according to the Census of 1961, held sway over about 45 per cent of the area of the country.

Bihar was the first state in the country to pass the Abolition of Zamindari System Act. Soon after the assumption of office by the Congress Ministry in 1946, the State Government introduced the 'Bihar State Acquisition of Zamindari Bill', 1947 in the Legislative Assembly. It was being passed finally by both Houses of the State Legislature (with certain amendments suggested by the Government of India relating to the acquisition of mines and minerals on the 6th of July, 1949 and was put on the Statute Book.

After the passing of this Act, measures were taken to execute it. But shortly the validity of the Act was challenged. The Patna High Court, in the special Bench case of Sir Kameshwar Singh Vs. The Province of Bihar, held the 'Bihar State Management of Estates and Tenures Act,' 1949 to be ultra vires. The Act was for a specific period as a preliminary step to the Zamindari Abolition scheme. As the Act was subsequently declared void and unconstitutional, so it was repealed and a new (piece of) legislation, called 'the Bihar Land Reforms Bill, 1949, was introduced. Inspite of the absolute majority of the Congress Party in the Bihar Legislative Assembly, the bill was not immediately passed. It was openly threatened on the floor of the Bihar Legislative Assembly in 1949 that if the Bill was passed, the 13 Lakhs Zamindars would turn Communist and uproot the Government. Their (landlords) opposition finally led to the sending of Bihar Lands Reforms Bill, 1950 to a Select Committee consisting of 37 members. The Committee was directed to submit its report by Jan 31, 1950. In 1950, the Bihar Land Reforms Bill, 1949, was passed and was sent for the consideration of the President of India under Article 31 (clause 4) of the Constitution of India. It received the assent of the President on 11th Sep. 1950 and was published as an Act, 'the Bihar Land Reforms Act' (Bihar Act XXX of 1950) in the State Gazettee.

The Act was to come in force on 25th Sept, 1950, but the High Court upheld the suit in favour of the Zamindars. It was held that the Act, except as regard Sec. 4 (B) and Sec. 23 (F) was Constitutionally valid.

The Hon'ble Justice Sheaver pointing to the shortcoming of the Act asked "on what principle, for instance, ought a proprietor or tenure holder, whose net income is Rs. 20,000, is given six years purchase". While a proprietor or tenure holder whose net income is Rs. 20,00 is given six years purchase? In respect of the two sections referred to above, the Court held the Act to be unconstitutional on the ground that it transgressed Article 14 of the Constitution and that it was clearly discriminating in character.

Thus, the Patna High Court declared that the Act contravened Article 14 of the Constitution of India. The verdict of High Court left the Government in a very helpless position. The State Governemnt then requested the Central Government suitably amend the Constitution in the light of the High Court's judgement.

The Constitution of India was for the first time amended in 1951, by inserting the new Article 31-A and 31-B. The amendmert spared the Act from all possible attacks on the ground of any infringement of Article 14.

The Zamindars did not keep silent rather they challenged the very validity of such an amendment of the constitution in the Supreme Court but this time they lost the suit. The drama did not end there. An alternative to block the reforms, legal proceedings, designed to test the constitutionality of the Bihar Land Reforms Act, 1950, was once more initiated by interested Zamindars and the matter eventually reached the Supreme Court.

After winning the legal battle, the State authorities in 1952 directed all the Zamindars to submit to the State Government all their rent rolls and related village records. But the State Government was handicaped with the refusal of the Zamindars to present the village papers. In 1954, the Zamindars again approached the Courts, this time individually to prevent the State from taking over their estates. Court injunctions were issued, according to which till the hearing of the cases and judgement, the landlords were to leave possession of their estates.

The Zamindars tried their best to prevent or atleast stall, the Abolition of Zamindari System. The reason behind it was the rich flow of income from the estates. Even a lesser Zamindari of Dumraon had an annual rental income of Rs. 1,00,000 according to its lawyer Dr. Sachhidanand Sinha, not to mention the big estates. The most vocal opposition within the Legislature came from Shyamanandan Sahay and Sir Chandreshwar Prasad Narain Sinha and outside the Assembly from Kamakhya Narain Singh, Raja of Ramgarh. The opposition was brought to the Courts by Maharajadhiraj Sir Kameshwar Singh of Darbhanga who was the biggest Zamindar of them all. They jointly came forward with the three tier attack—assaults on the tenants, wooing of Congress leaders and obstructing the implementa-tion of legislation in the Assembly and dilatory tactics in the Courts.'

Thus, it took more than eight years for the Supreme authority of the State, the State Legislatures to enact it. The Zamindar's interests used every means, at their disposal to prevent, delay, or dilute the legislation. In addition to the legal manoeuvers mentioned above, direct appeals were made to higher authority in the hope that national leadership might be induced to intervene to delay Zamindari Abolition Legislation, but all went in vain. First of all they called on Mahatma Gandhi to intervene in the matter. In a prayer meeting at Patna, Gandhiji deplored the growing lawlessness among the peasantry. But in his post-prayer speech Gandhiji spoke for the first time unreservedly against the Zamindari System and said that this system is bound to go.

In 1947, one group of Zamindars cabled Rajendra Prasad pleading to look into the matter. Several memorandum on behalf of the Zamindars were sent to the officials of the Government of Bihar and the Chief Minister Shri Krishna Sinha.

Maharaja Udai Pratap Nath Shah Deo of Chotanagpur protested the decision of the Government to introduce legislation designed to abolish all the Zamindari in the province. He said that the Zamindars are as much part of the nation as others are and they were never anti-national . . . . Numbers of Zamindars have taken part in various national and other progressive movements of the land and have taken active part in building the present nation . . . The interest of the raiyats and of the Zamindars are not antagonistic and they can be adjusted within the present social structure. He further made it clear that the rights and interests of the raiyats now-a-days are well protected by codified laws and the Zamindars have got no authority over them except the right to realize rent and the rent is an insignificant item in the budget of the raiyat . . . .

The man behind all these decisions was K.B. Sahay (then Revenue Minister). Rajendra Prasad wrote a long letter dated April, 27, 1947 from New Delhi in which he chastised the revenue minister for moving so rapidly in the direction of Zamindari Abolition Legislation without consulting adequately the Congress Working Committee. In his own words :—

> "Any hope that you may have of giving satisfaction to tenants by simply getting rid of the Zamindars is doomed to failure unless it is accomplished by some positive steps for the betterment of the tenants lot, but I gathered . . . that you were not thinking of the next step and that for the present you would be satisfied if you can remove the Zamindars. I have never been able to understand the justice or fairness of depriving a man of the management of his property. I can understand Abolition of Zamindari System. The Congress has sanctioned that, but I do not think there is any section in the Congress resolution for forcibly dispossessing people of their property before they have been compensated for it".

But K.B. Sahay did not change his approach. As he said "So far I am concerned, I felt that in order to rehabilitate the position of the Congress it is necessary that the Bill (relating to the Zamindari Abolition) should be proceeded with". Thus, the Land

Reforms Act faced many oppositions and rough weather inspite of the demand of the time. Leading English daily of Bihar, *"The Indian Nation"* wrote in favour of the intermediary interest. In the editorial of April 6, 1948 of the *'Indian Nation'*, the editor S. Sen while criticising the Revenue Minister said that "He (K.B. Sahay) is either one eyed or wilfully blind. He is impatient to see Zamindars out . . . .". Not only that the paper even threatened the Government decision. Later on, for this the *'Indian Nation'* had to abjectly apologised".

Even the landlords now tried to defame the pro-abolition leaders like K.B. Sahay. A day before the Abolition Bill was to be introduced in the Assembly, he was run over and seriously injured in a motor accident. His eagerness and strong will power for the abolition can be well traced as the 'Searchlight' mentioned, "Sahay came to the Assembly with a heavily bandaged forehead stained with blood". Perhaps symbolic of the struggle that had to be waged to achieve even this limited measures of agrarian reform. In reaction some of the largest and most conservative Zamindars joined Janta Party.

Inspite of emphatic and persistent appeals made to higher authorities, legal manoeuvers, and efforts made through the Janta Party, the Zamindari interest were not without representation within the national leadership of the Congress and in the Bihar Congress; the landholding interest were unable to prevent the enactment and subsequent validation of the Bihar Land Reforms Act, 1950. Through the Bihar Land Reforms Act, 1950, the Government of Bihar legally abolished the interest (1) of Zamindars and tenure holders, and (2) vested these interests in the state.

Main Provisions of the Act

The main features of the Bihar Land Reforms Act, 1950, have been considered under the following sub-heads :

(*a*) Intermediaries
(*b*) Aims and Object,
(*c*) Vestings of the Estates and Consequences,
(*d*) Management of Estates
(*e*) Assessment of Compensation.

(a) Intermediaries

The main object of the Bihar Land Reforms Act was to abolish the intermediaries between the Government and actual tillers of the soil. The Act seeks to bring the State into direct contact with the tenants by eliminating the intermediaries. This effected about 26 lakhs intermediaries and more than two crores of tenants brought into direct relationship with the State. It is, therefore, of interest to know what type of intermediaries were abolished. The Act only mentions a proprietor and tenure holder in this connection. The proprietor is at the top and a tenure holder is below him.

The following types of estates existed in Bihar during 1949-50.

Table 5.4

Estates	*No.*	*Revenue Demand*
1. Permanently settled estates (Revenue Paying)	205,977	1,08,09,085
2. Permanently settled estates (Revenue Free)	11,295	—
3. Temporarily settled estates	739	3,85,797
4. Government estates	421	15,28,977

The permanently settled revenue free estates were those which were exempted from payment of land revenue, because the proprietors of those estates had rendered some services to the previous rulers or to the British Government. Though the number of those estates was large yet the estates were small and the loss of the revenue was also small.

The Act mentioned only a proprietor and a tenure holder in this connection. The proprietor was above the tenure holder. Tenure holder means a person who had acquired from a proprietor or from any other tenure holder a right to hold land for the purpose of collecting rent or bringing it under cultivation by establishing tenants on it. It also included the successors interest of persons who had acquired such rights and a person who held such right in trust and, when a tenure holder was a minor or of unsound mind.

(b) Aims and Objects

The Act provided for "the transference to the state of the interests of proprietors and tenure holders in land and of the mortagages and leasses of such interests in trees, fruits, fisheries, Jalkars, ferries, hats, bazars, mines and minerals."

The Act also provided for the constitution of a Land Commission for the State of Bihar with powers to advise the state Government consequent upon such transference and for the matters connected therewith.

(c) Vesting of the Estates and Consequences

The Act of Bihar like those of U.P., Bengal, Mysore, Madhyra Pradesh, Madhya Bharat, Orissa and Assam provided for the issue of notifications in the Official Gazette for vesting different areas at different times. It is significant to note that in these states the Zamindari estates were not vested in Government with the enforcement of the Act, but provision had been made to vest different estates at different times. This provision had been made presumbly to suit local conditions and placate local interests as well. Another explanation was that the Government did not have adequate administrative machinery to take over all the Zamindaris. The phased manner of taking over the estates was open to discrimination and to appease fears, in this respect an amendment was subsequently introduced in the Bihar Act.

The Act provided that even interest of a particular Zamindar having a gross income above a certain amount was acquired, the interests of all those Zamindars whose income were with in that income group would be simultaneously notified for acquisition.

The Bihar Act followed the U.P. pattern with a few minor changes to suit the local variations with regard to the consequences of the vestings of estates with the State. Section 4 of the Act read partly as follows:—

> Such estates of tenure including the interests of the proprietor or tenure holder in any building or part of a building comprised in such estates or tenure or used primarily as office or Kutchery for the collection of rent of such estate or tenure, and his interest

> in trees, forests, fisheries, Jalkars, hats, bazars and ferries and all other sairiati interests as his interests in all sub-soil including any rights in mines and minerals.

It is, therefore, quoted that "Any rights in mines and minerals whether discovered or undiscovered or whether being worked or not inclusive of such rights of a leasee of mines and minerals, comprised in such estate or tenure (other than the interests of the raiyat and under raiyats), shall with effect from the date of vestings, vest absolutely in the state, free from all encumberances such proprietor of tenure holder shall cease to have any interest in such estate or tenure other than the interests expressly saved by or under the provision of this Act."

The government naturally made comprehensive provision regarding the mines, minerals and their leases because there are large mining areas in Bihar. The other provisions regarding the consequences of the vesting of estate in the state were as follows :—

> All arrears of rents, including royalties, would be recoverable by the state, arrears due with the tenure holders would be recoverable from the compensation money payable to such tenure holders.

Arrears of revenue and cesses with the Zamindars were recoverable by deduction from the compensation money". Force, if necessary could be applied to secure possession of the estates by the state. This unique provision in the Bihar Act was a display of strength of the government, perhaps to terrorise Zamindars who were offering opposition to the abolition. The Collector was given powers to annul settlement or lease of estates or tenures, and the transfer of any building used as office or kutchery by the Zamindars, such transfers or settlements had taken place after January, 1946.

The Government with the help of this provision wanted to salvage some of the losses it had suffered, when behind the cover of legal opposition the Zamindars were making false partitions and hasty transfers, so as to deprive the government from the use of the Kuthcery etc. It was also notable that as the rate of compensation was fixed on a progressive basis so partition of interests were going to increase the financial burden of compensation payment for the Government.

The Collector was empowered to forcefully enter on any land or building to seize such documents, registers etc. which were considered necessary for the management of over-taken estates. This provision again indicated the atmosphere of distrust between the Zamindars and the Government on the eve of the Abolition of Zamindari System.

Homesteads of proprietors and tenure holders were retained by them as tenants. Lands in *Khas* possession of proprietors and tenure holders were retained by them on payment of rents as raiyats having occupancy rights. The Zamindar was thus converted with one stroke of pen into occupancy raiyat with respect to the following :

(*i*) Private lands,

(*ii*) Privileged lands, and

(*iii*) Lands used for agricultural or horticultural purposes and cultivated by himself or by his own servants or by hired labour or with hired stock.

Such lands, the Act declares, "be deemed to be settled by the state with Land Reforms Act, 1950. Such proprietor or tenure holder as the case may be, were entitled to retain possession thereof and hold them as a raiyat under the state having occupancy rights in respect of such lands, subject to the payment of such fair and equitable rent as determined by the collector in the prescribed manner. Chowkidari, Chaknan or Goraiti Jagir or Napi Goraiti lands were not to be treated as lands under khas possession of the landlords. Building together with lands on which such building stood in the possession of proprietors and tenure-holders and used as goals were to be retained by the landlords on payment of rent.

The Bihar Land Reforms Act, 1950 Section 7(1) clause (3) added that this benefit could be claimed if and only if the State Government was satisfied that such building or structure was not constructed or used for the aforesaid purposes with the object of defeating any provision of this Act.

Mines worked by proprietors or tenure holder were deemed

to have been leased by the State Government to the proprietor or tenure holder as the case may be, on such terms and condition, as may be agreed upon between the State Government and the proprietor or tenure-holder. In case such agreements as were not reached at, the mines tribunal gave decision regarding them, subsisting leases of mines or minerals are to continue, only the State could step in the shoes of the proprietor or tenure-holder. The State Government was empowered to terminate leases by giving three months notice, if the leases had done no prospecting or development work before the commencement of the Act.

Bihar Government appointed Mines Tribunal for the purpose of settling disputes between the Government and the proprietor or tenure-holder of mines, fixing fair rents for buildings and lands appurtenant to mines and also for fixing compensation money when the State Government terminated the leases of mines or minerals prematurely.

The Government did not authorise the Collector to "take charge of any institution, religious or secular, if any trust or any building connected therewith or to interfere with the right of a trustee to apply the trust money to the objects of the trust.

The Bihar Government in general, left the management of the estates to the general revenue administration. Exception had, however, been made in villages where Village Panchayats had been established under Bihar Panchayati Raj Act, 1947. In such villages Government was empowered to entrust to a village panchayat, the management of the estates and tenures including trees, forest, fisheries, jalkars, hats, bazars and ferries comprised therein. Para 2 of chapter 3 of the Act dealing with the management of estates in the post abolition period is a proof of the very perfunctory attention that was given to this question by the Government under review.

At the outset, it may be made clear that except the Kashmir Government all State Government which had passed the Zamindari Abolition Act, had accepted the directive of the Constitution that no man shall be deprived of his property without payment of compensation. As a result, the Bihar Government accepted the obligation of paying compensation, for extinguishment of Zamindar's rights. The relevent provision had been examined from two angles, viz.

(*a*) the basis of compensation, and
(*b*) the rate of compensation.

The basis of compensation comprised of the net assets in U.P. and basic annual sum in Madras, in Bihar it was net income of a Zamindar. Section 19 of Bihar Act provided for the appointment of Compensation Officer, who calculated the net income of each proprietor and tenure holder. For the purpose of assessment and payment of compensation each member of a Joint Hindu Family was treated separately. The unit for determining, the amount of compensation was the individual proprietor, and each member of a joint Hindu Family formed one unit. But all the interests of one intermediary were to be treated Jointly. Thus compensation was to be paid on strictly sliding scale, making the individual proprietor as the unit for determing the amount of compensation. The Government had shown material financial favour to the Zamindars unlike Madhya Bharat Government who made estate as the unit for determining the amount of compensation. But by merging all the interests of intermediary, the Bihar Government took away with left hand what it gave with the right.

Computation of net income was done on the following lines :—

The Gross asset of the proprietor was to be calculated first, meant the aggregate of the rents, including all cesses which were payable in respect of the estates or tenures were of proprietors or tenure-holders.

To arrive at the net income of a proprietor or tenure-holder the following were deducted form the gross assets :—

(*a*) Sum payable as land revenue or rent including cesses to the State Government or to the immediately superior landlords by any sum payable as agricultural income tax.
(*b*) Any sum payable as income tax in respect of any income derived from such estate or tenure.
(*c*) Any sum payable as Chaukidari tax or Municipal tax.
(*d*) Cost of management of such estate or tenure at prescribed rates.

(e) Cost of works of benefit to the raiyat of such estates or tenure at prescribed rates.

The Bihar Government unlike the U.P., did not deduct 15% of the gross assets as 'irrecoverable arrears of rent.' In this respect, the Bihar Government was clearly more liberal to the Zamindars. It was still more liberal as compared to the Madras Act which made, 'the basic annual sum' as the basis of compensation, and the basic annual sum was one-third of the gross annual raiyatwari demand minus 5% of the gross raiyatwari demand or an account of establishment charges, deficiency in the collection of the like, and 3.1%, on account of maintenance of irrigation works in the estates.

The Zamindars were paying land revenue and cess. Besides these, agricultural income tax was imposed. In addition to these, the Zamindars had to incur costs in the management of their Zamindaris. The Cost of management varied depending on its size. Revenue, cess, agricultural income tax and cost of collection are deducted to arrive at the net Income of the Zamindars; an average of ten years from 1937 to 1947 was calculated. This average value was to be the amount of compensation paid to Zamindars or any other intermediate interests. All the different categories of intermediaries were paid compensation on the same principle i.e. the average of the market value of the net annual income which the holder of interest legally obtained for his right.

Another question connected with the rate of compensation was the payment of different rates of compensation for different incomes. The Government provided for payment of compensation at rates varying from three times the net income to twenty times the net income. The Flour Commission recommended that compensation should be paid at flat rate for all kinds of intermediary interests at a rate of 10.12. or 15 times the net income. The provision with regard to the payment of compensation under the Bihar Act was definitely unjust and opposed to any sound principle for the payment of compensation. The problem of livelihood for the smaller landlords, the problem of removal of inequality of wealth in the community, and the capacity to pay compensation were completely ignored.

In the case of a proprietor or tenure holder the compensation payable was in accordance with the following table 5.5 namely:—

Table 5.5

Amount of gross asset	*Rate*
1. Where the gross assets does not exceed Rs. 2,000	5 per cent of such gross asset.
2. Where the gross asset exceed Rs. 2,000 but does not exceed Rs. 5,000.	7.5 per cent, of such gross asset.
3. Where the gross asset exceeds Rs. 5,000 but does not exceed Rs. 10,000.	10 per centum of such gross asset.
4. Where the gross asset exceeds Rs. 10,000 but does not exceed Rs. 15,000.	12.5 per centum of such gross asset.
5. Where the gross asset exceeds Rs. 15,000.	Not less than 15 and not more than 20 per centum of such gross asset.

Cost of works of benefit to the ryots of an estate or tenure also be deducted from the gross income at the following rate as in the table 5.6 :—

Table 5.6

Amount of gross asset	*Rate*
1. Where the gross asset does not exceed Rs.5,000	4 per centum of such gross asset.
2. Where the gross asset exceeds Rs. 5,000 but does not exceeds Rs. 10,000.	6 per centum of such gross asset.
3. Where the gross asset exceeds Rs. 10,000 but does not exceeds Rs 15,000.	8 per centum of such gross interests.
4. Where the gross asset exceeds Rs. 15,000 but not does exceeds Rs. 20,000.	10 per centum of such gross asset.

Amount of gross asset	*Rate*
5. Where the gross asset exceeds Rs. 20,000.	12.5 per centum of such gross asset.

The Act laid down the following rates for payment of compensation to the different categories of Zamindars as given in the table 5.7 :—

Table 5.7

Amount of net Income	*Rate of Compensation Payable*
a. Where the net income does not exceed Rs. 500/-	Twenty times such income.
b. Where the net income exceeds Rs. 500/- but does not exceed Rs. 1250/-	Nineteen times such net income in any case but not less than the maximum amount under item (a) above.
c. Where the net income exceeds Rs. 1250/- but does not exceeds Rs. 2000/-	Eighteen times such net income but in any case not less than the maximum amount payable under item (b) above.
d. Where the net income exceeds Rs. 2000/-but does not exceeds Rs. 2750/-	Seventeen times such net income but in any case not less than the maximum amount payable under item (c) above.
e. Where the net income exceeds Rs. 2750/- but does not exceeds Rs. 3500/-	16 times such net income but in any case not less than the maximum amount payable under (d) above.
f. Where the net income exceeds Rs. 3500/- but does not exceeds Rs. 4250/-	15 times such net income but in any case not less then the maximum amount payable under (d) above.
g. Where the net income exceeds Rs. 4250/- but does not exceeds Rs. 5000/-	14 times such net income but in any case not less than the maximum amount payable item (f) above.
h. Where the net income exceeds Rs. 5000/- but does not	10 times such net income but in any case not less than the

Amount of net Income	*Rate of Compensation Payable*
exceeds Rs. 10,000/-	the maximum amount payable under item (g) above.
i. Where the net income exceeds Rs. 10,000/- but does not exceeds Rs. 20,000/-	8 times such net income but in any case not less than the maximum amount payable under items (h) above.
j. Where the net income exceeds Rs. 20,000/- but does not exceeds Rs. 50,000/-	6 times such net income but in any case not less than the maximum amount payable under item (i) above.
k. Where the net income exceeds Rs. 50,000/- but does not exceeds Rs. 100,000/-	4 times such net income but in any case not less than the maximum amount payable under item (j) above.
l. Where the net income exceeds Rs. 100,000/-	3 times such net income but in any case not less than the maximum amount payable under item (k) above.

Bihar dealt with the problem of determination of net income from mines and minerals. The gross income of a mine owner was calculated on the basis of past assessment of cess or income tax. The net income was deemed to be 5% of the gross annual income. It is clear that the provisions in regard to the determination of the net income of the mine-owners were very stringent. Tax evasion by the mine owners in past, gave the bitter fruit in the shape of low basis of compensation for the mine owners and land holders. Perhaps the pull of the capitalistic mine-owners had to be balanced by the democratic weight of the very large number of expropriated Zamindars and the personal animosity between the Revenue Minister Shri K.B. Sahay and the Raja of Ramgarh.

After the net income from mines was determined, the compensation officer fixed the amount of compensation by agreement with mine owner. Failing such agreement, the state government referred the case to the Mines tribunal. The award of the Mines Tribunal was the basis for computing compensation by the compensation officers.

The compensation officers were asked according to the Act to :—

1. Prepare and publish preliminary compensation assessment roll.
2. Send the assessment rolls to the proprietors or tenure holders by registered post with due acknowledge-ment.
3. Receive and consider objections to any entry in the draft compensation assessment roll and to dispose of complaints in such respects.
4. Finally publish the compensation assessment roll, after taking into account, the decision on the appeal, if any, to the Judge of the High Court, appointed to hear such appeals against the entry into draft compensation roll. Thus like the U.P. Act, the Bihar Act had provided for appeal to a higher office against the arbitraries of the compensaion officers.
5. Make a certificate stating the fact of such final publication and the date thereof.
6. Make correction of bonafied mistakes in the compensation roll, even after publication of the final compensation assessment roll.

The method of payment was decided after taking into consideration :—

(*i*) The capacity of the authority which pays compensation,
(*ii*) The nature of the asset for which compensation was paid,
(*iii*) The condition of the persons to whom compensation is to be paid, and
(*iv*) The general economic condition of the state and the magnitude of the amount involved.

The amount of compensation was either paid in cash or in bonds or partly in cash and partly in bonds. The bonds were either negotiable or non-negotiable and were payable in forty equal instalments and carried interest at 2.5% per annum with effect from the date of issue. Under the Madhya Bharat Zamindari Abolition Act, the compensation had to be paid in instalments not exceeding a period of ten years. The bonds were payable in thirty equal instalments in Madhya Pradesh, 20 equal instalments in Assam and equalised half yearly instalments over a period of forty years in U.P. It is thus clear as regards to the mode of payment in the Bihar and U.P. Acts were more indifferent to the financial plight of the intermediaries in the post abolition period. The Reserve Bank of India had also agreed that an interest as high as 3% may be made on the bonds in order to avoid the inflationary pressures of compensation payment in cash, the Bihar Government accepted the advice of the Reserve Bank of India and provided for the payment of compensation in cash or in bonds or partly in cash and partly in bonds, but kept the rate of interest on the bonds at a low level in view of the inflationary pressure in the economy in the post-abolition period, while the face value of the bonds had remained intact, their real value had suffered a great depreciation.

The Government also made provisions for an interim compensation to outgoing proprietors or tenure holders. The payment were made six monthly in accordance with the following tables 5.8 :—

Table 5.8

a. Where the approximate amount of compensation does not exceed Rs. 50,000/-	3% per annum of such approximate amount of compensation.
b. Where the approximate amount of compensation exceeds Rs. 50,000/-	2.5% per annum of such approximate amount of compensation subject to the maximum of Rs. 6,25,000 per annum.

The provisions of interim compensation were meant to give financial relief to the intermediaries immediately after abolition of their privileges. Such, payments were necessary to avoid undue hardships to the intermediaries inflicted, from delays, in the settlement of payments of compensation. In practice, however, the interim compensations were only nominally given for the Zamindars.

The Bihar Government also provided for the constitution of a

Tribunal which heard all the disputes regarding claims of compensation money. The Tribunal was consisted of three members including Chairman, who was a Judge of the High Court or a District Judge. The award of the Tribunal was final and conclusive and the Courts before which disputes about compensation money were pending, based their judgements on the aforesaid award of the Tribunal. When the scheme for Zamindari Abolition was being finalised, it was realised that some machinery should be provided for the settlement of the Zamindari debts.

Zamindari Abolition : survey and settlement operation

The object of the field bujharat was primarily to prepare a revenue roll i.e. a list of raiyats who had to pay revenue to Government or on whom rent was to be assessed. Instructions were also issued for extending the name of under raiyats held by them. Entries were made by the karamcharies which were checked up by Circle Inspectors and Circle Officers. A rough and ready record of rights was thus prepared for the entire State including certain diara area in which no survey had been done earlier.

The management of the acquired Zamindaries was done on the lines of Government Estates. Prior to the introduction of Zamindari Abolition Scheme, the State had no revenue machinery in rural areas except in the few Government estates. The state was divided into districts and sub-divisions, there being a Collector in-charge of a District and sub-divisional Officers in-charge at a sub-divisional level and this administrative machinery did not infiltrate lower down into villages. After the Abolition of Zamindari, the system changed considerably, the object being to have a raiyatwari system of revenue administration. The set up which had been brought into existence consisted of the village official called Karamchari, in-charge of each Halka consisting of 8-12 villages on the average. The Halka was the lowest unit of revenue administration. The whole State had been divided into 5970 *Halkas*, resulting in abrupt reduction in the Zamindars' assets. The reckless living of many Zamindars had brought them under the clutches of the money lenders. In view of the inevitable time-lag, between the vesting of the Estate and actual payment of compensation money, relief was considered to be urgent in this respect. As the Zamindarie's were a losing concern, the creditors who had lent so far, had awakened to the need of realising the loans as early as they could. The impatient attitude of money-lenders was driving the Zamindars to provide a machinery for a fair settlement of Zamindars debts.

The secured creditors were required to furnish full particulars and documents to the claim officers who were appointed for settlement of the debts. The creditors had to file their claim within six months of the date of vesting of the mortgaged estates, appointment of claim officers, whichever date was later. The claim officers had to scrutinise the claims of different creditors. They had to ascertain the amount of the principal originally advanced, and the amount of interest already paid and to set off towards the amount of the principal, any amount paid or realised as simple interest in excess of six per cent per annum or the stipulated rate of interest whichever was lower. In case the creditor had already received by way of interest, payment, a sum equal to the principal, no further interest was to be allowed.

Thus, some relief was given to the indebted Zamindars in the following way as :—

- *(a)* A ceiling was provided for the total interest payment.
- *(b)* The Zamindars who had been fleeced in the past by exhorbitant demands of the money-lenders were given a retributive justice. But on the whole, the relief provided to the Zamindars were meagre and nominal.

Appeal against the decision of the claim officer could be made before a board constituted by the Government, whose decision was final.

The Government under review also made provisions for the Bihar Land Commission in the Bihar Land Reforms Act. This unique feature was not present in the original abolition bill. The Commission consisted of the Revenue Minister as the Chairman and 11 members of whom five were elected from the Legislative Assembly, three from the Legislative Council, two persons were appointed by the State Government and one member was an official, who acted as the secretary to the

Commission appointed by the State Government.

The function of the Bihar Land Commission was to advise the State Government generally with regard to the agrarian policy which followed in administering the system of land tenure in the State. The Commission functioned purely as an advisory body, and it held such enquries as appeared to be necessary or desirable for its purposes.

The actual abolition of the Zamindaris started from 1952, after Articles 31 of the Constitution had been amended and the Supreme Court had upheld the validity of the Constitutional Amendment.

In the first phase of the abolition programme, the State Government abolished all the intermediaries having a gross annual income exceeding Rs. 50,000. The number of intermediaries abolished was 155. In the second phase, it was decided to abolish all intermediaries in the District of Gaya, Hazaribagh, Palamau and Darbhanga and necessary steps were taken to acquire the intermediary interest in these Districts.

Under the Bihar Land Reforms Act, 1950, it was necessary for the Government to issue a separate notification in respect of each individual intermediary, giving the details of all the intermediary interest held by him and the estate which was to be acquired. This made the progress of abolition very slow. The State Government therefore got the provisions of the law amended in this regard, which empowered the State Government to takeover all intermediary interests, situated within a particular area or throughout the state by a general notification after giving atleast three months notice by a proclamation. After this it became possible to proceed faster with the abolition of intermediaries.

The main difficulties which prevented speedier take over of intermediary interests in the State were the absence of an adequate revenue administrative machinery in rural areas, and the absence of reliable and up-to-date land records. Revenue village agencies had to be built up from the scratch, since there was hardly any revenue administration below the District level. There was a great dearth of subordinate personnel, of the ranks of the Tahsildars in the State, as this type of revenue officials did not exist. Recruitment programme for the junior civil service had to be greatly stepped up by the Government. The outgoing intermediaries did not deliver the revenue paper available with them or they did not themselves have full details of their intermediary interest. The survey and settlement operations were also conducted. The latest records were nearly thirty years old and the oldest over 50 years old as given in the table 5.9.

Table 5.9
Survey and Settlement Operation in Bihar (1892-1958)

District	*Initiation and completion dates at least Survey and Settlement Operation*
Patna	1907-1912
Gaya	1911-1918
Shahabad	1907-1916
Saran	1915-1919
Champaran	1913-1919
Muzaffarpur	1892-1899
Darbhanga	1896-1903
Bhagalpur	1902-1910
Monghyr	1905-1912
Purnea	1952-1958
Santhal Parganas	1922-1935
Saharsa	1902-1910
Ranchi	1927-1935
Hazaribagh	1908-1915
Palamau	1915-1920
Dhanbad	1918-1925
Singhbhum	1924-1938

Source : Revenue Department, Government of Bihar, August 1970.

Moreover, the state needed to initiate administrative reforms (particularly in the Revenue Department) so that there would be a machinery capable of coping with expanded responsibilities associated with the establishment of up-to-date land records and the collection of land revenue without the aid of intermediaries. After the abolition of Zamindaries, it became necessary to have information immediately regarding the area of land held by each raiyat and the rent payable by him, the extent of wastelands and village common lands and other information necessary for determination of compensation payable to intermediaries. As the revisional survey and settlement operations would have taken some times, the village reconstructed by field *bujharat* (identification) with reference to old entries recorded :—

1. One gazetted officer called an Anchal Adhikari in each Anchal, the whole State being divided into 597 anchals for the purpose.
2. One-non-gazetted officer called circle inspector, in each Anchal to assist the Anchal Adhikari, 6567 Karmcharies and 657 Circle Inspectors were appointed.

A provision was made by the State Government to entrust the management of the estate to the Executive Committee of Grampanchayat, on terms and conditions as the Government had fixed by general or special orders.

The Grampanchayats were remunerated for the work by payment of commission at certain percentage of the collection made, varying between 5% and 10%.

The Government appointed one subordinate Judge and Munsifs as claim officers for the purpose of receiving and disposing of claims—petitions filled by creditors, whose debts were secured by mortgage or were charged on the acquired Zamindaries.

In order to dispose of the compensation proceedings expenditiously, all Additional Collectors and Additional Sub-Divisional officers had been appointed as compensation officers.

The abolition of the intermediaries was the first major attempt in the programme of land reforms initiated by the Ministry under review. The success of this measure reaffirmed the faith in the Congress approach that far reaching changes in the agrarian structure were possible in legal peaceful manner.

The Zamindari System denoted land monopolies or concentration of land in a few hands. The slogan of 'down with landlordism' was really the slogan for a more equitable redistribution of land. But what was abolished in Bihar was just the intermediary interests.' The government took up the right of rent collection in its own Lands, with no relief to the kisans. Thus abolition of Zamindaries in reality meant 'State Landlordism' and when the rent collecting activities were taken away from the hands of Zamindars, they moved towards cultivation.

It was originally thought that the abolition of the intermediaries would increase the revenue of the state and thus help finance developmental works. In practice such hopes had been greatly belied, because the rent received by the Government had progressively increased, there was reduction in agricultural income tax receipts and stamp duties etc. It had been estimated that total compensation payable in Bihar was Rupees 158 crores plus rupees 80.98 crores in interest. The receipt from Agricultural Income tax had declined from Rs. 125 lakhs in 1946-47 to rupees 69 lakhs in 1950-51. The annual loss of income from stamp duty on account of Aamindari abolition was about Rupees 19 lakhs. Further, the State Government had to suffer the loss of the amount of cess on land revenue, which was paid by the Zamindars. This was amounted to about Rupees 35 lakhs. Thus the financial gains from the abolition of Zamindari were doubtful. Sri Dantwala had calculated that the net impact of Zamindari Abolition on Bihar Government revenue were a negative one. Again the controversy arose on the question of compensation. The Socialists and Communists alongwith the Sabhaites were not prepared for adequate compensation of the Zamindari, because they thought—Their (Zamindars) wealth is amassed only by exploiting the poor." Kisan Sabha openly declared that "Compensation is legal Dacoity."

But the Congress stand was in the favour of compensation. There was reason behind it. If the Congress would have not been liberal towards the landlords at this stage (when their Zamindari was seized) civil war might have taken place as Zamindars still had unbounded power and wealth.

It is clear that the Congress Party was not only a class party but it was the party of all classes (may be rich, poor, literate and illiterate). In the interest of the peasants, it abolished an age-old institution of landlordism but at the same time its duty was also towards the landlords. Obviously, these landlords were the pillars (financer) of Great National Freedom Struggle. It was shameful posture of the Congress Ministry to deprive them of the compensation for their worthy contribution to the national freedom movement. Important Congress leaders like Sardar Patel raised their voice in favour of compensation : "The Congress Government ..... were bound to pay adequate compensation by their election manifesto. They need not be afraid of the Socialists and communists to take away Zamindaries without paying compensation amounts to robbery .... Compensation must be adequate and not nominal." He invited attention to the proposals and said "The Maharajadhiraj of Darbhanga who had an annual income of Rs. 60 lakhs would get only Rs. 25 lakhs as compensation. How would they feel if they were put in his position?"

Even after the Zamindari was abolished some of the Congress leaders and officials were consciously or unconsciously acting as the agents of the landlords. On the occassion of the birth of the grandson of Babu Raghubans Prasad Singh of Kursela an elaborate celebration was held for four days and the finance minister A.N. Sinha, some Congress leaders and the District Magistrate of Purnea did not hesitate to participate in it. It is said that they were lavishly entertained.

Ambiguous Policy of the Leaders

The ambiguous policy of the ruling party introduced a stage of hesitancy and lack of expediency to the task. Even the Mahatma Gandhi did not have a clearcut view on Zamindari Abolition which can be well traced by his own statements delivered at Patna, April 1947 (It is already mentioned earlier).

Though Rajendra Prasad could not go publicly against the stated policy of the Congress (Abolition of Zamindari), yet he tried to delay the matter, He even warned the then Revenue Minister of Bihar, K.B. Sahay, "that the proposed legislation would affect the entire economic life of the province" and suggested that more time be given to think about it. But K.B. Sahay did not agree with Rajendra Prasad. Even the Chief Minister of Bihar, Shri Krishna Sinha warned the kisan workers that mischief makers among them will be treated as criminals while he was known as the supporter of abolition. Lastly, in May 1947 when they approved the Zamindari Abolition in Bihar it was too late to introduce the Bill in the Assembly session then. Thus the valuable time was gained for the Zamindars. Commenting on their attitude, the *Searchlight* in its editorial revealed .... "The Congress High Command and the Congress Ministry will be taking risk a great deal .... by appearing to be slow and hesitant".

The High Command announced that they have taken objection to the statement of the Bihar Chief Minister, Sri Krishna Sinha on the floor of the Legislative Assembly during the last session to the effect that the Bill could not be introduced as the sanction of the High Command was awaited. Whatever may be the reason the Bill was delayed and Zamindars got enough time to manipulate it.

After a lot of manipulation by the Zamindars, the abolition of Zamindaries in the state could not be ruled out. It paved the way for further agrarian reforms. As Mishra has noted that the abolition of parasitic landlordism cleared the path for further advance and post abolition reforms.

The basic urge for land reforms is based on the community's concern for equity and social justice in agrarian relation. In fact, the object behind the elimination of the intermediaries was to bind the peasants in direct contact with the state by conferring on them the right of ownership. Not only that, because of the measures for the first time tenants and the Zamindars came to the same platform gazing at each others eyes.

Indeed the State Government did all that was possible to do justice to the Zamindars and did its best to make the rigours of abolition as smooth as possible.

Notes & References

Ojha, G., *Land Problems and Land Reforms*, Delhi, 1972, p. 49.

Mclane, J.R., *Land Revenue and Peasant in South Asia*, New Delhi : Orient Longmans, 1977, p. 20.

Ghulam, Hussain, *Seir Mutagherin*, Vol. III, Madras, 1926, pp. 160-61.

Report of Sachhidananda Sinha on Land Reforms in Bihar.

Speech of K.B. Sahay, Revenue Minister, Bihar Legislative Assembly Debates, 1946, Vol. I, para-1, p. 71.

Report of the Land Reforms Committee 1946, p. 10.

Embree, A.T., *Charles Grant and British Rule in India*, London 1962, p. 115.

Hallet, Graham, *Economics of Agricultural Land Tenures*, London, 1960. p. 17.

Nanavati and Anajan, *Indian Rural Problems*, 1960, p. 200.

Sinha, R.N., *Bihar Tenantry*, Bombay, P.P.H., Bombay, 1968, p. 18.

Mishra, Madaneshwar, *Some Aspect of the Land Revenue History of Purnea District*, Patna, 1979.

Bihar Tenancy Act, 1885, *Land Development Report 1975*, pp. 21-27.

Bihar Tenancy Act of 1885, as reprinted in Government of India, Ministry of Food and Agriculture, Agricultural Legislation in India, VI, p. 31.

Revenue Department, Government of Bihar, June 1957. See also J. Allen *et.al.* (eds.). *Cambridge shorter History of India*, pp. 637-40.

Bihar Tenancy Act of 1872, 1886 and 1949, and Chotanagpur Tenancy Act of 1908, See India, Ministry of Food and Agriculture, *Agricultural Legislation in India*, VI. 31-174.

Chotanagpur Tenancy Act, (Act VI) of 1908.

Bihar Tenancy Act, 1885, Section 234, p. 39.

B.T. Act, 1885, Sec. 6.

Report of the Santhal Parganas Enquiry Committee, p. 10.

Santhal Parganas Settlement Regulation (Regulation 111 of 1872).

Chotanagpur Tenancy Act (Act VI of 1805).

Vide chapter V, Section 27, p. 32.

Santhal Parganas Settlement, Regulation III of 1812.

Chotanagpur Tenancy Act (Act VI of 1908).

Census of India, 1961 (Vol. I part XI-A (1) Land Tenures in India, pp. 18-45.

'Bihar Privileged Persons' Homestead Tenancy Act, 1948.

Bihar Legislative Assembly Debates, dated May 24, 1946, Vol. I, para-I, p. 113.

Speeches of K.B. Sahay, Minister for Revenue and Forest in the Bihar Legislative Assembly Debates, 1946, Vol. I, para I.

Bihar Legislative Assembly Debates 1946, Vol. I. para I. p. 72.

Bihar Wastelands (Proclamation) Cultivation and Improvement Act 1946, Chap. VII, B. Sec. 49, p. 56.

Mukherjee, Karuna, *Land Reforms*, p. 26.

Bihar Through Figures, 1952, p. 19.

Bihar Wastelands (Reclamation), Cultivation and Improvement Act, 1946, Chapter VIII, B. Section 49.

Bihar through figures, page 19.

Bihar Facts and Figure 1946-52, p. 23.

Nehru, Jawaharlal, *Glimpses of the World History*, New Delhi, 1934, p. 35.

Malviya, H.D., *Land Reforms in India*, New Delhi, 1955, p. 6.
Extract from the *Congress Election Manifesto*, 1946, p. 17-18.
Indian National Congress Resolution on Economic Policy and Programme, 1924-54 (AICC, New Delhi p. 23).
Government of Bihar Revenue Department File No. 15/44, 1944.
Indian National Congress, Resolution on Economic Policy and Programme 1924-54 (AICC, New Delhi, 1954) pp. 17-18.
Extract from the *Congress Election Manifesto*, 1946.
Article by Gyan Chand in *Indian Journal of Economics* Vol. IX, p. 487.
Warriner, D., *Land Reforms in Principle and Practice*, Oxford Clarendeon Press, 1969 pp. 156-65.
Bihar 1946-51 : A Brief Review, Director of Public Relations Bihar, p. 1.
Sinha, Ranjit, *The Law of Landlord and Tenant in Bengal, Bihar, Calcutta-1918*, p. 680.
Bihar, 1946-1951 : A Brief Review. Director of Public Relation, Bihar.
Jannuzi, F. Tomassan, *Agrarian Crisis in India, the case of Bihar*, p. 13.
Cited in Jannuzi's work based on the unpublished field of B.P.C.C. and several documents.
Searchlight, April 19, 1947.
Rajendra Prasad, First President of India, a man of conservative orientation, he was expected to give a sympathetic hearing to the pleas of zamindari interests.
Cited in Jannuzi's Agrarian Crisis in India, p. 15-16.
Letter from K.B. Sahay to Rajendra Prasad 15th May, 1947 cited in Valmiki Choudhary, *Op.cit.*, also see Jannuzi.
Searchlight, April 10, 1947. See also *Indian Nation, July 25*, 1947.
Secret Behind the Zamindari Abolition. *The Indian Nation*, Patna, March 26, 1947.
Searchlight, September 12, 1947.
Searchlight, September 13, 1947.
Indian Nation, April 6, 1948.
Roy, Ramashrey, *Dynamics of One Party Dominance in an Indian State*, Asian Survey (July 1958).
See Introduction : *Bihar Land Reforms Act, 1950 (Bihar Act 30 of 1950*, In the Bihar Local Acts, 22, 04.
Jain, S.C., *Agricultural Policy in India*, Bombay, 1965, p. 122.
Bihar Land Reforms Act, 1950, Problem.
Sahay, K.B., Revenue and Forest Minister cited in the proceedings of the *Bihar Legislative Assembly, Debates*, Vol. I, p. 78. Also see memorandum on Land Tenure System in Bihar prepared by the Revenue Deptt. Bihar 1956.

Prasad, Kedarnath, *Economics of a Backward Region in a Backward Economy : A Cases Study of Bihar* Vol. I, Calcutta, 1967, p. 415.

Preamble to the Bihar Land Reforms Act, 1950, Chapter I. Sec. 2, p. 21.

Bihar Land Reform Act, Chap. II. Section, 3-12, p. 11.

Bihar Land Reform Act, Chap. III, Sec. A, 3-12, p. 15.

Bihar Land Reform Act, 1950, See 4 (p). This section was absolutely declared illegal by the Supreme Court.

Bihar Land Reform Act, 1950, Section 5 (I), p. 23.

Articles 31 of the *Indian Constitution.*

Chap. III of the *Uttar Pradesh Zamindari Abolition and Land Reforms Act*, 1910.

Section 24-39 of *Madras Estates (Abolition and Conversion into Rayatwari) Act*, 1948.

Section 20 of the *Bihar Land Reforms Act 1950*, p. 120.

Report of the Land Revenue Flood Commission, Vol. I., p. 28.

Prasad Rao, M., *Land Reforms Under Congress*, p. 87.

Bihar Land Reforms Act, Vide Chapter VI, p. 56.

Report of the Progress of Land Reforms, Planning Commission, p. 180.

Bihar Land Reforms Act, 1950, Chap. IV, pp. 37-39.

Driver, P.N., *Problems of Zamindari and Land Tenure Reconstruction*, in India, Bombay, 1949, p. 313.

Revenue Department, Government of Bihar, August 1970.

Menon, V.K.N., *New Anchal 'Adhikari System in Bihar, Indian Journal of Public Administration*, no. 2 (April-June 1956).

Land Reforms Act, Bihar, 1950, Section 1.3.

Progress of Land Reforms, Planning Commission, p. 13.

Khusro, A.M., *Economic and Social Efforts of Jagirdari Abolition*, p. 115.

Dantwala, M.L., *Financial Implication of Land Reforms*, Zamindari Abolition, *Indian Journal of Agricultural Economics*, Vol. XXVII, No. 4. p. 28.

Bihar Through Figures 1952, p. 23.

Hunkar, 29 March, 1947.

Hunkar, 29 March, 1947.

Editorial, *Searchlight*, 27th July 1947 also question by Syt. Murli Manohar Prasad in the assembly, Bihar Legislative Assembly Progress, Sept. 1, 1948, Patna.

Searchlight, 27 October, 1947.

Searchlight, 29 May, 1947.

Seventh Year of Freedom, (AICC New Delhi), 1954 p. 305.

CHAPTER 6

AFTERMATH

The aftermath was characterized by great hope and relief both in the camps of Nationalist leaders as well as among poor peasants. It gave fresh impetus to the forces of equality, liberty and fraternity. The exploitative leverage of inconsiderate Zamindars were seen as vanishing and a new confidence dawned among peasants.

But as the study progresses and numerous after effects are evaluated, the result does not sound as encouraging as the initial euphoria suggested. The result, as would be seen, was at best mixed. In this chapter, an analytical study on the aftermath of the abolition of Zamindari has been discussed.

Upbringing oF Kisans

The foremost after-effect of the abolition was the upbringing of the kisans on the grave of the intermediaries. In common parlance, the Zamindari System denoted not only the picture of Zamindars as intermediaries or rent collectors but also a picture of land monopolies or concentration of land in a few hands. The 'down with landlordism' was really the slogan for a more equitable redistribution and possible now after a great struggle.

In practice, the abolition of Zamindari System in Bihar and all over India was just the 'intermediary interest'. The abolition of Zamindari thus began with a bang and ended with a whimper. It was merely the change of the crown from one (Zamindar) to another (State). As Mishra has pointed out that "the king stork log was dethroned and the king stork was placed on the pedestal."

The Government took up the right of rent collection in its own hands, but with no relief to the Kisan. The burden of the rent was not lessened, nor the severity of collection. Thus, the Act seems to be only a political stunt, "full of sound and fury, signifying nothing." Though it was reaffirmed the people's faith in the Congress, and its policy, but the far-reaching changes in the agrarian structure was possible in a legal, peaceful manner only, yet it did not solve the problem.

Rise of State Landlordism

After the abolition, the social oppression, exploitation and unrest did not end rather it made the situation more critical. The state became the 'landlord' and karmachari's, Circle Officers and B.D.Os, became its agent, frequently taking advantages from the Kisans and their products. In the post Zamindari days, there wre complaints in the Assembly of *Zoolums* of Karmachari's and Circle Officers which eclipsed the worst operation of the Zamindars. Thus, abolition of Zamindari in reality is meant only a 'State Landlordism'; it is not abolition, rather it is the perpetuation of landlordism on a higher level.

Breakdown of Old Harmony

One of the remarkable changes that the abolition brought about was the breaking of old harmony between the landlords and the tenants, because the rent collecting power of the Zamindars were seized and they fell to cultivation. As a result, there was spate of ejections and eviction. Commenting over the eviction problem Hare Krishan Konar, has well presented the picture, "that in Bihar there is the Bataidari Act," while in reality, he further said, "Bataidars are evicted at the sweet will of the owners. They have no *defacto* rights. They do not dare to demand the stipulated share. In reaction, tenants at will were dispossessed by the Zamindars. Thus, the abolition has made the agrarian scene more bleak. The forceable eviction of Bataidars went on in a big way. The Government did nothing to help them. On the other hand the police attacked the peasants in many places on the basis of one sided allegation of the landlords."

Mutual anger, hatred, distrust and suspicion became the order of the day. Villages have become divided house against themselves. The 'Factions' village of which Dr. Balwant Singh makes so much is completely of recent origin, a creation of the post abolition period.

Brake on the Progress of Village

The abolition closed the path to the road of progress in the villages. Zamindars, inspite of their hundred and thousand defects, were in a broad sense an institution and had a tradition of kindness and charity. Due to their generosity, benevolence and efforts, Primary, Middle, High Schools and Post Offices were running in the villages. Lamppost, repair of the roads and to some extent irrigations were also managed by them. The Zamindars used to help the tenants at the time of their daughters 'marriages, in ailment and in other social needs. Thus, the abolition buried an age of helpage and in place of it, state managed and centralized schemes took place, which are not at all concerned with the tenants day-to-day needs.

Changes in Rural Stratification

Abolition also brought some changes in the existing rural stratification system but these changes do not approximate the changes that were expected. One of the reasons could be that the policies of land reforms were not supported by all the contending pressure groups, within the ruling class. The rural poor were not articulate enough nor sufficiently organised to influence and implement the legislation. Therefore, the fruits of reform accrued mainly to certain intermediate social categories who were conscious enough to take opportunities offered by the state.

The class polarisation became more visible after the introduction of these Land Reform Legislation.

Some of the schemes started by the Government in fact, led to a much sharper polarisation and in places legitimized the emerging system of stratification. The schemes specifically introduced for all farmers and agricultrual labourer, *e.g.* the Small Farmer's Development Agency (SFDA), the Marginal

Farmers and the Agricultural Labourers Development Schemes (MFALDS), etc. benefitted a few from these categories.

Negative in Character

The abolition led to certain negative trends. Though it destroyed a particular class with bad reputation, yet the victims were mostly from the petty Zamindars who purchased the Zamindari with hard earned money. They had been the most vocal and active supporters of the Congress in the pre-independence days. The Congress Party lost the sympathy of the class forever who constituted its outposts in the villages. The big Zamindars hedged themselves against their rainy days by investing huge sum in industry, trade and commerce. The abolition of Zamindari was supposed to be a politically retributive measure, misfired. One of the bad effects to be judged is that a new immoral class of Petty contractors, Political sycophants and petty Officials took the place of old Zamindars. Thus, village politics became polluted and lost its sanctity and identity.

Large Ownership of the Landlord Broken

Real land reform is meant that the "economic power of landlords based on large ownership must be broken". Their lands must be distributed to the landless and poor peasants. "Land to the tiller" is the essence of land reforms. In a country like India and Bihar in particular with a huge landless and peasant population, the entire land of landlord should pass into the hands of the poor and landless peasants. No document and niceties should stand in the way. The landlords have enough properties, money and can manage alternative means of livelihood. Hence, it is a pertient question why they should be allowed to retain any land. But the abolition did not allow the tiller to own the land since 1951, because when talks about landlords started, they began to "manage" with their surplus lands by all fradulent means and fortify themselves by false documents. Anticipating the legislation, they adopted necessary means to evade ceiling by subtle methods; they even managed to get artificial divorcees to pose as seperate families.

No land reform legislation can be implemented if it is left mainly to the government administrative machinery. The indispensable condition for success in implementation is based on agricultural labourers, poor peasants, bataidars, who are really interested in land reforms, must be roused, their initiative and courage will have to be developed so that they can stand up before the power of the landlords, they must be asked to come forward to help the Government for implementing the reforms.

In Bihar, abolition of Zamindari did not contact the peasants with their organisation. In their absence the landlords (rich, powerful, intelligent and resourceful) who had links with the administration for generations together took the advantage. They prepared fake documents and even misused the process of law. Thus, the abolition of Zamindari was only on paper and not in the practice.

Failure of the object

The abolition did not achieve its goal and object. The Act, it was said, should bring the tillers into direct touch with the Government, but this claim was also misjudged. The Bihar Land Reforms Act only regulated the relationship between an outgoing proprietor and the State Government but not the proprietor and the third party (Tenant). There are serious loopholes in the Act. The outgoing Zamindars were permitted to retain their *sir* and Khudkast land. Such legal provisions prompted the Zamindars for enlargement of their estates through coercive transfers and illegal possession of ghairmazurua land. The provision to retain certain khas and khudkhast land by Zamindars prevented the process of breaking up land concentration in the agricultural sector. The Rent receiving class remained very much in the villages, who even today represents concentration of economic powers and exercises great influence on the community life. The social and economic barriers of pre-land reforms era very much exist today. From the tenants point of view, they were least benefitted by way of any reduction in rent. Although some illegal payments to ex-Zamindars have been stopped, they now suffered in other ways owing to the withdrawal of economic support provided by them. They were simple rentiers, who leased out most part of their lands to share croppers either on fixed cash rent or produce rent. In the present structural set up of the rural society, these rentiers are still an important factor. As Gyanchand affirms, "They are in fact landlords and they have the attitude and bearing of that class. They represent concentration of economic power in the villages and generally exercise great influence on account of their caste status. The working of the land Commission has been a flop. It is still not known what the Commission has done during these years."

Enactment of the Legislation

The main lacuna of the abolition was that the legislation appears to have been enacted in haste, without creating proper atmosphere, without studying the likely impact, the future implications, the manner in which the laws could be evaded, and without strengthening and overhauling the revenue administration which continued to be packed with officers having pro-landlord bias. As a result, when the Land Reforms Bill was presented in the Bihar Legislative Assembly, the opposition to it was most determined. In the Assembly, the opposition called the Bill as "Illegal, improper, unjust and unfair" due to the abolition.

Undemocratic

Due to abolition, democracy was at stake. Ahmad rightly picturise it "Democracy', it was said, 'was being killed outright; the Abolition Act was the "blackest law." Karuna Mukherjee while analysing the shortcomings of the Act (1950) characterised it as hasty, haphazard and makeshift, even opportunistic. The opposition's fury was quite natural against the Act.

Discriminatory

Shorn of the sentimental polorization, the opposition boiled down to the following :

(a) The Act was discriminatory against a particular of property, *viz.* Zamindari.
(b) There was not a single clause in it for the benefit of the masses.
(c) The rich will be made poorer, but the poor will remain where they are.

So the charge of discrimination was quite clear, as it was patently loaded against a particular interest which it abolished. But this charge was to some extent baseless as "any land reform proposal must be discriminatory against the vested interest in the land."

Destruction

Firstly, the charge posed by the opposition was that the reform entailed a negative approach, as it was destructive of an old institution. It was not constructive in the sense that the Ryotwari system was nothing, but actually new order visualised by it.

Secondly, most of the Indian leaders did not demand the abolition of the Zamindari tenure, and saw little difference between the Ryotwari tenure and the Zamindari tenure so far as the welfare of the ryot was concerned. Their indifference did not, however, spring primarily from a love for the landlord but from their belief that, as far as the evils of landlordism were concerned, there was little to choose between the Zamindari and Ryotwari systems, since both were just different forms of landlordism—one private landlordism and the other state landlordism. While under the former, rent was appropriated by the individual landlords, under the latter the Government came forward and appropriated it. For the cultivators, there was little to choose between the two systems. R.C. Dutt pointed out that the Ryotwari system had originated not in the East India Company's desire to save the ryot from the clutches of the landlord but in its desire to maximise own revenues by preventing interception of a part of the profits by intermediaries; the company had been jealous of the landlord's gains and not solicitous of the ryot's welfare. Under this system the Company had acquired "as good a grip over the cultivators as a slave, owner has over his slaves, and could take away all that was not needed to keep them alive." Some of the Indian leaders further maintained that, if anything, the Zamindari system had an edge over the Ryotwari system in two respects. For one, while the Government could legislate against the Zamindars to protect the ryot from undue enhancement of rent and other oppressions, it consistently refused to put any legal or other restrictions on its own powers of enhancing land revenue and determining its relations with the cultivator in other respects. Once a permanent settlement of revenue was granted, its benefits could be extended to the cultivators by imposing restrictions on the Zamindars or other superior holders right to enhance rents. In fact, the government could do so now with good grace, since it would have set up a good example in place of the existing policy of permitting, encouraging and even forcing the Zamindars to screw up rents. The second respect in which, according to some of the Indian leaders, the Zamindari tenure was superior to the Ryotwari tenure lay in the drain. They argued that, if the Ryot had to pay a heavy rent, it was better that he paid it to the Indian landlord, who expanded it within the country, rather than he paid it to the Government because of its alien character drained it out of the country.

Thirdly, some confusion was caused by the fact that some of the Indian leaders, being appalled at the manner in which the Indian people had been reduced to a uniformly low level of social existence without any outlets for their talents, looked wistfully upon the Zamindars as atleast one class of people who were able to keep up some standards of social and intellectual excellence. In their eyes the Zamindars appeared to serve the useful purpose of preventing the reduction of the entire Indian people to the dead level of an obscure and plebian existence. Moreover, a section of the Indian leadership was convinced that the people required leaders from a middle class, and it is appeared that the Zamindars might constitute this middle class as their natural leaders of the countryside. A long editorial explanation for defence of the Permanent Settlement of 1973 published by the 'Amrita Bazar Patrika' in its issue dated 20 January, 1871 makes interesting reading. It deserves reproduction as it gives us a good insight into the thought processes of Bengal and perhaps Indian nationalist opinion even though it was penned nearly a decade before. At the outset, the editorial laid down :

> "The rural masses as such were left untouched by the Act. The Act thus was much about rent collecting. It hit the landlord class in one respect, but it did not propose to ameliorate the status or condition of either the petty kisans or the landless labourers."

Complex Compensation Arrangements

One of the major defects of the abolition was the ground of compensation fixed by the Act and it was thoroughly complex. On strictly moral grounds no one can deny the need for "fair and equitable compensation". "Legal abolition of Zamindari, without the payment of compensation is a legalised robbery" which does not provide the basis for any civilised country or its Government's behaviour. In this case refusal to pay compensation would have shaken the people's faith in the Government itself, as the compensation was a just decision.

The compensation was only for the name, not for the substance. Not only that the payment began late and that too in driblets. There were thousands of ex-intermediaries of Bihar who had not initiated to receive compensation payment by the spring of 1968—sixteen years following initial attempts to implement the Act of 1950. The Land Reforms Implementation Committee of the National Development Council released a report in August, 1966 to the effect that the Government of Bihar "appeared" to be making all interim payments to 308,000 ex-Zamindars, that is to say about 65 per cent of the total number of ex-Zamindars in Bihar.

The report stated that these advance interim payments, amounted to a total of approximately Rs. 138,500,000 out of an estimated total due of Rs. 200,000,000. The committee had no information confirming the advance payment of up to 50 per cent of the estimated amount of compensation to any ex-intermediary. It was able to report that such payments could have been made in a limited number of cases as the amount of 50 per cent was determined only from about 36 per cent of the total number of cases. The Committee's report suggested the Government of Bihar to make payments by 1966 totalling approximately Rs. 158,000,000 to ex-intermediaries, either as payment of final compensation or 50 per cent of the estimated amount of compensation as due. The due amount had earlier been estimated to be in the neighbourhood of 1000 Crores rupees.

Another source provided contradictory data for the same general period ending in 1966. The Times of India Directory and Year book, 1967 suggested that "*ad interim*" payments to ex-intermediaries amounted to Rs. 178,00,000 and that additional amounts totaling Rs. 318,600,000 (of the estimated Rs. 1,000 Crore total compensation due) had been paid in bonds, in cash, or by adjustment of arrears of various Government dues. These figures were said to be valid through November, 1966.

Moreover, the unofficial records of August, 1970, Government of Bihar provided the data of compensation payments to ex-intermediaries as presented in the table 6.1 :—

Table 6.1
Compensation Payments to Ex-Intermediaries in Bihar

Year	*Compensation in Bonds and cash (Rupees)*	*Interim payments (Rupees)*
1953-54	—	78,000
1954-55	—	1,530,000
1955-56	—	3,090,000
1956-57	—	9,442,000
1957-58	—	16,882,000
1958-59	—	14,987,000
1959-60	—	18,317,000
1960-61	64,871,000	20,071,000
1961-62	57,486,000	18,672,000
1962-63	38,789,000	18,033,000
1963-64	22,065,000	18,346,000
1964-65	14,080,000	15,836,000
1965-66	15,597,000	15,682,000
1966-67	11,211,000	11,199,000
1967-68	9,916,000	13,307,000
1968-69	not available	
1969-70	not available	
	212,888,000	171,146,000

Thus discrepancies in the data are obvious; all available sources agree that compensation payment to ex-intermediaries have in no way approached the estimated Rs. 1,000 Crores total compensation due. Even the pivot of the Act, K.B. Sinha accepted during the General Election of 1967 that the state was far behind in making payments of any kind to ex-intermediares but also expressed doubt whether it would be paid according to the provisions of the Legislation. He further made it clear that "we wrote those (compensation) provisions into the bills, but with no feeling for them, I have no doubt that these provisions, will be scrapped in due course. And why not? If anything, the ex-Zamindars should be asked to pay compensation to the raiyats."

With the passage of time it appeared that the Government (non-congress or coalition Government) will stop all compensation payment to ex-intermediaries.

It is clear that the compensation was not only miserly, it was spread over unduly long number of years. The Government's escapist clauses which nominally gave compensation but really escaped the burden of such payments, led to displeasure among the-ex-zamindars.

Failure of the Rehabilitation Task

Again, the purpose behind the compensation was to rehabilitate the landlord class, it also did not succeed. Even the Taccavi loans (compensation money) were not easily obtainable. They had to make endless effort and buttering of the officials. Naturally, they were economically crippled, psychologically destablized, and frustrated physically and segregated.

At this stage, the Government should have taken up their (ex-Zamindars) rehabilitation task but it kept mum. Government was a mere silent spectator of their ruin. The Act consisted many bad features that made the situation more cumbersome.

Poor Revenue Collection

It was hoped that the abolition would increase the revenue of the state but in practice such collection of revenue continued to fall well below the estimated potential demand. Though the revenue Department reported yearly increase in income from land revenue from 1952, the first year in which the Act was implemented, yet related expenditure were also increasing as shown in the table below :—

Table 6.2
Bihar Land Revenue
Collection and Related Expenditures

Year	*Income*[a] *(Rupees)*	*Expenditure*[b] *(Rupees)*
1952-53	11,565,807	6,393,992
1953-54	15,133,356	14,023,631
1954-55	17,109,118	18,255,980
1955-56	35,414,331	24,161,414

On the basis of accomplishments through 1955-56, the Revenue Department predicted that income from rent collection might dramatically move ahead during 1956 to 1967 and approach 80,000,000 rupees close indeed to the published estimate that potential revenue demand (from land rent alone) would be 85,850,000 rupees; but this hope never came true.

Moreover, the revenue collection were poor initially (following the enactment and validation of the Bihar Land Reforms Act 1950) and varied enormously through the years as shown below in the table :—

Table 6.3
Bihar Land Revenue Demand and Collection

Year	*Current Demand (Rupees)*	*Current Collection of land rent (Ruppes)*
1.	*2.*	*3.*
1956-57	51,578,019	34,990,024
1957-58	56,322,465	30,088,201
1958-59	60,109,772	41,372,763
1959-60	63,181,979	40,387,383

1.	2.	3.
1960-61	67,659,208	44,561,189
1961-62	70,851,143	42,355,254
1962-63	72,755,082	53,184,784
1963-64	75,823,620	56,184,784
1964-65	76,217,364	60,048,956
1965-66	76,635,609	59,773,450
1966-67	77,199,679	13,296,370

Source : Government of Bihar, Revenue Department Land Ceiling Section.

G. Ojha says that the revenue of the State Government increased from Rs. 2.69 lakhs in 1952-53 to Rs. 14.99 lakhs in 1962-63.

Table 6.4
Magnitude of Compensation paid to Ex-intermediareis in Selected Permanently Settled States

States	*Acerage (in millions)* Rs.	*Total compensation (in million)* Rs.	*Per Acre compensation* Rs.
Bihar	39.64	1,510	39
West Bengal	28	560	20
Assam	167	37	22
U.P.	52.52	1,634	31
Madras	17.42	207	15

Source : Department of Revenue, Government of Bihar.

It is also to be noted that the pressure of compensation per acre was highest in Bihar in comparison to any other permanently settled State. The relative data are given in table 6.4. Bihar had to pay compensation at Rs. 39 per acre whereas Madras had to pay Rs. 15 per acre, Uttar Pradesh followed closely at Rs. 31 per acre.

These states had to finance the compensation to the divested intermediaries on the increase of the land revenue collection consequent upon the abolition of Zamindari. The table 6.5 gives the total revenue demand for the period 1952-53 to 1965-66.

Table 6.5
Magnitude of Compensation paid to Ex-intermediareis in Selected Permanently Settled States

States	*Acerage (in millions)* Rs.	*Total compen-sation (in million)* Rs.	*Per Acre compensation* Rs.
Bihar	39.64	1,510	39
West Bengal	28	560	20
Assam	167	37	22
U.P.	52.52	1,634	31
Madras	17.42	207	15

Source : Department of Revenue, Government of Bihar.

It is evident from the table that the revenue demand from land gradually increased since the abolition of intermediaries. It was the highest in 1962-63 at Rs. 14.99 crores. The declining trend thereafter might be attributed to draught or not favourable

Table 6.6
Total Demand of Rent during the Period (1952-1953 to 1965-1966)

Year	*Total demand (Rs. in lakhs)*
1952-53	269
1953-54	400
1954-55	488
1955-56	715
1956-57	774
1957-58	912
1958-59	1044
1959-60	1152
1961-62	1349
1962-63	1499
1963-64	1340
1964-65	1190
1965-66	117

Source : Department of Revenue, Government of Bihar.

agricultural years necessitating large scale rent remission.

However, this increase in revenue could not be utilised by the Government for development purposes, because it had to be paid as compensation to the intermediaries provided for in the Land Reforms Act.

Though the rent received by the Government was progressively increased, yet the question of reduction in agricultural income tax receipts and stamp duties was there. As M.L. Dantwala has rightly observed :

> "It has been estimated that total compensation payable in Bihar is rupees 158 crores plus Rs. 80.98 crores in the interest."

The receipts from agricultural income tax declined from Rs. 69 lakhs in 1950-51 to Rs. 18 lakhs in 1960-61.

Thus, the annual loss of income from stamp duty on account of Zamindari abolition placed at Rs. 19 lakhs. It was not the end; the State Governemnt had to suffer from the loss of the amount of cases on land revenue which was paid by the Zamindars (about 35 lakhs). Thus, Dantwala has rightly calculated that net impact of the Zamindari abolition on Bihar Government Revenue during the first and second plan is a negative one, to the tune of Rs. 155 lakhs. Therefore, the abolition did not bring any remarkable profit in the financial field.

Minimum Improvement in the National Wealth

The promise to improve the national wealth in the shape of trees, fronts, hat, bazars, fisheries, minerals, mines etc. also proved to be meaningless. In the assembly, K.B. Sahay (then Revenue Minister) while piloting the Land Reforms Bill opined that the Bill was absolutely necessary for improving the national wealth in the shape of forests, hats, bazars etc. But it is irony of fate that more than three decades have been passed (since the abolition of Zamindari) and still it is not clear as to how the Act helped in the improvement of the national wealth (hats, bazars, ferries etc.) whereas the mineral rights are concerned, it is alleged that the mineral interest secured very favourable term due to the intervention from the Central Government and this was possible from the political pulls and pressure tactics. Thus, the Bihar Land Reforms Bill was charged with applying a double standard for the mineral rights which were treated differently from other intermediary rights.

Bihar Land Reforms Act instead of improving the national wealth, led to destruction of trees and forest. It is to be pointed out that the toddy trees were fell in thousands on fear that the Government would lay claim to them., It is very peculiar that the 'Van Mahotsava' was begun in 1950, the very year when the Bihar Land Reforms Bill was inviting large scale destruction of trees by transference of forests to the Government from private hands. Commenting on it Vera Anesty has rightly referred to the ex-Zamindars who "cut down fruit groves and forest and hastily planted potatoes."

Negligence of Agriculture

One of the culminative effects of the Zamindari System was the neglect of agricultural improvement such as irrigation, drainage, etc. which adversely affected production. The system resulted in frittering away of the mineral and forest wealth of Bihar and had a very detrimental effect on the economy of the State after the abolition of the fetter that existed between the tenant and the State. Henceforth the Governemnt came to know the requirements of the agriculturist and restricted the exploitation of the minerals and forests resources of the State in an unbalanced manner.

The abolition of the intermediaries paved the way for an overall planning for the reconstruction of the agriculture, as the State got the benefits of the financial investments in the development schemes which hitherto had gone to Zamindar.

Simplification of Tenure

The abolition of the intermediaries has further resulted in the simplification of tenure and a uniform method of revenue administration. The abolition and associated legislation generally had the effect of simplying the tremendously varied and complex system of tenures which had so fascinated the British rulers of India and on which they in their turn piled further variety and complexity. According to the 1961 census, by far the most important impact of the these reforms on the pre-existing situation was that they had entered into a direct engagement with the Government to pay land revenue and had permanent rights in land. But at the same time the State needed to initiate administrative reforms (particularly in the Revenue Department) so that there would be a machinery capable of coping with expanded responsibilities associated with the establishment of up-to-date land records and the collection of revenue without the aid of intermediaries.

Illiteracy of the Masses

Another reason of the failure of abolition was the illiteracy of the masses. Gandhiji also emphasized the need for educating the villagers in making them conscious of their own potentialities. If they had been rendered unemployed or had been exploited, it was mostly due to ignorance which must be removed and the people made to understand that they need not live always as they had lived in the past and be unable to get out of the slough despondency. They should be made to know something of the outside world and how their land was being exploited. Therefore, it is a historical fact that any land reform can yield the desired results only if the people are educated. People must be aware of the pros and cons of the legislation. Otherwise, the ryots remain ignorant of their rights of which they are deprived in due course, or alternatively the ryots form exaggerated ideas of their rights and overstep the rightful limits, and when they take the law in their own hands and are defeated, frustration grips them. Thus, the proper education of the affected parties is the backbone to implementation of any legislation and it is the responsibility of the ruling party to give the message of the new changes to the villages. Only then any Act can be practised in the true sense.

Curbing of Feudal Set-up

The greatest benefit of the abolition is that it emancipated the 'agrarian structure' of a superfluous layer which had no organic connection. It's progressive importance from the stand point of history lies in the fact that it has certainly led to a considerable curbing of feudal and semi-feudal exploitation of the peasanty.

Jagjit Singh Lyallpuri, while presenting his report on the *Progress of the 'Land Reforms in India in the Trichur Silver Jubilee Session of the All India Kisan Sabha* (1981), said that "These legislations have considerably curbed the power of the old type feudal oppression of peasants, with productive services of any kind. Though the land system was not ever handled by it, yet a functionless element from the rural polity has been removed. The size of the sake income from land did not change but the party which had needlessly the largest slice of it was given the go by. That income must be used up for the welfare of the whole community. The Land Reforms Act *per se*, was barren as it set the stage for reaching changes and it brought uniformity in the choas of tenurial relations in the state. As the harbinger of great reforms to come, the Act was of inestimable benefits. Zamindars had stood as the symbols of a leisured rich class, when they fell down, it was brought home to society, that income must be linked with work and that the community was not going to tolerate parasitic living.

Direct Contact with State

The greatest benefit of the Land Reforms Act was that the State now reached into the villages, feeling concern with the day-to-day problems of the villagers, eager to reshape the whole rural atmosphere and in the shape of the impoverished revenue agency, a machinery was created for giving a facelift to the worn-out agrarian economy. Thus, the abolition of intermediaries has brought the tenants into direct relation with the State on an area of 2.2 crore acres of land. It has to some extent, created a sense of ownership in the minds of the tenants with a beneficial impact on the incentive to produce. Thus in the womb of the abolition lies the seeds of the welfare state.

The failure of intermediaries, Zamindars and tenure holders to provide the Governemnt with personal "estate records," further impeded the implementation of the Land Reforms Act of 1950. In many instances, the Zamindars withheld rent rolls pertaining to their intermediary interests. This was inspite of the fact Sections 56 and 57 of the Bihar Tenancy Act of 1885 had entitled a tenant to a rent receipt on payment of the rent and had stipulated that a landlord (Zamindar) should "prepare and retain a counterfoil of the reciept." But one and thousand grounds the landlords avoided it.

Assessment of the Land

The abolition created necessities to have information immediately regarding the area of land held by each raiyat and the rent payable by them. Hence, the *Bujharat* was introduced as the object of the field. *Bujharat* was primarily to prepare a revenue roll, i.e. a list of raiyats who has to pay revenue to the Government or on whom rent is to be assessed. Instructions were also issued for entering the name of under raiyat and the area held by them. Entries were made by the Karmachari's which were checked up by Circle Inspector and the Circle Officer. Thus a ready and rough record of rights was prepared for the entire state including certain *diara* area in which no Cadastral survey had been done previously. Therefore, by the beginning of 1963 survey and settlement operations were completed for the whole of Bihar.

Emergence of Panchayat Raj

Out of the seeds of the abolition, the Panchayat Raj system emerged, the attempt to develop a set of inter-connecting popular institutions at village, block and District level which would, amongst other things, take increasing responsibility for various aspects of the general drive for Community Development and help to build a new rural India from below. By 1963 Panchayat Raj was in operation in nine out of the fifteen states of the union, and in theory at any rate, extension and Community Development Workers became the co-ordinators for and executive officers of popularly elected institutions. It was being associated with the work of rent collection, management of village common land and supervision of small improvement words etc. It has been reported that about 900 panchayats in Bihar are collecting land revenues of the land. The Bihar Government has reported that they propose to utilise their agencies increasingly for the collection of land revenue. It is also to be noted that a provision was made in the Land Reform Act of 1950 that the State Government may entrust the management of the Estate to the Executive Committee of Grampanchayat on such terms and conditions as the Government may decide and fix by general or special orders.

Rise of Bureaucracy

Not only that, the grave of abolition brought a number of officials on the surface *viz*. Sub-judges, Munsifs, Circle Officers, Additional Sub-divisional Officers, Collectors and Additional Collectors, etc. Their appointment was being held for the purpose of receiving and disposing of claim petitions filed by creditors and for the purpose of compensation. One should not hesitate to note that the present set up of the bureaucracy is the most important contribution of the abolition.

Introduction of Capitalist Farming

One of the remarkable changes that drew our attention is the introduction of the capitalist farming. Now the only source of income of the ex-Zamindars was cultivation and they realised that if they did not take seriously to cultivation, even their landed property will in due course become a casualty to reforms legislation. Hence tractors were purchased and big mechanised farms with improved quality of seeds, manures, proper irrigation were seen emerging on the agrarian map.

Here again controversy arose : the Zamindari Abolition Act have not *per see* spurred landlords sufficiently to run their farms on a capitalist basis. True, the agrarian reform laws contained a proviso which excluded capitalist type landlord farm and plantations from the purview of reform. It is to be noted that capitalist type landlord farms in Zamindari areas covered a relatively small area. As regards tea, coffee and rubber plantations the total area in 1953-55 was less than 1.5 million acres out of 370 million under cultivation.

Again, the extension of Zamindars of *sir* lands through the eviction of tenants did not as a rule lead to setting up of large landlord farms; on the contrary many Zamindars who tried to establish capitalist farms on the land retained by them under the reform went bankrupt. H.D. Malviya stated in an article in the *AICC Economic Review* that in U.P. over 500 farms of ex-

Zamindars with a combined area of 200,000 acres were offered for sale. Same was the situation prevalent in Bihar. H.K. Konar said that the development of capitalism, particularly in the sphere of agriculture, is intimately related to the rural production, the Government tried for limited capitalistic development with the help of the landlords. But in reality it has not materalized. As Pradhan H. Prasad also reveals it, the essential condition of capitalism is yet to take root in Bihar's agriculture as the Dobb-Rudra condition of bondage enforced on direct producers through non-economic coercive methods mean that semi-feudal institution operate as a drain on development and that even primitive accumulation is not in evidence.

He further said that a theoretical model would facilitate the understanding of some of these implications of the 'semi feudal mode of production' wherein the surplus value is mainly appropriated through tenancy and usuary by the big peasantry and the landlords. Let us a have a model with a fixed quality of land and certain constant quality of fixed capital goods as pair of bullocks, plough, tractor, power tiller, Lift irrigation system etc. If we will drop the assumption that fixed capital per unit of land is constant, in that case if fixed capital rises, output and employment per unit of the land will also rise.

Though the capitalistic approach to the farming may not have achieved its goal due to many difficulties, yet it is quite clear that the reforms act popularised the capitalistic mode of farming.

Rural Violence

The abolition led deep rooted hatred and untold series of violence in rural society. Of course the consciousness created by the nationalist movement, the Peasant Movement and more importantly by the communistic movement to some extent has been able to mobilise the peasantry and strike some fear in the minds of the feudal elements that they cannot have it their way always. The movement has started penetrating to the landless poor whose major composition is scheduled castes. Indeed it signifies the changes from the old pattern of "landlord tenant set up" to the "upper class and the lower class set up." Though these classes were not organised for a collective action because of its wide dispersal of agricultural labour and the non-continuous nature of their employment yet the fact that there is a stir among them, and that there is some inchorate defiance among them is something that is to be credited to the Communist Party.

Chandwa Rupaspur in Bihar 1971 is the manifestation of the wrath and intense hatred of the landlord communities towards the agricultural labourers who happen to be scheduled castes. These attacks have been fierce, striking and inhuman. For example, rapings done in order to fiercely assert and demonstrate the power of the landed classes than to just satisfy the lust. In the post abolition era the scheduled caste men were shot dead in a moment because they refused to vote for a particular candidate in a panchayat election in 1971. Since then violence became the fate of the whole of the state.

As a result, in Bihar all these smart scheduled castes were impatient for revenge, and they launched attacks on them (upper class) at first sporadically and then on a mass basis. These attacks were counter attacked by the upper class people. Thus the reign of terror began to rule in the rural life.

The implementation of the above reaction is seen in Belchi, Bajitupur, Gijnur, Arwal, Nonhinagma, Baghaura-Dalelchak, Jehanabad and Sasaram brutal killings.

Though Mrs. Indira Gandhi was successfully able to pose as the champion of the down-trodden, yet the situation remained unchanged during her rule and upto now.

Division of Opinion

Abolition had divided Bihar Congressmen as well as the nationalist leaders into two different groups, a right wing and a left wing. Leaders like Mahatma Gandhi, Rajendra Prasad, Sardar Patel, S.K. Sinha, A.N. Sinha etc. wanted to introduce abolition in a phased manner. They were not in any hurry while Jawaharlal Nehru, Subhash Chandra Bose, Narendra Deo, Murarilal, Sampurnanand, K.B. Sahay, Sahajanand and several other kisan leaders wanted to do it at once. In 1937 the Bihar Congress Ministry decided to deal with this dilemma by concentrating on bringing more immediate relief to the tenants than by attempting any radical change. The bill reduced the amount of rent paid by the tenants to the level set in 1911. Some machinery was set up to settle a fair rent; it abolished arbitrary imposed rents by the landlords, stopped the arrest of tenants for arrears in rent and limited the interest on unpaid rents to 5%.

Important Land Legislation

The abolition also made the road easy for further Land Reforms. In order to meet the challenge of the time and the increasing rural discontent that resulted in a series of rural violence, the Government enacted a number of Land Legislations which strengthened further the position of tenants as against the landlords. The names of the important land legislations is given below :—

1. The Kosi Area (Restoration and Land to the Raiyats) Act, 1951 (Bihar Act XXX of 1951).
2. The Bihar Recovery of Arrears of Rent of outgoing proprietors and Tenure Holders (vested Estates and Tenures) Act, 1953 (Bihar III of 1953).
3. The Bihar Bhoodan Yajna Act, 1954 (Bihar Act II of 1954).
4. The Bihar Consolidation of Holdings and Prevention of Fragmentation Act 1956 (Bihar Act XXII of 1956).
5. The Bihar Land Reforms (Fixation of Ceiling Area and Acquisition of Surplus Land) Act 1962 (Bihar Act XII of 1962).
6. The Bihar Gramdan Act 1965 (Bihar Act IV of 1965)
7. The Bihar Urban Land Act, 1965 (Bihar Act V of 1966).
8. The Bihar Land Rent (Exemption from Payment) Act, 1970.
9. The Bihar Tenancy Act 1885.

Amendments in this Act from 1955 to 1970 are :

- *(i)* The Bihar Tenancy (Amendment) Act, 1955 (Act XIX 1955).
- *(ii)* The Bihar Tenancy (Second Amendment) Act, 1955 (Act XXIV of 1955).
- *(iii)* The Bihar Tenancy (Amendment) Act, 1958 (Act XVIII of 1958).

(iv) The Bihar Tenancy (Amendment) Act, 1959 (Act XXVII of 1959).

(v) The Bihar Tenancy (Amendment) Act, 1961 (Act XIV of 1961).

(vi) The Bihar Tenancy (Amendment) Act, 1962 (Act I of 1963).

(vii) The Bihar Tenancy (Amendment) Act, 1965 (Act II of 1965).

(viii) The Bihar Tenancy (Amendment) Act, 1967 (Act I of 1967).

(ix) The Bihar Tenancy Laws Amendment 1967 (Act IX of 1967).

(x) The Bihar Tenancy (Amendment) Act, 1969 (Act VII of 1969).

(xi) The Bihar Tenancy (Amendment) Act, 1970 (Act VI of 1970).

10. Consolidation of Holdings and Prevention of Fragmentation (Amendment) Act, 1970 (Act VII of 1970).
11. Bihar Privileged Persons Homestead Tenancy (Amendment) Act, 1970.

In the conclusion, it is to be said that we are on the threshbold of creating the old self-contained village communities which had a vigour, sanctity and vitality of their own. The danger is however that the Panchayats in most cases are dominated by old landlords. Thus, the revival of their power is a revival of the old Zamindari spirit. Still the villages are ruled by them. The Zamindar is dead, but long live the Zamindar in the new set up with a changed nomenclature (The Mukhia, the sarpanch, The Mantri of the samiti etc.) The approach of Cornwallis about 'natural leaders' of the soil had been best realised in the post-independence period, when the Zamindars were ripe for a change. In the changed situation it would have been much better if the old Zamindars would have accepted the newly organised socialistic pattern of the village life and the rural people should also accept them by trimming their feathers (power).

Though it was hoped that the abolition would bring a new dawn in the rural life yet it could not bring the desired change in the socio-economic set up which was prevalent for so long. In post-independence era the government did its best by enactment of a number of legislations. But the situation remains unchanged till today. The land reforms in real sense are possible only when the people become aware of their responsibility towards the society, state and country in that order.

Notes & References

Mishra, J., *Land Reforms in Bihar,* Patna, 1974. p. 95.

Khusro, A.M., *Economic and Social Efforts of Jagirdari Abolition* in *Hyderabad*. The Mass of evictions that followed the abolition of intermediaries in Hyderabad in turns by landed class appears as the 'ugliest blot, on the measures.'

Konar, Hare Krishna, *Agrarian Problems of India,* Calcutta, 1977.

Oomen, T.K., *Social Transformation in Rural India,* Delhi, 1984, p. 45.

Joshi, P.C., *Land Reforms in India,* New Delhi, 1970, p. 49.

Alexander, K.C., *Agrarian Unrest in Kuttanad, Kerala,* Behaviour Sciences and Community Development, Vol. III (1) 1973, also see F. Jannuzi, *Agrarian crisis India, The case of Bihar*, New Delhi, 1974, also cited in Geof Wood, "From Raiyat to rich peasant," *South Asian Review,* Vol. (1), 1973.

Jodha, M.S., "Special Programme for the Rural : The Constraining Framework," *Economic and Political Weekly,* Vol. III (13) 1973.

Ojha, Gyaneshwar, *Land Problem and Land Reform,* New Delhi, 1972, p. 284 also see J. Mishra, *Land Reform in Bihar,* p. 97.

Ojha, G., *Op.cit.,* p. 58 also see F.T. Jannuzi in *Agrarian crisis in India, a case of Bihar,* p. 32.

Ahmad's S.A. speech as reported in Legislative Assembly Debates, Bihar 1950, Vol. I., p. 24.

Donnells, C.J.O., "The Ruin of an Indian Province", *Journal of Poona Sarvajanik Sabha Quarterly from Jan. 1881* (Vol. III no. 3).

Dutta, R.C., *Economic History of India in the victorian Age, Op.cit* pp. 128-132-33 (Dutt quoted the following passage from a book by Henry St. John Tucker, one of the Directors of the Company.

Gupta, J.N., *Life and work of R.C. Dutt,* London, 1911, p. 60.

Benerjee, S.N., *A Nation in Making,* Calcutta, 1925, p. 39.

Ranade, M.G., *Essays on Indian Economics,* Bombay, 1898, pp. 287, 290; Dut, EHI, pp. 131-32, EHIT, p. 43.

Ranade, *Journal of Poona Sarvajanik Sabha*, 1881, (Vol. IV, No. 1) p. 9.

India, Planning Commission, implementation of land reform. A review by the Land Rform Implementation Committee of the National Development Council, p. 43.

Review by the Land Reforms Implementation Committee of the National Development Council, p. 44.

Times of India Directory and Year Book, 1967, ed. N.J. Nanporia, p. 410.

Sahay, K.B., Interview, Patna, Bihar, March 17, 1968.

Revenue Department Government of Bihar, June 1957.

Bihar Land Reform Act, 1950 Section 4, clause (a) In the Bihar Local Acts III, 2219.

Legislative Assembly Debates Bihar, 1950, Vol. I, Part 1, p. 31.

Anstey, Vera, "Land Reform in India", *Journal of Local Administration*, (Vol. I) No. 2.

Menon, V.K., "New Anchal Adhikar system in Bihar," *Indian Journal of Public Administration*, No. 2 (April-June 1956).

Choudhary, Valmiki, *Dr. Rajendra Prasad: Correspondence and Select Documents*, Vol. 5, p. 245. New Delhi, 1986.

Eighteenth Session of the All India Kisan Sabha (1961, New Delhi), pp. 37-38.

Cited in F.T. Jannuzi, p. 25 *Estates records*, are documents pertaining to their rights to land.

India, "Ministry of food and Agriculture" Agricultural Legislation in India VI, 66.

Progress of Land Reforms, Planning Commission, (1963) p. 189.

Third Plan, p. 332.

Land Reforms Act, Bihar, 1950, Sec. 13.

Kotovsky, G., *Agrarian Reforms in India*, p. 78.

Report of the Plantation Enquiry Commission, Vol. I-III (Delhi) Government of India.

Cited in Kotovsky, G., "*Asi*", Vol. X, No. 8" (November 1955), p. 605.

Malviya, H.D., Depressing Effects of Incomplete Land Reforms and Price instability on National Itput AKC Economic Review (July 1, 1957) p. 15.

Pradhan H. Prasad, "Towards a theory of tranformation of semi feudal Agriculture," *Economic and Political Weekly*, Aug. 1, 1987.

Seshadri, K., *Rural unrest in India*, New Delhi, 1983, p. 42-43.

Chandwa Rupaspur, (agriculture labourers) were burnt alive for having resisted unlawfull encroachment of their lands by landlords.

Notes by Rajendra Prasad on Bihar Tenancy Proposals in AICC p. 6. (1.1) 1937.

CONCLUSION

In a poor country like India in general and the State of Bihar in particular, the agrarian question is of paramount importance. The 'agrarian crisis is considered to be the main curse for pitiable economic condition of the state of Bihar. These curses came in forms of natural calamities such as droughts, floods, earthquake, epidemics, economic depression etc. and sometimes they were man made. The effect of natural calamities was short-lived but the man made calamities prolonged in forms of the parasitic intermediary system till today. Agriculture in Bihar had become a deficit economy and to every extent the Bihar cultivators laboured not for profit but for subsistence. One thing to be mentioned is that the common economic characteristics in respect of the agrarian structure observed in overpopulated economies like Bihar, is that the resources are limited in relation to demand. Population explosion and magnitude of unemployment are quite high in a disguised form. It made the situation very critical. The faulty land system had been mainly responsible for low yield of crops. These factors were responsible for deterioration of agrarian condition in Bihar prior to independence.

The colonial agrarian policy under the British rule was never peasant oriented. The non-agricultural sector was not developed enough to absorb the surplus labour force. As the Indian Cottage industries were undermined by the British, the mass of the handicraft men even lost their means of livelihood and they were reduced to the level of starvation. The landlords were not at all interested to increase the agricultural inputs and their raiyats had not enough money to invest in the farming. This resulted in a vacuum affecting the whole rural economic set up. It is also to be noted that some scholars have remarked with alarm about the distress caused to the Bihar agriculturist through fragmentation. Thus, the agrarian scene of Bihar during the period 1937-52 was the direct result of the combination of agricultural curses, which were further accentuated by the institution of joint family so common in Hindu Society.

The fragmentation entailed waste of land in boundaries, hedges and ploughways. In many tracts, efficiency of agriculture was due more to the small size and scattered nature of the holdings than to the ignorance or want of alertness on the part of the peasants. The illiteracy of the Bihar cultivators was another hurdle in the way of improvement of the State. Physical inefficiency of the peasant in the state was yet another curse coming in the way of developing agriculture.

In the early period, the principal aim of the rulers was to get the land cultivated as it was the permanent source of their income. The intermediary relationship in land was created through the changes in political situation when conquering rulers empowered their senior officials or near relatives with the right of revenue collection and general administration in far away places. This resulted in rackrenting of the landholders for their own gains by changing the holder every year. The chief and individual was connected with a limited land over which he acquired herditary rights, he always tried to convert this privilege into personal property. The situation, however, remained quiet and under control during the medieval period.

In the British rule, the existing land revenue system changed into a new one. Since they were wholly unfamiliar with the problem of land management in the country, they adopted a method of letting out Zamindari right to the highest bidder. The result was disastrous for the people. In due course, the land management the 'Permanent System of Land Tenure' better known as the Zamindari System (1973) was introduced. Thus a new Zamindari System of land ownership emerged in the agrarian scene. It transformed rural society, because it enacted proprietary rights for the Zamindars and placed the raiyats at the mercy of the former. There was no tie of love between the newly created class of persons and the actual tillers which necessiated the need for a change in the land system and made room for a series of reforms.

It dates back from the first genuine Kisan agitation (Indigo Planters) in Champaran for the abolition of Zamindari System. The period 1937-52 shows different factions among the Congress *viz*-right wing, left wing, divided over the question of agrarian problems. It was a period of historical significance when the Bihar Prantiya Kisan Sabha (BPKS) arose that paved the way for the rise of All India Kisan Sabha (AIKS). Though the Kisan Sabha charged the Congress as class collaborationist, yet it must be said that the Congress had awakened the kisans, provided them with a model for organisation, and methods of fighting. The freedom struggle brought awakening among the peasants which made them conscious of their own economic rights *vis-a-vis* the Zamindars. Once the peasants found that they could fight against the mighty British Raj, they felt encouraged to defy the Zamindars who lived at the sufferance of the British. The Faizpur Agrarian Programme of 1936 highlighted the need to do away with all the injustices in the land system. When the first Congress ministry came into power and decided to implement the election manifesto in which the promise of agrarian unrest was to be solved.

Organisational work of the ministry delayed a little bit to the implementation of the agrarian reform. It caused a great dissatisfaction among the political leaders. In reaction, different political groups emerged i.e. Socialists, Communist, Forward Block etc. Hence due to the oppositions pressure politics, different legislative and executive measures were taken by the Government to emancipate the people from the blood sucking groups (Zamindars). Thus the measure dealing with the agrarian problems came in the forefront of the Congress Government that resulted into a series of Tenancy Amendment Acts.

The suffering of the peasantry on the soil of Bihar is nicely described by F. Engels "It was peasants who supported the other strata of society, 'Princes, officials, nobles, clergymen patrician and burghers. No matter whose subject the peasant was—a prince's, an imperial baron's, bishops, a monastry's or a town's." It emphasised the awakening of the peasants, forms of peasantry, peasants reaction and differentiation of peasantry, causes behind the unrest viz—world economic depression, problem of rack-renting, produce rent system, fall in prices, rural indebtedness, illegal imposition, forced labour, underdeveloped economy, calamities, eviction and the bakasht problem.

The main objective is to present an extremely gloomy picture of rural life in the mid thirties that was full of pauperisation, misery, starvation and of utter despondency. This continual aggravation of exploitation of the peasantry as well as their social operation, in course of time became a system and feature of the then existing social life. Legal and illegal exaction, rackrenting, sub-infeudation, fragmentation of holdings, indebtedness, increasing taxation, decreasing real wages of agricultural labourers—all this created a very serious and intolerable situation in rural areas of Bihar leading to class struggle which seems to be a civil war like situation.

It was the urge of the society and demand for abolish of Zamindari System in Bihar. It is said the entire rural society was on the threshhold of the changes. It symbolises a new age of democracy on the grave of conservative elements. It was an age of emancipation of the tenancy from serfdom. Throughout the history of landlordism the raiyats had to bend at the will of the their lords. The landlords had impounded the raiyats cattle, posted peons on their houses, withdrawn the barbers, dhobies (washermen) carpenters and smiths. They were prevented from using village wells and pasture lands. By ploughing up the pathways and lands just infront of or behind their home-steads, they had brought or promoted civil suits or criminal complaints against them and resorted to actual physical force and wrongful confinements. It reveals that after a long drama in the midst of confusion, anger, dissatisfaction, the land reforms bill was passed. This bill received the assent of the President on 11th November, 1950. Thus, the Land Reforms Act 1950 came into force but it took a couple of years to execute it in true sense. Still it is hanging between the legislature and the bureacrates.

It is the turning point in the history of modern Bihar in particular India in general. The most important result was that it abolished the intermediaries system between the land and the tenants. It cleared the path for further advance and post-abolition reforms. It brought the peasants into direct contact with the state by conferring on them the right of ownership.

With the passing of the Land Reforms act, the peasants hoped that it would prove to be effective scissors to cut all the social diseases and distresses of their lives, but the agrarian reforms failed to solve the land problems through abolition of landlordism and redistribution of land to the tiller of the soil. The act did not even completely eliminate the semi-feudal exploitation of the peasantry.

After 40 years of the enactment of the agrarian Act the situation is remain the same. It needs further changes and improvement. Because its full solution and (if it is solved) the whole future, social, economic, and political trajectory of our state depends only upon the Land reforms.

The key to success of any political party is based on its land policy in an agricultural state. Since Bihar is an agricultural state, the Government policy should be in the direction of the upliftment of its peasant masses. For this the Government must have political will and determination to implement the Land Reforms Act in true sense. Strict instructions must be given to the administrative machinery to help the peasants and to take their co-operation. To execute the land legislation the police department has got a special role to play. Thus, with the co-operation of the law department, police department, and home department—land legislation can be carried out successfully. The people should also come forward to help the Government agencies in executing the law.

The major question that needs an immediate attention towards the solution of the land problems is the modernisation of our agriculture. For it is necessary to apply a broad strategy of science and technology-based agricultural development research and extension, development of irrigation particularly in backward areas should be emphasised.

In order to stabilise the fortunes of agriculture, control of flood and drought should be given the first priority in any plan for the economic development of Bihar. There should be implementation of an integrated scheme of flood control, irrigation and rural electrification so that the abundant water resources of Bihar can be well utilised in agriculture processes. Only by implementing said programmes the 'Green-Revolution' plan of the government can be fulfilled in the state in a true sense.

It is high time that the principle of rectangulation should be applied in the matter of consolidation which is the key factor for the spectacular achievement of the programme in Punjab. In Bihar it is necessary that the government should bear cost of consolidation in the initial stage, till the programme gains momentum.

Another step that should be taken in the field of the economic development is the creation of appropriate type of institutions. In order to supply necessary help to the agricultural and industrial sector, co-operative and banking institutions should be reshaped and developed with extensive branch facilities. The Block Development agencies must be made more effective. These institutions should be geared up to provide credit facilities, agricultural inputs and implements, marketing facilities etc. to the farmers, redistributive programmes, Food-for-Work, I.R.D.P. etc. should be carefully planned and executed on the required scale. This is needed to give additional income to the poor till the time that the trickle down effect reaches them.

There is an urgency to establish more industries on the basis of local industrial potentialities. Though Bihar is very rich in mineral resources yet it lags behind in industrialisation. In order to give employment to the agricultural labour force it will be a great solution. At present the production of total mineral resources is 40% percent on all-India calculation. Yet it gets only 14% of its royalty against its mineral resources. The Central Government should make policy efforts for export of quality products of Tisco, Telco, Bokaro etc. These products must be given sales tax instead of "Transfer of Stock" due to which we loose a large amount of money. The government can establish defence production, food-products and civil supply industries, mica, mangenese, and uranium based industries as well other industries. In Ranchi and Hazaribagh region we have special type of coal that can be used in the coal based fertiliser industry. Through establishment of above industries economically Bihar will be certainly more prosperous and it will definitely provide more employment. It is the best solution to utilise all those anti-social elements such as Naxalite, I.P.F., C.P.I., CPI(ML) and others who always threaten peace in the villages leading to several killings of innocent people and its counter action. For overall progress of the rural areas the development of infrastructure like transport, communication, power, health and housing programmes must be given priority by the Government.

Industrial growth can be stepped up with a 20% improvement in efficiency through organisational reform of public sector and through greater competition in private sector by careful liberalisation (excepting infant industries for a fixed period) and freer entry and exit of firms.

In Bihar, Family Planning programme, maternity and child welfare should be given special emphasis in order to check the population explosion. This will be done by opening health-cum-family planning centres at Panchayat level. But proper utilisation of existing human resources require that the plan should be implemented in such areas as rural employment, village based industries, stoppage of unproductive expenses like unemployment allowance etc. Adequate arrangement should be made for the education of the masses with a view to raising them intellectually, economically, culturally and morally to make them fit for the new work culture. These programmes will increase harmony in village areas.

These days a new 'Money order' culture is in practice all over Bihar. The human resources of Bihar are being utilised in other states like Punjab, Haryana, Bengal, Maharashtra, Delhi. The problem of alienation is acute. The government should check and provide proper employment to them at their native places which, in turn, will ensure the prosperity of the state.

The social equity is the best solution of the land reforms measures. The old dogmatism of the past should be replaced by diligence and enterprise; superstitions and social taboos should give way to scientific orientation. Conditions should thus be created in which every individual has an equal opportunity in the sphere of state activity and there is social security for all.

Apart from the land reforms policy initiated by the Government, a large number of programmes has already implemented for the village people such as '20 Point Programme', IRDP, NREP, PIREP, CSRE, RLEGP, DPAD, MNP, SFDA, MFALS, IIAP, IADP, HYVP, etc. and the latest 'Jawahar Rozgar Yojna'. The people of Bihar should be aware of taking advantage of the Government's welfare development programmes. There is complete absence of 'work culture' and enterprising activity. People do not discharge the work that may be assigned to them. There is an apt saying that the people hog the capital which are provided to them by the Government and they lack the initiative to multiply the capitals, which leads to further popularisation. The State's emancipation can only be achieved by removing the clouds of lethargy and indifference which have been hanging over the peasant. We must remove these clouds, identify ourselves with the peasant, we must feel that *'he is ours and we are his'*.

To sum up, the solution to the agrarian problems on a permanent basis can be elaborated in the following terms :—

1. Let the landlords be placed in a position in which they may not oppress the tenants but at the same time, let not the tenants be encouraged to set them at nought and defy them in matters of social delicacies.
2. Let the interest of the one be to love the other, and the interest of the other to respect him.

The agrarian unrest will remain on the surface unless the Government follow the solution presented for agrarian development in Bihar.

GLOSSARY

Abwab	:	Extra Taxes or Cess or Mahot
Amils	:	Collector of revenue
Arzees	:	Petitions
Bakasht	:	Any land other than the proprietor's private land
Bundibusht	:	Settlement
Cess	:	Extra taxes
Faujdar	:	Army holder
Gomasta	:	Agents
Gunj	:	Market place
Jama	:	Assessment
Khudkasht	:	Own cultivation
Mahajan	:	Money lender
Paikasht	:	Non-resident cultivation
Pottahas	:	Leases
Punyahya/ Pustbandi	:	A ceremony for inaugurating the revenue of the year.
Ryot	:	Peasant or Cultivator
Ryotwari	:	Tenure by cultivators who have permanent rights in land and who pay revenue direct to the Government.
Sair	:	Any levy or impost which is not revenue is 'Sair', its literal meaning is balance or remainder

Salamis	:	Presents, as a matter of honour but actually as a matter of custom.
Sanads	:	Grants, Patent
Taccavi	:	Direct loan from the Government
Talbana	:	Peon's Fee.
Tehsil/Taluk/ Taluka	:	Administrative sub-division of a District.
Tehsildar	:	Revenue official incharge of a tehsil.
Zamindar/ Jamindar	:	Generally an intermediary between the cultivators and the state, Zamindars were often recognised by the British as landlords.

APPENDICES

APPENDIX I

DIGEST OF THE LAND REVENUE HISTORY OF PERMANENTLY SETTLED AREAS IN BIHAR 1765 TO 1950

Year	*Event*	*Landowner's*	*Tenant's position*
1	2	3	4
1765	Grant of Diwani to the East India Company,	Revenue farmers with yearly renewals,	Collection of illegal cesses, fines and other imposts alongwith rent from the tenants was widespread.
1770	Great Bengal Famine.	Revenue farming system continued.	Rent became very burdensome.
1772	Quinquennial settlement introduced. The company took over the administration and management of revenue under its direct hands.	Highest bidders made revenue farmers for a term of five years.	Tenants suffered from oppression at the hands of the auction bidders.

1	2	3	4
1777	Order of the Court of Directors for annual settlements.	Annual settlement with the Zamindars	Tenants position did not improve.
1784	Pitt's India Act which directed the East India Company to adopt permanent rules for settlement and collection of revenue.		
1789-90	Decennial settlement.	Ten year settlement with the Zamindars.	Tenants continued to be harassed under burdens of exactions. No fixity of tenure.
1793	Decennial settlement made permanent.	Zamindars made proprietors of their estates. Government's demand of land revenue fixed in perpetuity. Sale of estate in case of non-payment of Revenue. Zamindari became heritable and tranferable.	The Governor-General-in-Council reserved the right to enact such Regulations as he may think necessary for the protection and welfare of the raiyats. The rights of the cultivators to the soil were left as uncertain, as unsettled, as undefined as they were found by the English at the time of

1	2	3	4
			the grant of the Diwani. All impositions under the name of 'abwabs' etc. were consolidated with the original rent and new 'abwabs' were prohibited. Leases (pattas) were not to be granted to the raiyats for a period exceeding ten years. This resulted in rack renting.
1799	'Haftam' or Seventh Regulation.	Power of distraint for enabling proprietors and farmers of land to realise their rents with greater punctuality.	Provision for distraining the property of the tenants, who defaulted in payment of rent, without sending notice to any Court of Justice or any public Officer. The crop, grains, cattle and other personal property of the tenants could be distrained. This power of distraint reduced the rights of tenants in land almost to nothing.
1812	Prohibition against leases by Zamindars for a period, longer than ten years, abolished.	Zamindars enabled to give leases for longer period.	Tenant's exploitation at the hands of the intermediaries or middlemen increased.
1819	Regulation VIII of 1819	This enabled the Zamindars	This gave further scope to create

1	2	3	4
	Legislative sanction given to 'Patini' tenure.	intermediaries which often descended to fourth degree. Growth of absenteeism.	exploitation of the tenants at the hands of a chain of middlemen.
1841	Act XII of 1841. Enlargement of the powers of purchasers at sales for arrears of Revenue.	The Zamindars who purchased at Revenue Sales were empowered by implication to en hance at discretion the rents exceptions.	All leases granted and encumbrances created by the defaulting Zamindars were voidable by the purchser. This affected the tenants whenever a Zamindari was sold for arrears of revenue. Rents were generally enhanced or tenants ejected.
1859	Rent Act (Act X of 1859)	Zamindar's rights regarding enhancement of rent or eviction curbed to some extent.	A well meaning attempt to grant rights of occupancy and protection against enhancement of rents of the raiyats and conferring certain other rights on the tenants.
1859	Act XI of 1859. Revenue Sale law	The purchaser of an entire estate in the permanently settled districts sold for the recovery of arrears due, were to acquire the estate free from all encumbrances, which might have	Occupancy right of most of the tenants annulled and subjected to enhancement of rents. Courts of justice failed to protect rights because interest in land had not been defined by law and could not be proved by evidence

1	2	3	4
		been imposed upon it after the settlement by the outgoing Zamindar. He was entitled to avoid and annul all under tenures and eject forthwith all under tenants with some exceptions.	of usage.
1885	Bengal Tenancy Act of 1885.	Zamindar's arbitrary power regarding eviction, enhancement of rents and levy of illegal cesses etc. curbed.	Tenants protected against eviction, enhancement of rents, levy of illegal cesses etc. to a great extent. Provision for construction of record of rights made. They were granted some more rights.
1901-08	Survey and Settlement Operation	Zamindars position regarding rent settled.	Tenant's rents settled. Their rights in land ascertained. Record of rights in land prepared.
1937-40	Tenancy Legislation under the first Congress Government in Bihar.	Zamindar's power in respect of exploitation of tenants further curtailed.	Reduction in rent to the level of 1911, restriction on enhancement of rents for a period of fifteen years.

1	2	3	4
			Reduction of rates of interest on arrears of rent to 6.25 per cent per annum. Some more rights granted to tenants.
1947	Bihar Privileged Persons' Homestead Tenancy Act, 1947.	The landowners were obliged to accept the right of the privileged tenants over homesteads.	The privileged tenants were granted protection over their homesteads.
1950	Bihar Land Reforms Act.	Intermediary interests in land abolished.	Tenants now had direct relationship with the State.
1951	Kosi Area (Restoration of Lands to Raiyats) Act.	Zamindars compelled to accept the rights of raiyats of Kosi flood affected area on the abandoned holdings.	Restoration to previous raiyats of certain lands which were sold for arrears of rent or from which they were ejected for arrears of rent for

APPENDIX-II

Agrarian Legislation at the time of separation of Bihar and Orissa from Bengal.

SURVEY AND BOUNDARIES:
BIHAR AREA

The following Bengal Act which was in force in Bengal Presidency at the time of separation of Bihar and Orissa from Bengal on April 1, 1912, continued to be in force in the newly created province of Bihar and Orissa, by virtue of Section 3 of the Bengal, Bihar and Orissa and Assam Laws Act, 1912 (Central Act 7 of 1912).

Bengal Act :

1. The Bengal Survey Act, 1875—Bengal Act 5 of 1875 as in force in Bhagalpur, Chotanagpur, Patna and Tirhut Divisions of Bengal Presidency on 31.3.1912.
   - 1.1 Adapted by the Government of India (Adaptation of Indian Laws) Order, 1937.
   - 1.2 Adapted by the Indian Independence (Adaptation of Bengal and Punjab Acts) Order, 1948.
   - 1.3 Adapted by the Adaptation of Laws Order, 1950.

LAND RECORDS
BIHAR AREA

The following Bengal Act which was in force in Bengal Presidency at the time of separation of Bihar and Orissa from Bengal on April 1, 1912, continued to be in force in the newly created province of Bihar and Orissa, by virtue of Section 3 of the Bengal, Bihar and Orissa and Assam Laws Act, 1912 (Central Act 7 of 1912).

Bengal Act :

1. The Land Records Maintenance Act, 1895—Bengal Act 3 of 1895 as in force in Bhagalpur, Chotanagpur, Patna and Tirhut Divisions of Bengal Presidency on 31.3.1912.

1.1 Adapted by the Government of India (Adaptation of Indian Laws) Order, 1937.

1.2 Adapted by the Adaptation of Laws Order, 1950.

KHARSAWAN STATE AREA
(Merged State)

Kharsawan Act :

1. The Kharsawan Record of Rights Act.

1.1 Repealed by Bihar Act 41 of 1951.

SERAIKELA STATE AREA
(Merged State)

Seraikela Act :

1. The Record of Rights of Seraikela Act, 1935—Seraikela Act 1 of 1935.

1.1 Repealed by Bihar Act 41 of 1951.

LAND REGISTRATION

BIHAR AREA

The following Bengal Regulation and the Bengal Act which were in force in Bengal Presidency at the time of separation of Bihar and Orissa from Bengal on April 1, 1912, continued to be in force in the newly created province of Bihar and Orissa, by virtue of Section 3 of the Bengal, Bihar and Assam Laws Act, 1912 (Central Act 7 of 19120.

Bengal Regulation :

1. The Bengal Revenue-free Lands Regulations, 1800-Bengal Regulation 8 of 1800 as in force in Bhagalpur, Chotanagpur, Patna and Tirhut Divisions of Bengal Presidency on 31.3.1912.

1.1 Adapted by the Government of India (Adaptation of Indian Laws) Order, 1937.

1.2 Adapted by the Adaptation of Laws Order, 1950.

Bengal Act :

1. The Land Registration Act, 1876-Bengal Act 7 of 1876 as in force in Bhagalpur, Chotanagpur, Patna and Tirhut Divisions of Bengal Presidency on 31.3.1912.
   - 1.1 Amended by Bihar and Orissa Act 3 of 1916.
   - 1.2 Adapted by the Government of India (Adaptation of India Laws) Order, 1937.
   - 1.3 Adapted by the Adaptation of Laws Order, 1950.
   - 1.4 Amended by Bihar Act 1 of 1951.
   - 1.5 Amended by Bihar Act 35 of 1953.

ATTACHMENT OF LAND

BIHAR AREA

The following Bengal Regulation and the British Act which were in force in Bengal Presidency at the time of separation of Bihar and Orissa from Bengal on April 1, 1912, continued to be in force in the newly created province of Bihar and Orissa, by virtue of Section 3 of the Bengal, Bihar and Orissa and Assam Laws Act, 1912 (Central Act 7 of 1912).

Bengal Regulation :

1. The Bengal Attached Estates Management Regulations, 1827-Bengal Regulations 5 of 1827 as in force in Bhagalpur, Chotanagpur, Patna and Tirhut Divisions of Bengal Presidency on 31.3.1912.

British Act

1. The Unlawful attachment Act, 1331-5 Edw. 3, C.9 as in force in Bhagalpur, Chotanagpur, Patna and Tirhut Divisions of Bengal Presidency on 31.3.1912.
   - 1.1 Repealed by Central Act 57 of 1960.
2. The Non-condemnation without due process Act, 1954-28 Edw. 3, C.3 as in force in Bhagalpur, Chotanagpur, Patna and Tirhut Divisions of Bengal Presidency on 31.3.1912.
   - 2.1 Repealed by Central Act 57 of 1960.

Central Act

1. The Small Cause Courts (Attachment of Immovable Property) Act, 1926-Central Act 1 of 1926.
   1.1 Repealed by Central Act 1 of 1938.

CESSES

BIHAR AREA

The following Bengal Act which was in force in Bengal Presidency at the time of separation of Bihar and Orissa from Bengal on April, 1, 1912, continued to be in force in the newly created province of Bihar and Orissa, by virtue of Section 3 of the Bengal, Bihar and Orissa and Assam Laws Act, 1912 (Central Act 7 of 1912).

Bengal Act :

1. The Cess Act, 1880-Bengal Act 9 of 1880 as in force in Bhagalpur, Chotanagpur, Patna and Tirhut Divisions of Bengal Presidency on 31.3.1912.
   1.1 Repealed in part and amended by Bihar and Orissa Act 1 of 1916.
   1.2 Amended by Bihar and Orissa Act 7 of 1934.
   1.3 Amended by Bihar Act 2 of 1936.
   1.4 Adapted by the Government of India (Adaptation of Indian Laws) Order, 1937.
   1.5 Repealed in part and amended by Bihar Act 2 of 1939.
   1.6 Amended by Bihar Act 3 of 1942.
      1.6.1 Repealed by Bihar Act 24 of 1944
   1.7 Amended by Bihar Act 11 of 1944
      1.7.1 Repealed by Bihar Act 24 of 1947
   1.8 Amended by Bihar Act 9 of 1947
   1.9 Amended by Bihar Act 21 of 1947
   1.10 Amended by Bihar Act 24 of 1948
   1.11 Adapted by the Indian Independence (Adaptation of Bengal and Punjab Acts) Order, 1948.
   1.12 Adapted by the Adaptation of Laws Order, 1950.
   1.13 Amended by Bihar Act 37 of 1951
   1.14 Repealed in part and amended by Bihar Act 9 of 1952.

1.15 Amended by Bihar Act 17 of 1954.
1.16 Amended by Bihar Ordinance 5 of 1956
 1.16.1 Repealed by Bihar Act 4 of 1957.
1.17 Amended by Bihar Act 4 of 1957.

Bihar Act

1. The Bihar Refund of Cess Act, 1940-Bihar Act 7 of 1940
 1.1 Amended by Bihar Act 3 of 1941
 1.2 Amended by Bihar Act 2 of 1943

Central Act

1. The Agricultural Produce Cess Act, 1940-Central Act 27 of 1940.
 1.1 Adapted by the Indian Independence (Adaptation of Central Acts and Ordinances) Order, 1948
 1.2. Amended by Central Act 62 of 1956

MERGED STATE AREA

Bengal Act

1. The Cess Act, 1880—Bengal Act 9 of 1880 as in force in Bihar area of Bihar State.
 1.1 Application extended to the merged states of Kharsawan and Seraikela by Bihar Act 19 of 1961.

AGRICULTURAL INCOME-TAX

BIHAR AREA

Bihar Acts

1. The Bihar Agricultural Income Tax Act, 1938—Bihar Act 7 of 1938.
 1.1 Amended by Bihar Act 5 of 1939
 1.2 Amended by Bihar Act 9 of 1939
 1.3 Amended by Bihar Act 1 of 1940
 1.4 Amended by Bihar Act 1 of 1942
 1.5 Amended by Bihar Act 4 of 1944
 1.6 Repealed by Bihar Act 32 of 1948
2. The Bihar Agricultural Income-Tax Act, 1948-Bihar Act 32 of 1948.

2.1 Amended by Bihar Act 9 of 1949
2.2 Amended by Bihar Act 21 of 1949
2.3 Adapted by the Adaptation of Laws Order, 1950
2.4 Amended by Bihar Act 17 of 1950
2.5 Amended by Bihar Act 7 of 1951
2.6 Amended by Bihar Act 9 of 1953
2.7 Amended by Bihar Act 11 of 1954
2.8 Amended by Bihar Act 12 of 1959

MERGED STATES AREA

Bihar Act

1. The Bihar Agricultural Income-Tax Act, 1948—Bihar Act 32 of 1948 as in force in Bihar area of Bihar State.
   1.1 Application extended to the merged states of Kharsawan and Seraikela by Bihar Act 23 of 1949.
   1.2 Adapted by the Adaptation of Laws Order, 1950
   1.3 Amended by Bihar Act 17 of 1950
   1.4 Amended by Bihar Act 7 of 1951
   1.5 Amended by Bihar Act 9 of 1953
   1.6 Amended by Bihar Act 11 of 1954
   1.7 Amended by Bihar Act 12 of 1959

RIGHTS IN LAND

Bihar Area

The following Bengal Regulations, Bengal Acts, Central Acts and the British Acts which were in force in Bengal Presidency at the time of separation of Bihar and Orissa from Bengal on April, 1, 1912, continued to be in force in the newly created province of Bihar and Orissa, by virtue of Section 3 of the Bengal, Bihar and Orissa and Assam Laws Act, 1912 (Central Act 7 of 1912).

Bengal Regulations

1. The Bengal Permanent Settlement Regulation, 1793—Bengal Regulation 1 of 1793 as in force in Bhagalpur, Chotanagpur, Patna and Tirhut Divisions of Bengal Presidency on 31.3.1912
   1.1 Adapted by the Government of India (Adaptation of

Indian Laws) Order, 1937.

1.2 Adapted by the Adaptation of Laws Order, 1950

2. The Bengal Decennial Settlement Regulation, 1793-Bengal Regulation 8 of 1793 as in force in Bhagalpur, Chotanagpur, Patna and Tirhut Divisions of Bengal Presidency on 31.3.1912.

2.1 Adapted by the Government of India (Adaptation of Indian Laws) Order, 1937

2.2 Adapted by the Indian Independence (Adaptation of Bengal and Punjab Acts) Order, 1948.

2.3. Adapted by the Adaptation of Laws Order, 1950

3. The Bengal Revenue-free Lands (Non-Badshahi Grants) Regulation, 1793-Bengal Regulation 19 of 1793 as in force in Bhagalpur, Chotanagpur, Patna and Tirhut Divisions of Bengal Presidency on 31.3.1912.

3.1 Adapted by the Government of India (Adaptation of Indian Laws) Order, 1937

3.2 Adapted by the Indian Independence (Adaptation of Bengal and Punjab Acts) Order, 1948.

3.3 Adapted by the Adaptation of Laws Order, 1950

4. The Bengal Revenue-free Lands (Badshahi Grants) Regulation, 1893-Bengal Regulation 37 of 1793 as in force in Bhagalpur, Chotanagpur, Patna and Tirhut Divisions of Bengal Presidency on 31.3.1912.

4.1 Adapted by the Government of India (Adaptation of Indian Laws) Order, 1937

4.2 Adapted by the Adaptation of Laws Order, 1950

5. The Bengal Ghatwali Lands Regulation, 1814—Bengal Regulation 29 of 1814 as in force in Barabhum Pargana in the district of Manbhum and the Santhal Parganas in the Bengal Presidency on 31.3.1912.

5.1 Adapted by the Government of India (Adaptation of Indian Laws) Order, 1937.

5.2 Adapted by the Adaptation of Laws Order, 1950

6. The Bengal Patni Talukas Regulation, 1819-Bengal Regulation 8 of 1819 as in force in Bhagalpur, Chotanagpur, Patna and Tirhut Divisions of Bengal Presidency on 31.3.1912

6.1 Adapted by the Government of India (Adaptation of Indian Laws) Order, 1937

6.2 Repealed in part and amended by Central Act 15 of 1940

6.3 Adapted by the Adaptation of Laws Order, 1950

7. The Bengal Patni Talukas Regulation, 1820—Bengal Regulations 1 of 1820 as in force in Bhagalpur, Chotanagpur, Patna and Tirhut Divisions of Bengal Presidency on 31.3.1912

8. The Bengal Land Revenue Settlement (Resumed Kanungos and Revenue-free Lands) Regulation, 1825-Bengal Regulation 13 of 1825 as in force in Bhagalpur, Chotanagpur, Patna and Tirhut Divisions of Bengal Presidency on 31.3.1912.

8.1 Adapted by the Government of India (Adaptation of Indian Laws) Order, 1937

8.2 Adapted by the Indian Independence (Adaptation of Bengal and Punjab Acts), 1948

8.3 Adapted by the Adaptation of Laws Order, 1950

9. The Bengal Revenue-free Lands Regulation, 1825-Bengal Regulation 14 of 1825 as in force in Bhgalpur, Chotanagpur, Patna and Tirhut Divisions of Bengal Presidency on 31.3.1912

9.1 Adapted by the Government of India (Adaptation of Indian Laws) Order, 1947

9.2 Adapted by the Indian Independence (Adaptation of Bengal and Punjab Acts) Order, 1948

9.3 Adapted by the Adaptation of Laws Order, 1950

10. The Bengal Land Revenue Assessment (Resumed Lands) Regulation, 1828—Bengal Regulation 3 of 1828 as in force in Bhagalpur, Chotanagpur, Patna and Tirhut Divisions of Bengal Presidency on 31.3.1912

10.1 Adapted by the Government of India (Adaptation of Indian Laws) Order, 1937

10.2 Adapted by the Adaptation of Laws Order, 1950

Bengal Acts

1. The Estates Partition Act, 1897—Benal Act 5 of 1897 as in force in Bhagalpur, Chotanagpur, Patna and Tirhut Divisions of Bengal Presidency on 31.3.1912.
   - 1.1 Amended by Bihar and Orissa Act 3 of 1916
   - 1.2 Adapted by the Government of India (Adaptation of Indian Laws) Order, 1937
   - 1.3 Adapted by the Adaptation of Laws Order, 1950
2. The Bengal Settled Estates Act, 1905-Bengal Act 3 of 1904 as in force in Bhagalpur, Chotanagpur, Patna and Tirhut Divisions of Bengal Presidency on 31.3.1912.
   - 2.1 Repealed in part by Central Act 38 of 1920.
   - 2.2 Adapted by the Government of India (Adaptation of India Laws) Order, 1937.
   - 2.3 Adapted by the Adaptation of Laws Order, 1950

Central Acts

1. The Property in Land Act, 1837—Central Act 4 of 1837 as in force in Bhagalpur, Chotanagpur, Patna and Tirhut Divisions of Bengal Presidency on 31.3.1912
   - 1.1 Repealed by the Adaptation of Laws Order, 1950
   - 1.2 The Landlord's Public Charges and Duties Act, 1855-Central Act 2 of 1853 as in force in Bhagalpur, Chotanagpur, Patna and Tirhut Divisions of Bengal Presidency on 31.3.1912.
   - 2.1 Repealed by the Adaptation of Laws Order, 1950.
3. The Bengal Ghatwali Lands Act, 1859—Central Act 5 of 1859 as in force in Bhagalpur, Chotanagpur, Patna and Tirhut Divisions of Bengal Presidency on 31.3.1912.
   - 3.1 Adapted by the Government of India (Adaptation of Indian Laws) Order, 1937.

British Act

1. The Grantees of Reversions Act, 1540—32 Hen. 8, C. 34 as in force in Bhagalpur, Chotanagpur, Patna and Tirhut Divisions of Bengal Presidency on 31.3.1912.

MERGED STATES AREA

Central Act

1. The Property in Land Act, 1837—Central Act 4 of 1837 as in force in Bihar.
   1.1 Application extended to the merged states of Kharsawan and Seraikela by Bihar Act 23 of 1949

ABOLITION OF INTERMEDIARY RIGHTS

BIHAR STATE

Bihar Act

1. The Bihar Abolition of Zamindari Act, 1948—Bihar Act 18 of 1949.
   1.1 Repealed by Bihar Act 9 of 1950.
2. The Bihar State Management of Estate and Tenures Act, 1949—Bihar Act 21 of 1949.
   2.1 Adapted by the Adaptation of Laws Order, 1950
   2.2 Declared *ultra vires* by the Patna High Court
3. The Barahiya Tal Lands (Declaration of Possession) Act, 1950—Bihar Act 26 of 1950.
   3.1 Declared *ultra vires* by the Patna High Court.
4. The Bihar Land Reforms Act, 1950—Bihar Act 30 of 1950.
   4.1 Amended by Bihar Ordinance 3 of 1954.
      4.1.1 Repealed by Bihar Act 28 of 1954.
   4.2 Amended by Bihar Act 20 of 1954.
   4.3 Amended by Bihar Act 28 of 1954.
   4.4 Amended by Bihar Act 16 of 1959.
   4.5 Amended by Bihar Act 2 of 1961.
5. The Bihar Continuance of Certificate Proceedings and Indemnity (State Management of Estates and Tenures) Act, 1950—Bihar Act 32 of 1950.
6. The Sathi Lands (Restoration) Act, 1950—Bihar Act 34 of 1950.
7. The Bihar Recovery of Arrears of Rents of out going Proprietors and Tenure-holders (Vested Estates and Tenures) Act, 1953—Bihar Act 3 of 1953.
8. The Bihar Disqualified Owners' (Management of Property) Act, 1955—Bihar Act 2 of 1955.

Bihar Ordinance

1. The Bihar Continuance of Certificate Proceedings and Indemnity (State Management of Estates and Tenures) Ordinance, 1950—Bihar Ordinance 3 of 1950
   1.1 Repealed by Bihar Act 32 of 1950
2. The Bihar Recovery of Arrears of Rents of Out going Proprietors and Tenure-holders (Vested Estates and Tenures) Ordinance, 1952—Bihar Ordinance 6 of 1952
   2.1 Repealed by Bihar Act 3 of 1953

ENDOWMENT AND TRUSTS

BIHAR AREA

The following Bengal Regulation, Central Act and the British Acts which were in force in Bengal Presidency at the time of separation of Bihar and Orissa from Bengal on April 1, 1912, continued to be in force in the newly created province of Bihar and Orissa, by virtue of Section 3 of the Bengal, Bihar and Orissa and Assam Laws Act, 1912 (Central Act 7 of 1912).

Bengal Regulation

The Bengal Charitable Endowment, Public buildings and Estates Regulation, 1810-Bengal Regulation 19 of 1810 as in force in Bhagalpur, Chotanagpur, Patna and Tirhut Divisions of Bengal Presidency on 31.3.1912.

1.1 Amended by Bihar and Orissa Act 3 of 1916.
1.2 Adapted by the Government of India (Adaptation of India Laws) Order, 1937.
1.3 Amended by Bihar Act 8 of 1948.
1.4 Adapted by the Adaptation of Laws Order, 1950.
1.5 Amended by Bihar Act I of 1951.

Central Act

1. The Religious Endowments Act, 1863—Central Act 20 of 1863 as in force in Bhagalpur, Chotanagpur, Patna and Tirhut Divisions of Bengal Presidency on 31.3.1912.
   1.1 Amended by Bihar Act 8 of 1948.

1.2 Application to religious trusts in Bihar barred by Bihar Act 1 of 1951.

British Acts

1. The Prevention of Frauds and Perjuries Act, 1677-29 Chas. 2, c. 3 as in force in Bhagalpur, Chotanagpur, Patna and Tirhut Divisions of Bengal Presidency on 31.3.1912.
   1.1 Repealed by Central Act 57 of 1960.
2. The Trusts Act, 1893-56 & 57 Vict., c. 53 as in force in Bhagalpur, Chotanagpur, Patna and Tirhut Divisions of Bengal Presidency on 31.3.1912.

MERGED STATES AREA

Central Act

1. The Religious Endowments Act, 1863—Central Act 20 of 1863 as in force in Bihar area of Bihar State.
   1.1 Application extended to the merged states of Kharsawan and Seraikela by Bihar Act 23 of 1949.
   1.2 Application to religious trusts in Bihar barred by Bihar Act 1 of 1951.

BIHAR STATE

Central Act

1. The Wakf Act, 1954—Central Act 29 of 1954.

LAND GRANTS

Bihar Area

The following British Act which was in force in Bengal Presidency at the time of separation of Bihar and Orissa from Bengal on April 1, 1912, continued to be in force in the newly created province of Bihar and Orissa, by virtue of Section 3 of the Bengal, Bihar and Orissa and Assam Laws Act, 1912 (Central Act 7 of 1912)

British Act

1. The Act of Settlement, 1701-12 & W.3, C.2. as in force in

Bhagalpur, Chotanagpur, Patna and Tirhut Divisions of Bengal Presidency on 31.3.1912.

1.1 Repealed by Central Act 57 of 1960.

HINDU WOMEN'S RIGHT TO PROPERTY IN AGRICULTURAL LAND

BIHAR AREA

Central Act

1. The Hindu Women's Right to Property Act, 1937—Central Act 18 of 1937 as amended by Central Act 11 of 1938.

   1.1 Application extended to agricultural lands by Bihar Act 6 of 1942.

      1.1.1 Re-enacted by Bihar Act 21 of 1948

   1.2 Adapted by the Adaptation of Laws Order, 1950

MERGED STATES AREA

Central Act

1. The Hindu's Women's Right to Property Act, 1937—Central Act 18 of 1937 as in force in Bihar area of Bihar State.

   1.1 Application extended to the merged states of Kharsawan and Seraikela by Bihar Act 23 of 1949.

   1.2 Adapted by the Adaptation of Laws Order, 1950.

SALE OF LAND

Bihar Area

The following Bengal Regulation and the Central Acts which were in force in Bengal Presidency at the time of separation of Bihar and Orissa from Bengal on April 1, 1912, continued to be in force in the newly created province of Bihar and Orissa, by virtue of Section 3 of the Bengal, Bihar and Orissa and Assam Laws Act, 1912 (Central Act 7 of 1912).

Bengal Regulation

1. The Bengal Government Indemnity Regulation, 1822—Bengal Regulation 11 of 1822 as in force in Bhagalpur, Chotanagpur, Patna and Tirhut Divisions of Bengal Presidency on 31.3.1912.
   1.1 Adapted by the Government of India (Adaptation of Indian Laws) Order, 1937.
   1.2 Adapted by the Adaptation of Laws Order, 1950.

Central Acts

1. The Bengal Land Revenue Sales Act, 1841—Central Act 12 of 1841 as in force in Bhagalpur, Chotanagpur, Patna and Tirhut Divisions of Bengal Presidency on 31.3.1912.
2. The Forfeited Deposits Act, 1850—Central Act 25 of 1850 as in force in Bhagalpur, Chotanagpur, Patna and Tirhut Divisions of Bengal Presidency on 31.3.1912.
3. The Rent Recovery Act, 1853—Central Act 6 of 1853 as in force in Bhagalpur, Chotanagpur, Patna and Tirhut Divisions of Bengal Presidency on 31.3.1912.
   3.1 Adapted by the Government of India (Adaptation of Indian Laws) Order, 1937.
   3.2 Adapted by the Adaptation of Laws Order, 1950.
4. The Bengal Land-revenue Sales Act, 1859—Central Act 11 of 1859 as in force in Bhagalpur, Chotanagpur, Patna and Tirhut Divisions of Bengal Presidency on 31.3.1912.
   4.1 Adapted by the Government of India (Adaptation of Indian Laws) Order, 1937.
   4.2 Adapted by the Adaptation of Laws Order, 1950.

TRANSFER OF LAND

Bihar Area

The following Central Act which was in force in Bengal Presidency at the time of separation of Bihar and Orissa from Bengal on Apirl 1, 1912, continued to be in force in the newly created province of Bihar and Orissa, by virtue of section 3 of the Bengal, Bihar and Orissa and Assam Laws Act, 1912 (Central Act 7 of 1912).

Central Act

1. The Conveyance of Land Act, 1854—Central Act 31 of 1854 as in force in Bhagalpur, Chotanagpur, Patna and Tirhut Divisions of Bengal Presidency on 31.3.1912.
   1.1 Repealed by Central Act 48 of 1952.

PARTITION OF LAND

Bihar Area

The following Bengal Regulation and the Bengal Act which were in force in Bengal Presidency at the time of separation of Bihar and Orissa from Bengal on April 1, 1912, continued to be in force in the newly created province of Bihar and Orissa, by virtue of Section 3 of the Bengal, Bihar and Orissa and Assam Laws Act, 1912 (Central Act 7 of 1912).

Bengal Regulations

1. The Bengal Inheritance Regulation 1793—Bengal Regulation 11 of 1793 as in force in Bhagalpur, Chotanagpur, Patna and Tirhut Divisions of Bengal Presidency on 31.3.1912.
   1.1 Adapted by the Government of India (Adaptation of Indian Laws) Order, 1937.
2. The Bengal Inheritance Regulation, 1800—Bengal Regulation 10 of 1800 as in force in Bhagalpur, Chotanagpur, Patna and Tirhut Divisions of Bengal Presidency on 31.3.1912.

Bengal Act

1. The Estates Partition Act, 1897—Bengal Act 5 of 1897 as in force in Bhagalpur, Chotanagpur, Patna and Tirhut Divisions of Bengal Presidency on 31.3.1912.
   1.1 Amended by Bihar and Orissa Act 3 of 1916.
   1.2 Adapted by the Government of India (Adaptation of India Laws) Order, 1927.
   1.3 Adapted by the Adaptation of Laws Order, 1950.

COURT OF WARDS

Bihar Area

The following Bengal Act which was in force in Bengal Presidency at the time of separation of Bihar and Orissa from Bengal on April 1, 1912, continued to be in force in the newly created province of Bihar and Orissa, by virtue of Section 3 of the Bengal, Bihar and Orissa and Assam Laws Act, 1912 (Central Act 7 of 1912)

Bengal Act

1. The Court of Wards Act, 1879—Bengal Act 9 of 1879 as in force in Bhagalpur, Chotanagpur, Patna and Tirhut Divisions of Bengal Presidency on 31.3.1912.
   1.1 Reported in part and amended by Bihar and Orissa Act 3 of 1916.
   1.2 Amended by Bihar Act 1 of 1936.
   1.3 Adapted by the Government of India (Adaptation of Indian Laws) Order, 1937.
   1.4 Amended by Bihar Act 4 of 1940.
   1.5 Adapted by the Indian Independence (Adaptation of Bengal and Punjab Acts) Order, 1948.
   1.6 Adapted by the Adaptation of Laws Order, 1950

LAND DISPUTES

Bihar Area

The following Bengal Regulation and the Central Acts which were in force in Bengal Presidency at the time of separation of Bihar and Orissa from Bengal on April 1, 1912, continued to be in force in the newly created province of Bihar and Orissa, by virtue of Section 3 of the Bengal, Bihar and Orissa and Assam Laws Act, 1912 (Central Act 7 of 1912).

Bengal Regulation

1. The Bengal Alluvium and Diluvion Regulation, 1825—Bengal Regulation 11 of 1825 as in force in Bhagalpur, Chotanagpur, Patna and Tirhut Divisions of Bengal Presidency on 31.3.1912.
   - 1.1 Adapted by the Government of Indian (Adaptation of Indian Laws) Order, 1937.
   - 1.2 Adapted by the Adaptation of Laws Order, 1950.

Central Acts

1. The Bengal Alluvion and Diluvion Act, 1847—Central Act 9 of 1847 as in force in Bhagalpur, Chotanagpur, Patna and Tirhut Divisions of Bengal Presidency on 31.3.1912.
   - 1.1 Adapted by the Government of India (Adaptation of Indian Laws) Order, 1937.
   - 1.2 Amended by Bihar Act 4 of 1942.
     - 1.2.1 Repealed by Bihar Act 15 of 1948.
   - 1.3. Adapted by the Indian Independence (Adaptation of Central Acts and Ordinance) Order, 1948.
   - 1.4 Amended by Bihar Act 15 of 1948.
   - 1.5 Adapted by the Adaptation of Laws Order, 1950.
2. The Bengal Alluvial Land Settlement Act, 1858—Central Act 31 of 1858 as in force in Bhagalpur, Chotanagpur, Patna and Tirhut Divisions of Bengal Presidency on 31.3.1912.

Bihar Act

1. The Bihar Basasth Disputes Settlement Act, 1947—Bihar Act 13 of 1947.
   - 1.1 Amended by Bihar Ordinance 4 of 1948.
     - 1.1.1 Repealed by Bihar Act 4 of 1949.
   - 1.2 Amended by Bihar Act 27 of 1948.
     - 1.2.1 Application extended to all the Scheduled Areas by Bihar Regulation 1 of 1951.
     - 1.2.2. Application extended to the Districts of Hazaribagh, Manbhum, Palamau (excluding Lateha sub-division), and Godda and

Deoghar sub-divisions of the Santhal Parganas, by Bihar Act 24 of 1951.

1.3 Amended by Bihar Act 4 of 1949.

1.4 Adapted by the Adaptation of 1950 Laws Order, 1950.

1.5 Amended by Bihar Act 22 of 1950.

1.6 Amended by Bihar Act 29 of 1953.

LAND ENCROACHMENT

BIHAR STATE

Bihar Acts

1. The Bihar Land Encroachment Act, 1950—Bihar Act 31 of 1950.
   1.1 Amended by Bihar Act 29 of 1951.
   1.2 Amended by Bihar Act 25 of 1952.
   1.3 Repealed by Bihar Act 15 of 1956.
2. The Bihar Public Land Encroachment Act, 1956—Bihar Act 15 of 1956.
   2.1 Amended by Bihar Act 19 of 1960.

EASEMENTS

MERGED STATED AREA

Central Act

1. The Indian Easement Act, 1882—Central Act 5 of 1882.
   1.1 Application extended partially to the merged states of Kharsawan and Seraikela by Bihar Act 23 of 1949.
   1.2 Amended by Central Act 36 of 1963.

LAND ACQUISITION

Bihar Area

The following Central Acts which were in force in Bengal Presidency at the time of separation of Bihar and Orissa from Bengal on April 1, 1912, continued to be in force in the newly created province of Bihar and Orissa, by virtue of Section 3 of the

Bengal, Bihar and Orissa and Assam Laws Act 1912 (Central Act 7 of 1912).

Central Acts

1. The Land Acquisition (Mines) Act, 1885—Central Act 18 of 1885 as in force in Bhagalpur, Chotanagpur, Patna and Tirhut Divisions of Bengal Presidency on 31.3.1912
   - 1.1 Repealed in part and amended by Central Act 38 of 1920.
   - 1.2 Repealed in part by Central Act 20 of 1937.
   - 1.3 Adapted by the Indian Independence (Adaptation of Central Acts and Ordinance) Order, 1948.
   - 1.4 Adapted by the Adaptation of Laws Order, 1950.
   - 1.5 Adapted by the Adaptation of Laws (No. 2) Order, 1956.
2. The Land Acquisition Act, 1894—Central Act 1 of 1894 as in force in Bhagalpur, Chotanagpur, Patna and Tirhut Divisions of Bengal Presidency on 31.3.1912.
   - 2.1 Repealed in part by Central Act 4 of 1914.
   - 2.2 Repealed in part and amended by Central Act 10 of 1914.
   - 2.3 Amended by Central Act 17 of 1919.
   - 2.4 Repealed in part and amended by Central Act 38 of 1920.
   - 2.5 Amended by Central Act 10 of 1921.
   - 2.7 Repealed in part and amended by Central Act 38 of 1923.
   - 2.8 Amended by Central Act 10 of 1921.
   - 2.9 Amended by Bihar and Orissa Act 4 of 1934.
   - 2.10 Adapted by the Government of India (Adaptation of Indian Laws) Order, 1937.
   - 2.11 Amended by Central Act 1 of 1938.
   - 2.12 Amended by Bihar Act 8 of 1946.
   - 2.13 Adapted by the Indian Independence (Adaptation of Central Acts and Ordinance) Order, 1948.
   - 2.14 Amended by Bihar Act 19 of 1948.
   - 2.15 Amended by Bihar Act 23 of 1948.
   - 2.16 Adapted by the Adaptation of Laws Order, 1950

2.17 Amended by Bihar Act 7 of 1951.
    2.17.1 Repealed by Bihar Act 11 of 1961.
2.18 Amended by Bihar Act 17 of 1951.
    2.18.1 Repealed by Bihar Act 11 of 1961.
2.19 Amended by Bihar Act 35 of 1951.
2.20 Amended by Central Act 22 of 1954.
2.21 Adapted by the Adaptation of Laws (No. 2) Order, 1956.
2.22 Amended by Bihar Act 21 of 1956.
    2.22.1 Repealed by Bihar Act 11 of 1961.
2.23 Amended by the Bihar Act 34 of 1956.
    2.23.1 Repealed by Bihar Act 11 of 1961.
2.24 Amended by Bihar Act 11 of 1961.
2.25 Amended by Central Ordinance 3 of 1962.
2.26 Amended by Central Act 31 of 1962.

Central Act

1. The Requisitioned Land (Continuance of Powers) Act, 1947—Central Act 17 of 1947.
    1.1 Amended by Central Act 9 of 1951.
    1.2 Adapted by the Indian Independence (Adaptation of Central Acts and Ordinances) Order, 1948.
    1.3 Repealed by Central Act 30 of 1952.

Central Ordinance

1. The Requisitioned Land (Continuance of Powers) Ordinance, 1946—Central Ordinance 19 of 1946.
    1.1 Repealed by Central Act 17 of 1947.

MERGED STATES AREA

Central Acts

1. The Land Acquisition (Mines) Act, 1885—Central Act 18 of 1885 as in force in Bihar area of Bihar State.
    1.1 Application extended to the merged states of Kharsawan and Seraikela by Bihar Act 23 of 1949.
    1.2 Application extended to the merged state area by Central Act 59 of 1949

1.3 Adapted by the Adaptation of Laws Order, 1950.
1.4 Adapted by the Adaptation of Laws (No. 2) Order, 1956

2. The Land Acquisition Act, 1894—Central Act 1 of 1894 as in force in Bihar area of Bihar State.
   2.1 Application extended to the merged states of Kharsawan and Seraikela by Bihar Act 23 of 1949.
   2.2 Application extended to the merged states area by Central Act 59 of 1949.
   2.3 Adapted by the Adaptation of Laws Order, 1950.
   2.4 Repealed by Bihar Act 11 of 1961.
   2.5 Amended by Bihar Act 17 of 1951.
      2.5.1 Repealed by Bihar Act 11 of 1961.
   2.6 Amended by Bihar Act 35 of 1951.
      2.6.1 Repealed by Bihar Act 11 of 1961.
   2.7 Amended by Central Act 22 of 1954.
   2.8 Adapted by the Adaptation of Laws (No. 2) Order, 1956.
   2.9 Amended by Bihar Act 21 of 1961.
   2.10 Amended by Bihar Act 34 of 1956.
      2.10.1 Repealed by Bihar Act 11 of 1961.
   2.11 Amended by Bihar Act 11 of 1961.
   2.12 Amended by Central Ordinance 3 of 1961.
      2.12.1 Repealed by Central Act 31 of 1962.
   2.13 Amended by Central Act 31 of 1962.

BIHAR STATE

Bihar Acts

1. The Bihar Displaced Persons Rehabilitation (Acquisition of Land) Act, 1950—Bihar Act 38 of 1950.

Central Acts

1. The Requisitioned Land (Apportionment of Compensation) Act, 1949—Central Act 51 of 1949.
   1.1 Application extended to the districts of Hazaribagh and Manbhum, Sadar sub-division of the Palamau district, Dhalbhum sub-division of the Singhbum

district, and Godda and Deoghar sub-divisions of the Santhal Parganas District, by the Absorbed Areas (Laws) Act, 1954 (Central Act 20 of 1954.

2. The State Acquisition of Land for Union purposes (Validation) Act, 1954—Central Act 23 of 1954.
3. The Wakf Act, 1954—Central Act 29 of 1954.
4. The Petroleum Pipelines (Acquisition of Right of User in Land) Act, 1962—Central Act 56 of 1962.

LAND RESTORATION

BIHAR AREA

Bihar Acts

1. The Bihar Restoration of Bakasht Lands and Reduction of Arrears of Rent Act, 1938—Bihar Act 9 of 1938.
   1.1 Adapted by the Adaptation of Laws Order, 1950.
2. The Bihar Restoration of Agricultural Land. (Temporary Provisions) Act, 1945—Bihar Act 4 of 1945.
3. The Ranchi District Tana Bhagat Raiyat's Agricultural Lands Restoration Act, 1947—Bihar Act 2 of 1948.
   3.1 Adapted by the Adaptation of Laws Order, 1950.
   3.2 Amended by Bihar Act 26 of 1951.
   3.3 Amended by Bihar Act 18 of 1956.
   3.4 Amended by Bihar Act 3 of 1960.
   3.5 Amended by Bihar Act 26 of 1962.
4. The Barahiya Tal Lands (Declaration of Possession) Act, 1950—Bihar Act 26 of 1950.
5. The Sathi Lands (Restoration) Act, 1950—Bihar Act 34 of 1950.
6. The Kosi Area (Restoration of Lands of Raiyats) Act, 1951—Bihar Act 30 of 1951.

CEILING ON LAND HOLDINGS

BIHAR STATE

Bihar State

1. The Bihar Land Reforms (Fixation of Ceiling area and

Acquisition of Surplus Land) Act, 1961—Bihar Act 12 of 1962.

1.1 Amended by Bihar Act 18 of 1962.

PREVENTION OF FRAGMENTATION, AND CONSOLIDATION OF HOLDINGS

BIHAR STATE

Bihar Act

1. The Bihar Consolidation of Holdings and Prevention of Fragmentation Act, 1956—Bihar Act 22 of 1956

TENANCY

BIHAR STATE

The following Bengal Regulations, Bengal Acts and the Central Acts which were in force in Bengal Presidency at the time of separation of Bihar and Orissa from Bengal on April 1, 1912, continued to be in force in the newly created province of Bihar and Orissa, by virtue of Section 3 of the Bengal, Bihar and Orissa and Assam Laws Act, 1912 (Central Act 7 of 1912).

Bengal Regulation

1. The Bengal Ghatwali Lands Regulation, 1814—Bengal Regulation 29 of 1814 as in force in Santhal and Barabhum Parganas in Chotanagpur Division of Bengal Presidency on 31.3.1912.
   1.1 Adapted by the Government of India (Adaptation of Indian Laws) Order, 1936.
   1.2 Adapted by the Adaptation of Laws Order, 1950.

Bengal Acts

1. The Chota Nagpur Tenures Act, 1869—Bengal Act 2 of 1896.
   1.1 Repealed in part by Central Act 7 of 1870.
   1.2 Adapted by the Government of India (Adaptation of Indian Laws) Order, 1937.
   1.3 Adapted by the Adaptation of Laws Order, 1950.

2. The Chotanagpur Tenancy Act, 1908—Bengal Act 6 of 1908.
   - 2.1 Amended by Bihar and Orissa Act 4 of 1914.
   - 2.2 Amended by Bihar and Orissa Act 6 of 1920.
     - 2.2.1 Amended by Bihar and Orissa Act 7 of 1920.
   - 2.3 Amended by Central and Orissa Act 5 of 1923.
   - 2.4 Amended by Bihar and Orissa Act 5 of 1923.
   - 2.5 Amended by Bihar and Orissa Act 3 of 1929.
   - 2.6 Adapted by the Government of India (Adaptation of Indian Laws) Order, 1937.
   - 2.7 Amended by Bihar Act 2 of 1938.
   - 2.8 Amended by Bihar Act 3 of 1940.
   - 2.9 Amended by Bihar Act 14 of 1944.
   - 2.10 Amended by Bihar Act 15 of 1946.
   - 2.11 Repealed in part and amended by Bihar Act 20 of 1947.
   - 2.12 Repealed in part by Bihar Act 21 of 1947.
   - 2.13 Amended by Bihar Act 25 of 1947.
   - 2.14 Amended by Bihar Act 11 of 1950.
     - 2.14.1 Application extended to all the Scheduled Areas by Bihar Regulation 1 of 1951.
     - 2.14.2 Application extended to the Districts of Hazaribagh, Manbhum, Palamau (excluding Latehar sub-division), and Dhalbhum sub-division of the Singhbhum district, by Bihar Act 24 of 1951.
   - 2.15 Adapted by the Adaptation of Laws Order, 1950.
   - 2.16 Amended by Bihar Act 12 of 1955.
   - 2.17 Amended by Bihar Ordinance 4 of 1955.
   - 2.18 Amended by Bihar Act 20 of 1955.
     - 2.18.1 Amended by Bihar Act 8 of 1961.
   - 2.19 Amended by Bihar Act 27 of 1959.

Central Acts

1. The Bengal Ghatwali Lands Act, 1859—Central Act 5 of 1859 as in force in Santhal Parganas in Chotanagpur Division of Bengal Presidency on 31.3.1912.
   - 1.1 Adapted by the Government of India (Adaptation of Indian Laws) Order, 1937.

1.2 Adapted by the Adaptation of Laws Order, 1950.

2. The Bengal Tenancy Act, 1885—Central Act 8 of 1885 as in force in Bhagalpur, Chotanagpur, Patna and Tirhut Divisions of Bengal Presidency on 31.3.1912.
   - 2.1 Amended by Bihar and Orissa Act 4 of 1916.
   - 2.2 Amended by Bihar and Orissa Act 3 of 1916.
   - 2.3 Amended and validated by Bihar and Orissa Act 9 of 1920.
   - 2.4 Repealed in part and amended by Central Act 38 of 1920.
   - 2.5 Amended by Bihar and Orissa Act 8 of 1934.
   - 2.6 Amended by Bihar and Orissa Act 7 of 1935.
   - 2.7 Amended by Bihar Act 8 of 1937.
   - 2.8 Adapted by the Government of India (Adaptation of Indian Laws) Order, 1937.
   - 2.9 Repealed in part and amended by Bihar Act 11 of 1938.
   - 2.10 Amended in Kosi Diara by Bihar Act 13 of 1939.
   - 2.11 Amended by Bihar Act 2 of 1940.
     - 2.11.1 Repealed by Bihar Act 20 of 1948.
   - 2.12 Amended by Bihar Act 2 of 1941.
     - 2.12.1 Repealed by Bihar Act 20 of 1948.
   - 2.13 Amended by Bihar Act 2 of 1944.
     - 2.13.1 Repealed by Bihar Act 20 of 1948.
   - 2.14 Amended by Bihar Act 13 of 1944.
   - 2.15 Amended by Bihar Act 13 of 1946.
   - 2.16 Amended by Bihar Act 14 of 1946.
   - 2.17 Amended by Bihar Act 23 of 1947.
   - 2.18 Amended by Bihar Act 20 of 1948.
   - 2.19 Adapted by the Adaptation of Laws Order 1950.
   - 2.20 Amended by Bihar Act 41 of 1950.
   - 2.21 Amended by Bihar Ordinance 3 of 1955.
     - 2.21.1 Repealed by Bihar Act 19 of 1955.
   - 2.22 Amended by Bihar Ordinance 6 of 1955.
     - 2.22.1 Repealed by Bihar Act of 19 of 1955.
   - 2.23 Amended by Bihar Act 19 of 1955.
     - 2.23.1 Amended by Bihar Act 8 of 1961.
     - 2.23.2 Amended by Bihar Act 5 of 1963.

- 2.24 Amended by Bihar Act 24 of 1955.
- 2.25 Amended by Bihar Act 18 of 1958.
- 2.26 Amended by Bihar Act 14 of 1961.
- 2.27 Amended by Bihar Act 1 of 1963.

Bihar and Orissa Acts

1. The Champaran Agrarian Act, 1918—Bihar and Orissa Act 1 of 1918.
   - 1.1 Amended by Bihar Act 10 of 1938.
   - 1.2 Adapted by the Adaptation of Laws Order, 1950.
2. The Chotanagpur Tenure Holders' Rent Account Act, 1929—Bihar and Orissa Act 1 of 1929.
   - 2.1 Adapted by the Government of India (Adaptation of Indian Laws) Order, 1937.
   - 2.2 Amended by Bihar Act 14 of 1939.
   - 2.3 Adapted by the Adaptation of Laws Order, 1950.

The following Bengal Acts in force in Bihar area of Bengal Presidency were repealed before the formation of the province of Bihar and Orissa on April 1, 1912.

Bengal Acts

1. The Chotanagpur Landlord and Tenant Procedure Act, 1879—Bengal Act 1 of 1879.
   - 1.1 Repealed in part by Central Act 1 of 1903.
   - 1.2 Amended by Bengal Act 5 of 1905.
   - 1.3 Amended by Bengal Act 5 of 1905.
   - 1.4 Repealed by Bengal Act 6 of 1908.
2. The Chotanagpur Commutation Act, 1897—Bengal Act 4 of 1897.
   - 2.1 Repealed in part by Central Act 1 of 1903.
   - 2.2 Amended by Bengal Act 5 of 1903.
   - 2.3 Repealed by Bengal Act 6 of 1908.

MERGED STATES AREA

Bengal Act

1. The Chotanagpur Tenancy Act, 1908—Bengal Act 6 of 1908 as in force in Bihar area of Bihar State.

1.1 Application extended to the merged states of Kharsawan and Seraikela by Bihar Act 41 of 1951.

1.2 Amended by Bihar Ordinance 4 of 1955.

  1.2.1 Amended by Bihar Act 5 of 1963.

1.3 Amended by Bihar Act 20 of 1955.

  1.3.1 Amended by Bihar Act 8 of 1961.

1.4 Amended by Bihar Act 27 of 1959.

BIHAR STATE

Bihar Acts

1. The Santhal Parganas Tenancy (Supplementary Provisions) Act, 1949—Bihar Act, 14 of 1949.

   1.1 Adapted by the Adaptation of Laws Order, 1950.

   1.2 Amended by Bihar Act 11 of 1951.

   1.3 Amended by Bihar Ordinance 5 of 1955.

     1.3.1 Repealed by Bihar Act 21 of 1955.

   1.4 Amended by Bihar Act 21 of 1955.

     1.4.1 Amended by Bihar Act 8 of 1961.

     1.4.2 Amended by Bihar Act 5 of 1963.

2. The Bihar Rent (Commutation Proceedings) Validating Act, 1950-Bihar Act 23 of 1950.

3. The Bihar Emergency Cultivation and Irrigation (Temporary Provisions) Act, 1951—Bihar Act 3 of 1951.

   3.1 Amended by Bihar Act 21 of 1951.

   3.2 Amended by Bihar Act 21 of 1953.

   3.3 Amended by Bihar Act 3 of 1955.

4. The Bihar Emergency Cultivation and Irrigation (Temporary Provisions) Act, 1955—Bihar Act 22 of 1955.

Bihar Ordinance

1. The Bihar Emergency Cultivation and Irrigation (Temporary Provisions) Ordinance, 1950—Bihar Ordinance 5 of 1950.

   1.1 Repealed by Bihar Act 3 of 1951.

2. The Bihar Emergency Cultivation and Irrigation (Temporary Provisions) Ordinance, 1955—Bihar Ordinance 7 of 1955.

2.1 Repealed by Bihar Act 22 of 1955.

AGRICULTURAL LABOUR

BIHAR AREA

Bihar and Orissa Act

1. The Bihar and Orissa Kamiauti Agreements Act, 1920—Bihar and Orissa Act 8 of 1920.
   1.1 Adapted by the Adaptation of Laws Order, 1950.

BHOODAN AND GRAMDAN

BIHAR STATE

Bihar Act

1. The Bihar Bhoodan Yojna Act, 1954—Bihar Act 22 of 1954.
   1.1 Amended by Bihar Act 15 of 1959.

LAND IMPROVEMENT

BIHAR AREA

The following Bengal Acts and the Central Acts which were in force in Bengal Presidency at the time of separation of Bihar and Orissa from Bengal on April 1, 1912 continued to be in force in the newly created province of Bihar and Orissa, by virtue of Section 3 of the Bengal, Bihar and Orissa and Assam Laws Act, 1912 (Central Act 7 of 1912).

Bengal Act

1. The Bengal Drainage Act, 1880, Bengal Act 6 of 1880 as in force in Bhagalpur, Chotanagpur, Patna and Tirhut Divisions of Bengal Presidency on 31.3.1912.
   1.1 Amended by Bihar and Orissa Act 3 of 1916.

Central Act

1. The Land Improvement Loans Act, 1883—Central Act 19 of 1883 as in force in Bhagalpur, Chotanagpur, Patna

and Tirhut Divisions of Bengal Presidency on 31.3.1912.

The following amending act which was enacted before 31.3.1912 was affected by subsequent legislation as shown below:

1. Amending Act—Central Act 18 of 1899.
   1.1 Repealed in part by Central Act 10 of 1914.
   1.1 Repealed in part and amended by Central Act 4 of 1914.
   1.2 Adapted by the Government of India (Adaptation of Indian Laws) Order, 1937.
   1.3 Adapted by the Indian Independence (Adaptation of Central Acts and Ordinances) Order, 1948.

Bihar Act

1. The Bihar Waste Lands (Reclamation, Cultivation and Improvement) Act, 1946—Bihar Act 16 of 1946.
   1.1 Adapted by the Adaptation of Laws Order, 1950.

MERGED STATES AREA

Bihar Act

1. The Bihar Waste Lands (Reclamation, Cultivation and Improvement) Act, 1946—Bihar Act 16 of 1946 as in force in Bihar area of Bihar State.
   1.1 Application extended to the merged states of Kharsawan and Seraikela by Bihar Act 23 of 1949.
   1.2 Adapted by the Adaptation of Laws Order, 1950.

Central Act

1. The Land Improvement Loans Act, 1883—Central Act 19 of 1883 as in force in Bihar area of Bihar State.
   1.1 Application extended to the merged states of Kharsawan and Seraikela by Bihar Act 23 of 1949.

LAND UTILIZATION
BIHAR AREA

Bihar Act

1. The Bihar Restriction of Uses of Land Act, 1946—Bihar Act 8 of 1946.

1.1 Repealed by Bihar Act 23 of 1948.

BIHAR STATE

Bihar Act

1. The Bihar Restriction of Uses of Land Act, 1948—Bihar Act 23 of 1948.
   1.1 Adapted by the Adaptation of Laws Order, 1950.

WASTE LANDS

Bihar Area

The following Central Act which was in force in Bengal Presidency at the time of separation of Bihar and Orissa from Bengal on April 1, 1912, continued to be in force in the newly created province of Bihar and Orissa, by virtue of Section 3 of the Bengal, Bihar and Orissa and Assam Laws Act, 1912 (Central Act 7 of 1912).

Central Act

1. The Waste Lands (Claims) Act, 1863—Central Act 23 of 1863 as in force in Bhagalpur, Chotanagpur, Patna and Tirhut Divisions of Bengal Presidency on 31.3.1912.
   1.1 Repealed in part and amended by Central Act 4 of 1914.
   1.2 Repealed in part by Central Act 10 of 1914.
   1.3 Adapted by the Government of India (Adaptation of Indian Laws) Order, 1937.
   1.4 Repealed in part by the Indian Independence (Adaptation of Central Acts and Ordinances) Order, 1948.
   1.5 Adapted by the Adaptation of Laws (No. 2) Order, 1956.

MERGED STATES AREA

Central Act

1. The Waste Lands (Claims) Act, 1863—Central Act 23 of 1863 as in force in Bihar area of Bihar State.

1.1 Application extended to the merged states of Kharsawan and Seraikela Bihar Act 23 of 1949.
1.2 Application extended to the merged states of Kharsawan and Seraikela by Central Act 59 of 1949.
1.3 Adapted by the Adaptation of Laws (No. 2) Order, 1956.

FORESTS

Bihar Area

The following Central Act which was in force in Bengal Presidency at the time of separation of Bihar and Orissa from Bengal on April 1, 1912, continued to be in force in the newly created province of Bihar and Orissa, by virtue of Section 3 of the Bengal, Bihar and Orissa and Assam Laws Act, 1912 (Central Act 7 of 1912).

Central Act

1. The Indian Forests Act, 1878—Central Act 7 of 1912 as in force in Bhagalpur, Chotanagpur, Patna and Tirhut Divisions of Bengal Presidency on 31.3.1912.

The following amending Act which was enacted before 31.3.1912 was subsequently repealed as shown below.

1. Amending Act Central Act 5 of 1901.
   1.1 Repealed by Central Act 10 of 1914.
   1.1 Amended by Central Act 10 of 1914.
   1.2 Amended by Central Act 1 of 1918.
   1.3 Repealed by Central Act 16 of 1927.

Bihar Acts

1. The Bihar Private Forests Act, 1946—Bihar Act 3 of 1946.
   1.1 Repealed by Bihar Act 9 of 1948.
2. The Bihar Private Forests Act, 1947—Bihar Act 9 of 1948.
   2.1 Amended by Private Forests Act, 1947—Bihar Act 9 of 1948.
   2.2 Adapted by the Adaptation of Laws Order, 1950.
   2.3 Amended by Bihar Act 12 of 1950.
      2.3.1 Application extended to all the Scheduled

Areas by Bihar Regulation 1 of 1951.

2.3.2 Application extended to the districts of Hazaribagh, Manbhum, Palamau (excluding Latehar sub-division), Godda and Deoghar sub-divisions of the Santhal Parganas, and Dhalbhum sub-division of the Singhbhum districts, by Bihar Act 24 of 1951.

Central Act

1. The Indian Forests Act, 1927-Central Act 16 of 1927.
   1.1 Amended by Central Act 26 of 1930.
   1.2 Amended by Central Act 3 of 1933.
   1.3 Amended by Bihar and Orissa Act 3 of 1934.
   1.4 Amended by Bihar and Orissa Act 9 of 1945.
   1.5 Adapted by the Government of India (Adaptation of Indian Laws) Order, 1937.
   1.6 Amended by Central Act 8 of 1938.
   1.7 Repealed in part and amended by Central Act 2 of 1948.
   1.8 Adapted by the Adaptation of Laws Order, 1950.
   1.9 Adapted by the Adaptation of Laws (No. 3) Order, 1956.

MERGED STATES AREA

Bihar Act

1. The Bihar Private Forests Act, 1947—Bihar Act 9 of 1948 as in force in Bihar area of Bihar State.
   1.1 Application extended to the merged states of Kharsawan and Seraikela by Bihar Act 23 of 1949.
   1.2 Amended by Bihar Act 1 of 1950.
   1.3 Adapted by the Adaptation of Laws Order, 1950.
   1.4 Amended by Bihar Act 12 of 1950.

Central Acts

1. The Indian Forests Act, 1927—Central Act 16 of 1927 as in force in Bihar Area of Bihar State.
   1.1 Application extended to the merged states of

Kharsawan and Seraikela by Bihar Act 23 of 1949.

1.2 Application extended to the merged states area by Central Act 59 of 1949.

1.3 Adapted by the Adaptation of Laws Order, 1950.

1.4 Adapted by the Adaptation of Laws (No. 3) Order, 1956.

BIHAR STATE

Bihar Act

1. The Bihar Private Forests (Validating) Act, 1949—Bihar Act 12 of 1949.

   1.1 Adapted by the Adaptation of Laws Order, 1950.

APPENDIX III

Changes Effected Through Agrarian Reforms

States	*Major External Stimuli*	*Measures Taken*	*Nature of Change*	*Type of Leadership*	*Adaptive Function Divi-*	*Latent Functions*
1947 to date	Land reforms initiated by state	Acquisition and abolition of estates; imposition of land ceilings; the Regulation of tenancy	Disappearance rich and/or absentee landlords, emergence of prosperous owner cultivators	Politicians mainly of the ruling parties, administrative leadership associated with implementation	Division of land formation of fictitious cooperative, indulgence in fake divorces (old equilibrium continues)	Aspirations of rural poor soar high, disappearance of traditional employer-employee relations, incresed frustration of the rural poor, indulgence of rural rich inconspicuous consumption.
1951 to date	Agrarian reforms initiated by the non-violent Bhudan, Gram-	Recieve donation from the landed, distributing land to the land	Continuance of rich landlords as the land is communally	Leader of the movement largely a political,	Donations of barren unproductive lands, dona-	Entry of land into the market blocked land ceilling

States	Major External Stimuli	Measures Taken	Nature of Change	Type of Leadership	Adaptive Function	Latent Functions
	dan movement.	less, initiating co-oprative farming, rendering ownership in land communal, in theory	owned but not individually distributed, emergence of a prosperous cultivating class as special funds are available to Gramdan Villages.	constructive workers at the village level.	tion to one's kith and kin, (Old equilibrium continues).	measures escaped, agriculture income tax avoided, feeling of deprivation among the poor increases
1964 to date	Agrarian reforms initiated through violent agrarian movement sponsored by political parties of leftist pursuasions	Forceful occupation of excess government and private land; protecting the rights of share croppers; raising the wages of agricultural labourers.	New intergroup relations based on the class develops in the place of traditional patron-client relations, landed aristocracy loses their erstwhile	Politicians of opposition parties, local level leadership, in the form of peoples courts; land tribunals etc.	Formal agencies of social control (e.g. police, court etc.) are envoked to deal with the problem, the bargaing power of agricultural	Violent incidents increase, the landed and landless hostile to each other, agricultural labourers lose their traditional security; anomie sets

States	*Major External Stimuli*	*Measures Taken*	*Nature of Change*	*Type of Leadership*	*Adaptive Function*	*Latent Functions*
			status and privileges.		workers increases, the farmers organise themselves for self-protection (disequilibrium sets in)	in agrarian relations.

? It is not suggested that land reforms initiated by states as a post-independence phenomenon.

APPENDIX IV

THE PROGRAMME FOR RURAL DEVELOPMENT RUNNING IN THE COUNTRY

1. Agricultural Development Branches.
2. Agro Service Centres.
3. Antyodaya.
4. Applied Nutrition Programme.
5. Bharat Agro-Industries Foundation Programme.
6. Command Area Development Programme.
7. Community Banking centres.
8. Community Development Project.
9. Crash Scheme For Rural Employment.
10. Desert Development Programme.
11. District Industries Centres.
12. Drought Prone Area Programme.
13. Extension Education And Training Scheme.
14. Family Welfare Programme.
15. Farm Clinics.
16. Food for Works Programme.
17. Gram Vikas Kendra.
18. Half a Million Jobs Programme.
19. High Yielding Varieties Programme.
20. Hill Area Development Programme.
21. Intensive Agricultural Area Programme.
22. Intensive Agricultural District Programme.
23. Integrated Rural Development Programme.
24. Lead Bank Scheme.
25. Marginal Farmer And Agricultural Labour Schemes.
26. Minimum Needs Programme.
27. Multi Service Agency.
28. National Rural Employment Programme.
29. Panchayat Raj.
30. Pilot Intensive Rural Employment Project.
31. Pilot Integrated Rural Employment Programme.
32. Rural Landless Employment Guarantee Programme.
33. Rural Manpower Programme.

34. Rural Service Centre.
35. Rural Works Programme.
36. Small Farmers Development Agency.
37. Special Animal Husbandry Programme.
38. Special Area Programme.
39. Special Component Programme.
40. Training For Youth and Self Employment.
41. Tribal Development Agency.
42. Twenty-Point Programme.

BIBLIOGRAPHY

Published official Sources :

Agriculture, Land Reforms and Economic Development, Preface by Lange.

All India Kisan Sabha. All India Kisan Committee Meeting at Vithalnagar, Bihta, Patna 1938.

Atkinsons Kumaon Gazetteers quoted in *Baden Powell*.

BDR 1974 Vol. 13 dated 6th June 1794.

BOR, Prog. 17th Jan. 1793 Letter from :

(1) Board of Revenue, Collector, Shahabad to the board.

(2) BOR. Prog. 2nd July 1793, Letter from Collector, Shahabad to the Board.

Bengal Act of 1908, (A 8 modified upto the 15th Nov. 1965) Patna, 1966.

Bihar & Orissa Banking Enquiry Committee, Patna.

Bihar Bakasht Disputes Settlement Act, 1947, in the Bihar Land Reforms Act, 1936, 1953, Vol. IV (Patna-1955).

Bihar Directorate of Public Relations, Bihar 1946-1951.

Bihar Directorate of Statistics and Evaluation : Bihar-Ek-Jhalak, 1980.

Bihar Government and its work, Government of Bihar, Review of Post 18 Months by Information Officers.

Bihar : Note on the Kisan Movement in Bihar.

Bihar Prantiya Kisan Sabha Ki Report, Nov. 1921, Nov., 1945 (B.P.K.S.R.) estimated by Swami Sahajanand Saraswati.

Bihar Tenancy Act, 1885, Patna-1975.

Bihar through the figures 1952.

Brett, G.T., Report of administration of the police in the Province of

Bihar 1938 Patna Supdt. Government Printing Press 1939.
Census of India 1921-61.
Census of India 1961, Vol. V. Bihar Part, II-A, General population table.
Champaran District Gazetteer (1907).
Chotanagpur Tenancy Act 1908.
Congress Bulletin, Report of the General Secretaries AICC, Allahabad, A.L.J. Press, Allahabad.
Congress Election Manifesto 1946.
Darbhanga District Gazetteer (1907).
Derpost, Van : *Economics of Agriculture* 1937.
Election Manifesto of the Congress Party 1936.
First Five-year Plan, Agricultural Legislation in India. Vol. II, Consolidation of Holdings 1950.
Fortnightly report of the Patna Commissioner for the period ending 11th April 1936, *Searchlight*, 1st April 1936.
Fortnightly report of the Patna Commissioner for the period ending 13 Nov., 1936.
Fortnightly report of the Patna commissioner for the period ending 17, Dec., 1937.
Final report of survey & settlement operation in the Purnea dist.
Final report of the survey & settlement operations in the Makshudpur estate, in the dist. of Gaya, 1900-1904, Calcutta, 1907.
Final report on the rent settlement operation under Sec. 112, Bihar Tenancy Act in 11 Sub-division of the Patna, Gaya, Sahabad & Monghyr, Patna-1943.
G.B. Land revenue administrative report for 1939-40, pp. 12-13 and for 1940-41 pp. 11-12.
I.N.C. 1988 Resolution of XIV.
1989 Resolution of VI.
1893 Resolution of X.
1904 Resolution of II.
INC Resolution on economic policy and programme, New Delhi-1954.
India-A reference annual 1985.
India Ministry of Food and Agriculture : Agricultural Labour Enquiry Committee. Vol. I. New Delhi.
India. Ministry of Food and Agriculture : Agricultural Wages in India, Vol. I. New Delhi.
Indian National Congress Resolution on Economic policy and programme, 49th Congress Session at Lucknow, April 12-14, 1936.

India. Note on Land Transfers and Agricultural Indebtedness in India Calcutta-1895.
James, Selection from the correspondence of revenue chiefs of Bihar.
Klonov, V. European conference on rural life (1939), Document No. (League of Nations).
Krishnan, H.R., Account of the Bakasht struggle, Report on enquiry, 29 Aug., 1939.
Letter from Collector of Bhagalpur to Major Lunas, Bhagalpur Dist. Records, Vol. V.
Memorandum and land tenure system in Bihar prepared by the revenue department Bihar, 1956.
Muzaffarpur old records 1789.
Murphy, P.W. : Final report on the survey and settlement operation in the dist. of Monghyr (South) 1905-12) Supd. Ranchi.
Original rent in the public register minute of share, 18th June 1789, Fifth report Vol II.
Proceedings of Bihar Legislative Assembly of 1938.
Proceedings of Bihar Legislative Assembly of 1946.
Proceedings of Bihar Legislative Assembly of 1949.
Proceedings of Bihar Legislative Assembly of 1950.
Report at the 45th Session at the Indian National Congress held in Karanchi in 1931.
Report at the General Secretaries 45th Indian National Congress.
Report of Sachidananda Sinha on land reforms in India.
Report of the Bihar provincial Kisan Sabha. Nov. 1929 to 1955.
Report of the General Secretaries AICC, New Delhi. Sept. 1938.
Report of the General Secretaries, I.N.C. Jan. 1937 to Feb., 1938.
Report of the land reforms committee 1946.
Report of the Land revenue flood Commission Vol. 1, p. 28.
Report of the plantation enquiry commission, Vol. III (Delhi) Govt. of India.
Report of the Royal Commission on Agriculture in India (Linlithgow Commission) 1928.
Report of the Santhal Parganas enquiry Committee.
Reported U.N.S. Land Reforms Committee 1946 (Defects in Agrarian Structure is obstacles to economic development).
Report on political events in Bihar for the second half of the Jan. 1938.
Report on the progress of land reforms, Planning Commission.
U.N.O. Land reforms defects in agrarian structure, as obstacles to economic development, 1951.
Williams, R.A.E., Final report on the rent settlement operations 1937-1941.

Unpublished Official Sources :

Agrarian Situation in Bihar or Orissa, Kisan sabha File no. 34/1931, BSCRO Patna.

A Letter from collector Arrah to the commissioner, Patna division, Home special, file no. 6/1936.

All India Kisan Conference, Gaya, Govt. of Bihar, Home Political Dept. (Special), File no. 217/1939.

B.K. Ghokhle, Commissioner of Monghyr, to J.L. Merriman, Commissioner of Bhagalpur.

Confidential diary of the Supd. of Police Monghyr, dated 17th April 1936.

D.I.G. Police to Chief Secretary, Govt. of Bihar & Orissa, 20 Jan. 1921 Pol. spl. File 21 1921.

Govt. of Bihar & Orissa Revenue Department file No. 1199/IVL-57 R. Dated the 6th Dec. 1921.

Govt. of Bihar Home Political Dept. (Special), File No. 42 (III) 1939.

Govt. of Bihar, Home Political Department (Special), File No. 68/ 1936.

Govt. of Bihar Revenue Department, File No. 15/44, 1944.

Home Special, File No. 25 (VII).

Home Special, Confidential File No. 29 (VII) 1939.

Home political, file no. 34/1931 Manifesto of B.P.K.S.

Home Political, File No. 6/1936 (Part III-B).

Home Special, File *Op.cit* letter from the Magistrate of & to the commissioner of Patna 10th July 1936.

Home Special, Confidential file no. 29 (VIII) 1939 containing a note on p. 9. para I.

Letter of the collector of Monghyr dated 4 Jan. 1939 to Russells C.S. to the Govt. of Bihar, Govt. of Bihar Home Political Department (Special), File No. 29 (II) 1939.

Letter of the Collector of Monghyr, dated 11-12, Feb. 1939, to Russells, Chief Secretary.

Rajendra Prasad's Letter to Ram Dayalu Sinha, Dec. 7, 1937.

Rajendra Prasad's paper, file no. 111/37 NMML.

Unpublished Ph.D. Thesis :

Brown, J.M., *Gandhi in India.* (1915-20) : University of Cambridge, 1968.

Hauser, Walter—*The Bihar Provincial Kisan sabha and the Congress,* University of Chicago, 1961.

Books

Annoymous, *Bihar Kisan Sabha Comes of Ages*, Congress Socialist, Vol. III, (New Series, no. 4, 22 Jan. 1938.

Banerjee, S.N. *A Nation in Making*, Calcutta, 1925.

Basu, D.D., *Ruin of Indian Trade and Industries*, Calcutta, 1935.

Bhatia, B.M., *Famines in India*, Bombay, 1967.

Beams, John, *Memoirs of a Bengal Civilians*, London, 1961.

Briggs, Ferishta, *Trans. J. Briggs*. Vol. I. London, 1829.

Chaudhary, S.B. *Civil rebellion India*, Calcutta, 1957.

Chaudhary, Valmiki., *Dr. Rajendra Prasad Correspondence and select documents*, Vol. III (Jan. to July) New Delhi, 1980.

Choudhary, V.C.P., *The creation of Modern Bihar*, Darbhanga, 1964.

Das, Arvind N., *Agrarian unrest and socio economic change in Bihar*, New Delhi, 1980.

Desai, A.R. (ed.), *Peasants struggle in India*, Delhi, 1979.

Dhanagre, D.N., *Peasant movements in India*, New Delhi, 1983.

Diwakar, R.R., *Bihar Through the Ages*, Calcutta, 1958.

Driver, P.N. *Problems of zamindari and Land Tenure Reconstruction in India*, Bombay 1949.

Dutta, Romesh, *Economic History of India*, Vol. I, New Delhi, 1976.

Dutta, K.K., *Freedom Movement in Bihar*, Patna, 1957.

Dutta, K.K., *Mahatma Gandhi in Bihar*, (Speeches and writings), Patna, 1969.

Dutta, K.K., *The Santhal Insurrection of 1955-57*, Calcutta, 1940.

Dutt, R.C., *The Economic History of India Under early British Rule*, London, 1956.

Dutt, R.C., *Economic History of India during Victorian Age*, (6th ed.) London, 1906.

Empree, A.T., *Charles grant and British Rute in India*, London, 1962.

Fei, Hsiao Tung., *Peasants Life in China*, 1938 (a field study of country life in they angtze valley) 1980.

Field, C.D., *Land Holding and the relation of Landlord and Tenant in various countries*, (2nd). Calcutta, 1885.

Gandhi, M.K., *An Autobiography*, Ahmadabad, repairing 1963.

Ghosal, H.R., *Two Mughal Farmans In Indian History Congress Progress*, Patna, 1950.

Gupta, J.N., *Life and work of R.C. Dutt*, London, 1911.

Guha, Ranjit., *A Rule of Property for Bengal*, Paris, 1963.

Gupta, M.P. *The Indian National Congress*, Delhi, 1985.

Gupta, Sulekh., *Agrarian Relations and Early British Rule in India*, Bombay, 1963.

Gupta, Rakesh K., *Bihar Peasantry and the Kisan Sabhas,* New Delhi, 1982.

Gyanchand, *Socialist Transformation of Indian Economy,* New Delhi, 1965.

Hallet, Graham., *The Economics of Agricultural Land Tenures,* London, 1960.

Hand, J.R., *Early English administration in Bihar,* Calcutta, 1894.

Heningham Stephen, *Peasant Movement in Colonial India,* Canberra, 1982.

Hume, A.O., *Hints on Agricultural Reforms in India,* Calcutta, 1870.

Hunter, W.W. *The Annals of Rural Bengal,* Calcutta, 1965.

Hossain, Gholam, *The Seir Mutagherin,* Vol. III, Madras, 1926.

Jain, A.P., *Abolition of zamindari,* Bihar, 1945.

Jain, S.C., *Agricultural Policy in India,* Bombay, 1965.

Jannuzi, F. Tomasson., *Agrarian Crisis in India,* The case of Bihar, New Delhi, 1974.

Johnson, Chalmens, *Peasant Nationalism and Communist Party, Stanford,* 1962.

Joshi, G.V., *Notes on Agriculture,* Bombay, 1894.

Joshi, P.C. *Land Reforms in India,* New Delhi, 1970.

Kling, Blair B., *The blue mutiny,* London, 1966.

Konar, Harekrishna, *Agrarian Problems of India,* Calcutta, 1977.

Kotovsky, G., *Agrarian Reforms in India.* Delhi, 1964.

Kumar, Shiv, *Peasantry and the Indian National Congress Movement* Meerut, 1980.

Limaye, Madhu, *Evolution of Socialist Party,* Hyderabad, 1952.

Lorenzo, A.H. *Agricultural Conditions in Northern India,* 1948.

Low, D.A. (ed)., *Congress and the Raj* Facets of the Indian Struggle (1917-47) London, 1977, New Delhi, 1977.

Malviya, H.D., *Land Reforms in India,* New Delhi, 1955.

Martin., *New India 1885,* London, 1969.

Mclane, J.R., *Land Revenue and Peasant in South Asia,* New Delhi, 1977.

Mishra, Girish., *Agrarian Problems of Permanent Settlement,* A case Study of Champaran, New Delhi, 1978.

Mishra, Jagannath, *Land Reforms in Bihar,* Patna, 1974.

Mishra, Madaneshwar, *Some aspects of the Land Revenue History of Purnea district,* Patna, 1979.

Mitra, N.N. (ed)., *The Indian Annual Register Jan.-June, 1939,* Calcutta, 1938.

Mitra, Vimal. *Muzrim Hazir,* T.V. Serial (1989)

Mukherjee, R.K., *Land Problem of India,* Calcutta, 1933.

Mukherjee, R.K. (ed)., *Economic Problems of India,* Calcutta, 1940.

Mukherjee, Karuna, *Land Reforms*, Calcutta.
Nanda, B.R. *Socialism in India*, Delhi, 1972.
Nanavati and Anjaria, *The Indian Rural Problems*, Bombay, 1960.
Neale, Walter C., *Economic Changes in Rural India Land Tenure and Reforms in Uttar Pradesh*, London, 1962.
N.L. Nanporia., *Times of India Directory & year book 1967*, Delhi, 1968.
Nehru, Jawaharlal, *Autobiography*, New Delhi, 1936.
Nehru, Jawaharlal, *Discovery of India*, Calcutta, 1946
Nehru, Jawaharlal, *Glimpses of the World History* New Delhi, 1984.
Ojha, Gyaneshwar, *Land Problems and Land Reforms*, New Delhi, 1972
Ojha, P.N. (ed)., *History of Indian National Congress in Bihar*, Patna, 1985.
Oomen, T.K. *Social Transformation in Rural India*, Delhi, 1984.
Pio, Lin (ed)., *Quotations from chairman Mao Tse-Tung*, Peking 1970.
Prasad, Kedarnath, *The Economics of a Backward Region in a Backward Economy*, Calcutta, 1967
Prasad, Rajendra, *Autobiography*, Bombay, 1957.
Powell, B.H. Baden., *The Land Systems of British India*, Vol. I, II, III, Oxford, 1892.
Ram Krishna, *Dynamics of a Rural Society*, Berlin.
Ranga, N.G. & Saraswati, Swami Sahajanand, *Agrarian Revolts*, in A.R. Desai (ed.) Peasant Struggle in India. Delhi, 1979.
Rasul, M.A., *A History of the All Indian Kisan Sabha*, Calcutta, 1974.
Ray, S.C. (Comp), *Land Revenue administration in India*, Calcutta, 1915.
Ray, S.C., *The permanent settlement in Bengal*, Calcutta, 1915.
Rousseau, Jean Jacques., *Social Contract*, 1762.
Roy, Ajit Gopal (ed)., *The Bihar Tenancy Act 1885*, (Act VIII of 1885), Patna, 1969.
Roy, Ramashray, *Dynamics of one party dominance in an Indian State*, Asian Survey July, 1958.
Sankrityayan, Rahul, *Naye Bharat ke Naye Neta*, (in Hindi) Vol. I, Allahabad, 1973.
Saraswati, Sahajanand Swami *Kranti aur Samyukta Morcha*, Patna, 1943.
Saraswati, Sahajanand, *Mera Jeevan Sangarsh*, Patna, 1952.
Seal, Anil, *The Emergence of Indian Nationalism Competition and collaboration in the later nineteenth century*, London, 1968.
Sen, Sunil, *Agrarian Relation in India, 1946 to 1947*, New Delhi, 1972.
Seshadri, K., *Rural unrest in India*, New Delhi, 1983.
Sharma, G.P. *Congress and the Peasant Movement in Bihar*, Bombay, 1985.
Shelvankar, *Problems of India*, Penguin, 1940.
Singh, Charan, *Abolition of Zamindari*, Allahabad, 1947.

Sinha, Indradeep, *Marxism and the Peasantry*, New Delhi, 1982.
Sinha, Indradeep, *Bihar Main Congress Party Ka Vikas*, (in Hindi) Patna, n.d.
Singh, K. Suresh, *The Dust Storm and hanging mist*, Calcutta, 1965.
Sinha, Sachidanand, *Some Eminent Behari Contemporaries*, Patna, 1944.
Sinha, N.K., *The Economic History of Bengal*, from plassey to the permanent settlement Vol. II. Calcutta, 1962.
Sinha, Ranjit, *The Law of Landlord and Tenant in Bengal, Bihar*, Calcutta, 1918.
Sinha, R.N., *Bihar Tenancy*, Bombay, 1968.
Sitarammya, P., *The History of the Indian National Congress*, Vol. II, Bombay, 1947.
Tarachand, *History of Freedom Movement in India*, Vol IV. Delhi, 1960.
Tendulkar, D.C., *Gandhi in Champaran*, Delhi, 1960.
Thakur, D., *Politics of Land Reforms in Indian with special Reference to Bihar*, Patna, 1988.
Tomlinson, R.R., *Indian National Congress and the Raj*, London, 1976.
Wasi, S.M., *Bihar in 1937-38*, Patna, 1941.
Warriner, D., *Land Reform in principle and practice*, Oxford, 1969.

Index